DANCE, GENDER AND CULTURE

ONE WEEK LOAN

Dance, Gender and Culture

Edited by

Helen Thomas

Senior Lecturer in Sociology at Goldsmiths College
University of London

First published 1993 by
MACMILLAN PRESS LTD
Houndmills, Basingstoke, Hampshire RG21 2XS
and London
Companies and representatives
throughout the world

ISBN 0–333–51374–6 hardcover
ISBN 0–333–63759–3 paperback

A catalogue record for this book is available
from the British Library.

11 10   9   8   7   6   5   4
04 03 02 01 00 99 98

Printed and bound in Great Britain by
Antony Rowe Ltd
Chippenham, Wiltshire

In memory of
Lizzie and Steve McDonald

Contents

PART THREE   THEORY/CRITICISM

List of Plates

Notes on the Contributors

Roger Copeland is Professor of Theater and Dance at Oberlin College in the US. His books include *What Is Dance?* and the forthcoming *Cunningham's Legacy*. He has published over one hundred articles about dance, theatre and film in a wide variety of publications that include the *New York Times, Dance Theatre Journal, New Republic, Partisan Review, American Theatre, Drama Review*, and *Journal of Aesthetics and Art Criticism*.

Richard Dyer teaches film studies at the University of Warwick. He has published widely on film, popular culture and lesbian and gay rights issues. His books include *Heavenly Bodies: Film Stars and Society, Only Entertainment* and *The Matter of Images: Essays on Representation*. He is currently developing work on the construction of dominant but invisible identities, heterosexuality and whiteness.

Andrée Grau is an anthropologist and a Benesh notator. She is a senior research associate in the Department of Dance Studies at Roehampton Institute. She teaches anthropology of dance at the London School of Contemporary Dance and in the Ethnomusicology Centre at Goldsmiths College, University of London. Her publications have appeared in *Dance Research, Dance Research Journal, Man, Popular Music* and *Visual Anthropology*.

Judith Lynne-Hanna is a senior research scholar at the University of Maryland and a consultant in the arts, education, health and social policy. She has written extensively on dance and her major publications include *To Dance Is Human, The Performer–Audience Connection, Dance, Sex and Gender* and *Dance and Stress*.

Cynthia J. Novack is a dancer and choreographer with The Richard Bull Dance Theatre. A trained anthropologist, she is an Associate Professor of dance at Wesleyan University. She is the author of *Sharing the Dance, Contact Improvisation and American Culture*.

Zagba Oyortey is an arts administrator and a cultural journalist who holds an MA in art criticism. He publishes in specialist magazines and newspapers. He is currently researching into the role of black dance in the United Kingdom.

Ted Polhemus is an anthropologist who has published widely on fashion and dress. His books include *The Body as a Medium of Expression* (co-editor), *Social Aspects of the Human Body* (editor), *Fashion and Anti-Fashion* (co-author), *Body Styles*, and *Popstyles* (co-author). He has written programmes for television and radio and is at present working on a television series entitled *Across a Crowded Room.*

Valerie Rimmer teaches at the Laban Centre for Movement and Dance, where she is currently working on her doctoral thesis in dance studies. She has published several articles on dance in the *Laban Papers.*

Ana Sanchez-Colberg is a practising dancer and choreographer who performs regularly in the UK and Europe. She has published an article on Pina Bausch in a forthcoming edition of *Parallel Lines.* She has recently been awarded a Ph.D. from the Laban Centre for Movement and Dance.

Lesley-Anne Sayers is a writer and dance historian specialising in British dance history and the history of dance criticism. She writes regularly on dance, contributing to various publications, including *Dance Theatre Journal, World Ballet and Dance, Laban Papers, Dancing Times, New Dance* and in *The Dictionary of Ballet and Classical Dance.*

Helen Thomas is a senior lecturer in Sociology at Goldsmiths College, University of London. She has published articles on dance in *Dance* and *Issues in Architecture, Art and Design.* She is the author of *Equal Opportunities in the Mechanical Media,* a large-scale survey commissioned by Equity. She has recently completed a new book entitled *Dance, Modernity and Culture,* and is the research director of *Unequal Pay for Equal Parts,* a further survey of men and women actors, funded by the Leverhulme Trust.

David Walsh is a senior lecturer in Sociology at Goldsmiths College, University of London. His previous publications include *New Directions in Sociological Theory* and *Rationality, Education and the Social*

Organisation of Knowledge. He is currently working on a book on Emile Durkheim.

Andrew Ward has taught sociology at Goldsmiths College, University of London, Oxford Polytechnic, and Ealing College, London. His current interests rest with cultural studies methodologies. He is now corporate relations manager at Thames Valley University, but he still occasionally dances.

Introduction

The papers in this collection were written specially for this edition. To my knowledge this is the first time that an anthology such as this has been produced by a major British publishing house. Although the central theme throughout, as the title suggests, is dance and gender, there is no intention to offer a coherent or unified viewpoint of the topic. The writers come from a number of different areas of expertise: sociology, film studies, dance criticism, journalism, dance performance and dance anthropology. However, although there is diversity, the selection is not random – I wanted the book to bring together writers who had an interest in dance but were not dance specialists; those whose work fell under the umbrella of dance scholarship with a social science or cultural studies influence, and those who were trying explicitly to combine dance with another discipline. I considered that this interdisciplinary and intradisciplinary approach was essential if the concerns of the book were to be achieved. These concerns, it must be said, are mine, not necessarily the individual contributors' and they encompass more than the title suggests.

The aims of this compilation are as follows: to explore the possibilities of a number of ways in which dance and gender intersect within particular cultural contexts; to demonstrate that dance can provide a rich resource for subject areas like sociology, cultural/film studies and feminism, which have all but ignored it; to show that dance scholarship can benefit from the insights which the aforementioned disciplines have to offer; and to indicate that, although it might help, it is not always necessary to be a dancer in order to write about dance in an illuminating manner.

Dance as an activity and as a performance art has occupied a marginal role in academic thought. Indeed, most academic texts on dance begin by bemoaning the lack of systematic work in this area. Tutors, also, are only too aware of the problems of finding a body of reference material on dance that is directly suitable for their students' requirements. The reasons for this gap are complex and to pursue them in any detail would take this anthology away from its focus of attention. Therefore, while three of the papers (Polhemus, Ward, Thomas) do topicalise the issue of the marginalisation of dance in particular areas (sociology, sub-cultural analysis, feminism), it does not constitute a dominant theme in the book as a whole. The focal point in this collection is directed towards the positive as opposed to the negative. The major concern is to demonstrate how dance forms and dance contexts can speak of and to gender differences within particular socio-cultural environments; to indicate that dance is a worthy site for a broad range of academic inquiry as opposed to concentrating on the reasons why there has been a lack of systematic research on dance.

I do not wish to suggest that the forms and contexts discussed in this anthology are all-encompassing. Indeed, the majority of the papers consider social and/or performance dance within the Western tradition. But, in order to get away from that ethno-centrism, three of the papers (Grau, Hanna and Oyortey) con-sider the relationship(s) between dance and gender in other dance traditions (Tiwi, classical Indian dance, African dance in the UK). Moreover, two Western dance forms (social dance, ballet) are discussed by anthropologists (Polhemus, Novack).

Neither would I wish it to be implied from the collection that what constitutes dance in one culture is necessarily the same as that in another. There is enough evidence from dance anthro-pologists to show that, for example, what one culture might term play, another culture would call dance. The discussions here, however, are not oriented towards the philosophical issue of 'what is dance?' – again because it would divert attention away from the intended aims of the project. The papers (Dyer, Copeland, Sanchez-Colberg, Novack, Sayers, Rimmer) that specifically address dance aesthetics and/or dance criticism of particular forms (Hollywood musical, postmodern dance, *Tanztheater*, ballet) are concerned to examine these in terms of the representations of gender they invoke and the ideologies they encapsulate.

Just as the collection addresses a variety of dance forms and dance contexts, so there is no single theoretical overview of gender being adhered to throughout. I use the term 'gender' deliberately to refer to differences between men and women that are socially acquired, in contrast to 'sex' which has come to be taken to refer to distinctions founded on biological determinants. The current interest in the analyses of gender differences owes much to the past two decades or so of feminism. Feminists, however, do not speak with one voice, they come from different theoretical and political positions. Despite the fact that feminists are in general agreement that women are oppressed, there is argument and debate as to the character of this subjugation, its causes, analyses, mechanisms and the appropriate remedies. Given the incursions that feminism has made into the social sciences, the humanities and the arts, it is not surprising that the papers in this volume either draw explicitly from this emergent tradition, or have been influenced by it. What is surprising, however, is that feminist interests in the representation of women's bodies, have not focused on dance as a site for analysis, given the centrality of the body in dance and, as two of the papers point out (Polhemus, Thomas), the importance of the body as a symbol of society. Hopefully, this collection will go some way to doing just that.

Over half of the papers concentrate primarily on women and femininity and/or sexuality in the context of their discussions on dance. Some (Copeland, Rimmer, Sanchez-Colberg, Novack) use particular feminist perspectives or theoretical formulations that have influenced feminism (French feminism, psychonalytic theory, cultural studies), as tools of analysis. Others (Ward, Novack, Thomas, Sayers) draw on feminist perspectives in a more general manner. Some papers (Grau, Polhemus, Oyortey) focus on both men and women, thus extending the discussion to include a consideration of images of masculinity and femininity in dance traditions (social dance, Tiwi, African dance in the UK). While others (Dyer, Walsh) extend the discussion further by topicalising heterosexuality and gay subculture in particular dance genres (Hollywood musical, disco).

There is no intention of imposing a singular or unified version of culture throughout the collection and apart from the first paper (Polhemus), the concept is not addressed explicitly. Nevertheless, two meanings of the word predominate and often the individual papers slip between the two: 'culture as a way of life', which is a feature of the anthropological and sociological traditions (Polhemus, Ward, Grau, Walsh, Oyortey); and the more restricted stratified version of culture (high culture v. popular culture), which stems from the English literary tradition and refers to standards of excellence, particularly in the arts. It should be pointed out, however, that those papers which deal with dance as art (Novack, Thomas, Hanna, Copeland, Sanchez-Colberg, Oyortey, Rimmer) do not necessarily afford it a privileged status and indeed some (Novack, Rimmer) seek to draw out the inherent ideological implications. Similarly, those who offer interpretations of popular or mass cultural forms (Ward, Dyer, Walsh) do not see these as inferior or denigrated aspects of culture.

The anthology is divided into three sections which virtually speak for themselves; Cultural Studies, Ethnography and Theory/Criticism. Generally speaking, we would expect to find popular and/or entertainment dance under the Cultural Studies heading, dances from different cultures, usually non-Western, under Ethnography and dance as a performance art under Theory/Criticism. It is almost as if the first and the third sections encapsulate the opposite poles in the cultural stratification tradition, while the second section encompasses the concept of 'culture as a way of life'. However, to a certain extent, I have tried to debunk the conventions by putting some topics in categories where they would not normally be expected to reside. Thus, for example, classical ballet turns up in Cultural Studies and African dance is discussed in the Theory section. Generally, ballet would be restricted to the Theory section and African dance would be placed in the Ethnography section. Moreover, the Ethnography section draws on performance dance as well as social and popular dance from anthropological and sociological perspectives. Thus, once again, it is diversity rather than singularity that is at work.

I would like to thank the individual contributors for enabling me to bring together a stimulating collection which, hopefully, will be read by dance students and their tutors, as well as students and tutors from other disciplines who are interested in dance but do not know where to begin to look for relevant reference material. I would also like to thank Macmillan for saying yes to my initial proposal, thus enabling another book on dance to be placed on the shelves of book shops to help fill that aforementioned gap.

HELEN THOMAS

Part One
Cultural Studies

1 Dance, Gender and Culture

TED POLHEMUS

At the most fundamental level of analysis, dance, gender and culture are one and the same thing. In order to demonstrate this provocative contention, however, it is necessary that we examine each of these subjects separately.

First *culture*. Putting aside a class-based view which presupposes that culture is possessed only by an educated élite, I will here use this term in a properly anthropological sense to encompass everything which the members of a social group (*any* social group) have in common – everything which they share and which contributes to and generates their sense of 'we-ness'. Culture is the glue which holds peoples together.

World view, religion, cosmology, an ethical system and language are some of the most obvious components of culture. Especially obvious to us is language which traditionally has been seen as the cornerstone, sometimes even the totality, of culture. It would, of course, be foolish to dismiss out of hand the significance of verbal language as an essential component of the social cement which is culture. Throughout human history verbal language has served as a marker of the boundaries of social groups and as a depository of any social group's tradition and history. It is, however, just as foolish to presume that verbal language is the *only* significant socio-cultural marker and depository.

Our own socio-cultural tradition (which for want of a better term is usually called 'the West') has always ascribed a particular importance to verbal language; an importance which some anthropologists have increasingly come to suspect is not shared by other peoples. There is, therefore, a growing suspicion that our 'In the beginning was the Word', logocentric world view has biased our perception of *all* cultural systems.[1] It is not my wish to debate here the relative importance of verbal communication or to suggest that verbal language is not a major component of culture. What does seem appropriate here and now (in a book on this subject and in light of recent develop-

3

ments in the social sciences) is to underline and celebrate the significance of non-verbal communicative systems–especially what might be termed *physical culture.*

From the moment of birth an individual begins the long and complex task of learning how to use his or her physical body. This is obvious and we note in 'baby books' significant moments of this process such as the first time a baby manages to stand or walk. What is less obvious, but by no means less important, is the fact that such physical development is a cultural as well as a biological phenomenon. *How* one should stand, walk, hold the body, etc. differs from one society to the next and in a fast changing society such as our own, from one era to the next.

Thus, for example, while everyone would readily agree that all physiologically normal human beings develop, for example, bipedal locomotion, it is less often appreciated that not only is the style of such locomotion specific to a given social group or era, but furthermore, that such stylistic differences – just like differences between verbal languages or dialects – are essential markers of 'Our Way of Life' and depositories of 'Our' tradition. To be a Masai, a Hopi, an Xingu, etc. is to comport oneself like a Masai, a Hopi or a Xingu. To put a foot wrong, that is, to move one's body in a stylistically inappropriate manner, is to step outside the boundaries of one's culture.

If it is difficult for us to accept the implications of this line of thought it is simply because we – like all the world's peoples – consign everything to do with our bodies to the domain of the 'natural'. That is to say, that territory which is beyond the reach of culture. Always and everywhere the way 'we' walk, sit, squat, lean against a wall, stand, sleep, copulate, and so forth is seen as *the* way the body *'naturally'* behaves. This is not only because one's physical self is existentially omnipresent, it is also because 'the body' is inevitably caught up in a symbolic congruence with 'the social body' of one's society; a congruence which is so complete that it has the effect of blinkering us to the cross-cultural relativity of corporal experience.

This is a complex problem which has been discussed at length by the anthropologist Mary Douglas (1970) and by myself in other works (1975, 1978, 1988). For our present purposes let us simply concentrate on the practical entailment of the interplay between the physical body and the social body; namely, that such symbolic interfacing inevitably consigns physiological behaviours to a domain which is 'natural' and, therefore, apparently outside of human intervention. (The precise, mirror-like replication of the human body in the social body – and vice versa – gives each of these levels of experience a patina of objective reality which is mutually reifying.)

In the terminology of our own culture's world view, this means that physical behaviour is classified as biological and genetic rather than socio-cultural and learned. Although this particular distinction may be unique to us, the bottom line of such classification is the same as that found in any traditional, tribal or peasant society – to consign physical behaviours to the realm of the 'natural' and immutable. But while the tendency to classify the physiological as 'natural' might itself be 'natural' it is rather amazing that we who have been uniquely exposed to so much cross-cultural experience should persist in this view. If not through first-hand experience, at least through the medium of ethnographic films we have seen how people from other societies use their bodies differently than we do and yet we persist in placing physicality outside the bounds of culture.

And most surprising of all, anthropologists who have studied other societies first hand and extensively are often the most persistent offenders. Indeed, anthropology itself has traditionally been divided between, on the one hand, 'physical anthropology' which deals with the evolution of the human body and, on the other hand, 'social' or 'cultural' anthropology which deals with human social organisation and its products and artefacts. Thankfully there have been important exceptions and these individuals have pointed the way towards a study of humankind which would explore the interface between the socio-cultural and the physical levels of experience.

Margaret Mead, for example, in her work with Gregory Bateson (1942) and Francis Cooke Macgregor (1951) has shown not only that the members of traditional Balinese society learn to use their bodies in a style which is radically different from our own, but also that such physical behaviour is an intrinsic and fundamental part of Balinese culture. For Mead and her co-authors the essence of 'Balinese character' is Balinese style comportment.

While Mead and her colleagues concentrated on providing us with a magnificently detailed understanding of the interplay of physical and socio-cultural experience in one society, a few others in the social sciences have sought to develop a general theory of this interface which is applicable to all of humankind. Two students of Emile Durkheim's, Robert Hertz (1960) and Marcel Mauss (1972) are important pioneers. In America, Ray Birdwhistell's advances in the study of kinesics (1971) have helped us to recognise not only that physical behaviour is cross-culturally variable but that such behaviour is also, and more importantly, a key component of human expressive and communicative systems.[2]

In light of such work it seems pertinent that the social sciences re-examine the meaning of the word 'culture'. Culture is not exclusively nor, I would suggest, even primarily encoded and transmitted by means of words or artefacts. At least in so far as an individual's first and most rudimentary experience of his or her society is via bodily manipulation and physical education in its broadest sense, the deepest and most fundamental foundations of being a member of a particular society are inevitably corporal. Muscular tonus, stance, basic movement styles, gestures and so forth once learned are, like any physical activity, remarkably resistant to change and constitute not only the essential component of personal identity but of social and cultural identity as well. Furthermore, movement and other physical styles are in any society imbued with symbolic meaning with the result that how we use and move our bodies is inevitably the occasion for the transmission of all sorts and various levels of socio-cultural information including, most importantly, those meanings which exceed the limits of verbal language.[3]

At its core, therefore, culture not only includes a physical dimension, it *is* a physical style system which signifies (embodies) what it means to be a member of a particular society. Mead and colleagues have shown how this works for the Balinese – that a particular way of holding one's body, of relaxing, of squatting, of walking and so forth is the very essence of being Balinese.

Our society is more complex and difficult to see in these terms because it is actually a loose conglomerate of many different, competing socio-cultural groups. Nevertheless, 'Western Society' offers us many examples of the central position of physical style within cultural systems. Consider, for example, the clash which occurred in the sixties between the hippies and 'Straight Society': The essence of hippiness was symbolically expressed in the form of a physicality which was 'laid-back', 'loose' and 'easy' while 'Straight Society' was just that – 'rigid', 'up-tight', 'square' and 'up-right'. Where one personally stood in relationship to this clash of cultures was precisely encapsulated in how one walked down the street, sat in a chair, leaned against a wall or moved on a dance floor.

Which brings us to our second subject: Dance. While physical culture may be viewed as a crystallisation – an embodiment – of the most deeply rooted and fundamental level of what it means to be a member of a particular society, dance might be seen as a second stage of this process – a schema, an abstraction or stylising of physical culture. There is impressive evidence to support both of these assumptions in the research which was generated by the Choreometrics Project.

Choreometrics, defined as 'the measure of dance or dance as a measure of culture',[4] began as an offshoot of the cantometrics project which the anthropologist Alan Lomax set up to explore cross-cultural differences and similarities of music style.[5] In essays in their book *Folk Song Style and Culture* Lomax and his team tell us that the choreometrics project set out to test the hypothesis that 'dance itself is an adumbration of or derived communication about life, focused on those favoured dynamic patterns which most successfully and frequently animated the everyday activity of most of the people in a culture'.[6] That,

> dance is the most repetitious, redundant, and formally or-
> ganized system of body communication present in a culture
> (Hanna 1965). The dance is composed of those gestures,
> postures, movements, and movement qualities most charac-
> teristic and most essential to the activity of everyday, and thus
> crucial to cultural continuity . . . In dance those postures and
> qualities of movement should be discovered which are so
> familiar, so acceptable, or for some reason so important to a
> particular human community that all will take pleasure in
> continually watching or repeating them. These patterns of
> action ought to be of maximal importance to the actual physi-
> cal survival of the culture and thus should be esteemed not
> merely as desirable, but as necessary as breath and food.[7]

To test this hypothesis the choreometrics team created a cod-ing system for scoring the primary parameters of dance (shape of transition, shape of main activity, energy of transition, energy of main activity, degree of variation, spread of flow through body).

They then, after viewing film of dance from some 43 cultures from around the world, scored each of these according to these parameters. There is not room here to discuss in detail either their methodology or their results[8] but two principle findings deserve note:

First, in all societies studied by the Choreometrics Project there was found to be an intrinsic relationship between dance styles and everyday movement styles. That is, dance could indeed be described as a stylistisation of everyday movement qualities.

Second, the dance styles of the societies investigated by the Choreometrics Project seemed to reflect and embody the overall culture of that society. That is, dance styles, instead of being arbitrary, constitute a 'natural' expression of the cultural system within which they are found.

In other words: Dance is a stylised, highly redundant schema of a people's overall physical culture which is itself the embodiment of that particular people's unique way of life – their culture in the broadest sense of the term. Dance is the metaphysics of culture.

Lomax and his colleagues most frequently demonstrate this view in rather simplistic terms which seek to show how the movement patterns necessitated by a peoples' techniques of food gathering and preparation shape their styles of dance movement. Thus, for example, an Eskimo's forceful downward striking movement in fishing is shown to be translated into similar movement patterns in Eskimo dance while the dance of the Tadjik peoples of the Near and Middle East is shown to be an abstraction of the movement patterns required by these people's agricultural endeavours. But while such specific examples are highly convincing, I am wary of such examples being extrapolated into an overall theory of dance-physical culture which would proceed purely along the lines of a means of production reductionism. Culture is always a multi-faceted system which incorporates a complexity of symbolic codes which while inevitably 'practical' are rarely reducible to the straightforward practicality of obtaining and preparing something to eat.

A culture is a blueprint for a way of living. As such it must, of course, prescribe a means of obtaining foodstuffs, but it must also prescribe patterns of kinship, ethics, political organisation, religion, cosmology and all the other systems which taken together organise and structure a way of life. If everyday movement patterns and dance are an embodiment of culture then one must expect that they embody *all* of these systems – many of which are far removed from the concrete techniques of food production and preparation and which, it could be argued, may even shape these techniques themselves.

These criticisms, however, do not necessarily invalidate the work of the choreometrics team, but rather, serve as a spur to a second stage of research. The objective of this second stage would be to show how the full complexity of any cultural system is embodied and given form in a style of everyday movement (physical culture) which, in turn, is abstracted into the dance style of that people. For now we must rely for 'proof' of this thesis upon the work of Mead, Bateson and Macgregor which, as we have seen, so clearly demonstrates precisely this for one cultural system, the Balinese. For the time being, it is only in this kind of work that we rise above the simplistic and obvious to appreciate the full, rich interface of a way of life, a style of everyday movement and the adumbration of the latter in the form of dance. Moreover, the work of Mead and her colleagues does not deny the fact that within any social system there is to be found a pluralism of everyday movement/dance styles and cultural possibilities.

The most important factor to emerge from the above is that to understand and appreciate the implications of even a single moment of dance movement it is necessary to possess a full understanding of the complexities of the socio-cultural system in which it is found. Because dance is a system of signification which possesses roots which permeate to the core of culture, it is necessary, if we wish to decode its meanings, to appreciate that a way of life (a culture) is much more than a way of filling one's stomach.

Thus far I have tried to show that dance is a liqueur which is distilled of the stuff of culture. It remains for us to explore the issue of gender in relation to dance and culture.

Traditionally, culture has been viewed as a single, coherent, objective entity; a 'thing' which exists on its own. Perhaps this view derives from a misunderstanding of Durkheim's axiom that a society is 'more than the sum of its parts' – a facile misinterpretation which credits socio-cultural systems with an objective reality (a 'thing-ness') which the French sociologist never intended.[9] For, ironically, while culture is the definitive shared, intersubjective experience its reality is, in the final analysis, always subjective – from the perspective of a particular individual. 'Our Culture' is always a synthesis of my or yours or Joe Bloggs's understanding of 'Our Culture' and, obviously, if you or I or Joe (or Jane) Bloggs are experiencing 'Our' culture from radically different perspectives then this will in turn affect not only our vision of our culture, but – because culture exists only in our intersubjective visions of it – culture itself.

Let us, therefore, outline the most fundamental differences of perspective which generate a disjunction of that which we commonly take to be uniform and objective. In any society and at any point in human history there have always been two significant categories of experience which inevitably and profoundly distort any individual's subjective perception of cultural reality: age and gender.

In any society a ten-year-old will always perceive his or her culture differently than will a 70-year-old. However, given that a 70-year-old will have had the experience of having been a ten-year-old, the significance of this subjective distinction will eventually be diminished, at least for those individuals who reach old age. Gender, however, is more problematic. No matter how long we may live, no matter how rich and varied are our experiences, no matter how much we might strive to be 'objective', all of us are either male or female and none of us have ever truly experienced life from the perspective of the gender which we are not.[10] Even those few individuals in modern society who have changed sex can never know what it is like to have grown up as a member of the sex which – physiologically speaking – they have become.

Gender is a primary and insurmountable existential division which must inevitably define cultural experience and the perception of cultural reality. Again, it is surprising how often this simple fact of life has been ignored by anthropologists and sociologists. A male anthropologist conducting fieldwork amongst tribe X will find that the 'woman's world' of the X are off-limits to his investigations. Likewise a female anthropologist studying the same tribe on another occasion will find that the 'men's world' of the X is similarly beyond her reach. Yet, typically, both these anthropologists will report on the X's culture as if it were a single, unisex phenomenon.

Logically, because life can only be experienced from the perspective of one particular gender and because culture (ultimately) exists only in the mind's eye of particular individuals, all of the world's cultures must be multiplied by two: the male culture and the female culture.

Because of this fact of life we must slightly revise our understanding of the interface between culture and dance. A culture is that which is shared by all of the members of a society. In practice, however, the possibilities of such intersubjectivity will always be limited by differences of gender. For this reason, it is necessary to distinguish between male and female cultural realities within the context of any social group. For both male and female cultural realities the processes of cultural expression and signification will be the same as those discussed above; culture in its broadest sense is embodied in the form of physical culture and this in turn is stylised and schematised in the form of dance. However, while this process itself may be unrelated to gender, the end results always are: the cultural reality which, for example, Masai (etc.) men express in their dance will be a different cultural reality than that which Masai (etc.) women express in their dance.

In emphasising the obvious role that gender must play in the definition of cultural reality I do not want to fall into a physiological reductionism. Gender is itself, of course, culturally defined. We are not referring here simply to differences of genital equipment and so forth. However, the fact that, in any society, 'maleness' and 'femaleness' is a socio-cultural-physiological phenomenon and the fact that gender roles differ considerably from one society to another, does not alter the fact that *for any given individual* the experience of gender identity is an absolute boundary which is existentially insurmountable. Some distinction between the sexes is universal in all human societies, and inevitably, therefore, culture is bifurcated into male culture and female culture.

Dance – the distillation of culture into its most metaphysical form – always embodies and identifies this gender-generated division of cultural realities. Whenever men and women dance together, therefore, cultures collide: male culture and female culture. Nor is it necessary, of course, for men and women to actually dance together for such collisions to occur. In societies where men and women dance separately a simple comparison of their respective dance styles instantly alerts us (and them, the participants) to their intrinsic gender-culture differences. The men's dance style is a crystallisation of what it means to be a male member of their culture. The women's dance style is a crystallisation of what it means to be a female member of that culture. Indeed, in some tribal societies the cultures which the men and women dance are so different that it is as if the two sexes came from different worlds – which is, of course, precisely the case.

I do not doubt, on the other hand, that some 'unisex' cultures could be found in which dance and cultural realities exhibit few gender-specific differences. The majority of socio-cultural systems probably exist somewhere in the middle of this kline between the sexually dymorphic and the unisex. In our own culture, in recent times, we have seen the most unusual phenomenon: extreme fluctuations in the degree of gender differentiation of cultural systems. Such a phenomenon, especially given the comparatively short time-span within which it has occurred, must be unique in human history.

When I was a teenager growing up in an American suburb in the late 1950s and early 1960s I was taught to dance at school, against my will, I might add. Whether 'slow' or 'fast' these dance steps and the macho behavioural activities which framed dance movement per se had one thing in common: the male led. The male chose with whom he would dance. The male (if the female consented to dance with him – for she always had, if nothing else, the terrible power of rejection) physically supported the female. The male determined the rhythm and the style of their relationship in time and space. The female – as in 'real life' – followed his lead.[11]

At the time that I had just about managed to do this, a social revolution occurred – a revolution of gender and culture which was spelled out on the dance-floors of America and Britain long before such things were written or spoken about. Suddenly males did not ask girls to dance, nor did they define the rhythm and style of the encounter. As with hippy clothing and adornment styles, dance was heralding a brave new unisex world.

However, when the film *Saturday Night Fever* was released in the late 1970s, it became clear, beyond a shadow of a doubt, that this new world would never become a reality, if, indeed, it ever was such for even an alternative minority. Here we saw a complete return at least in terms of gender differentiation to the norms of dance, behaviour and culture which existed prior to the unisex experiments of the late 1960s. The male asks the girl to be his partner. The male physically supports the female. The male sets the pace and style of the dance; the male is the centre of attention.

'Disco', despite its 'alternative' popular connotations (i.e. one's parents saw it as completely opposed to the dance styles of their day) brought a return of Western society's traditional assumptions of gender. There may be less touching and therefore less possibilities of the male physically supporting the female and the business of males asking females to dance may be less verbal and formal, but simply by observing a disco dance-floor in, say, the Costa Brava, it is clear that here we have returned to a dance/cultural system where men lead and women follow. For example, the male approaches the female on the dance floor, makes eye contact, checks for rejection or approval while the female, if and when the situation becomes one of a couple dancing together, marks time until she can respond to the style and rhythm of dance established by the male.

Disco and the male/female cultures which it embodies, however, are not all-embracing and since *Saturday Night Fever* we have also seen the rise of various alternative subcultures which continue the unisex direction of the hippies in dance, body decoration and world view. One is thinking here of punks, gothics, the New Psychedelics and so forth. For example, the 'pogo' dance of the punks, like their adornment styles, makes little or no distinction between male and female.

This must serve to remind us that 'the West' is no longer, if indeed it ever was, a single cultural system. Aside from Normal Western Male Culture and Normal Western Female Culture there is also to be taken into consideration an ever-increasing cultural pluralism in the form of the new 'tribes' – each with its own values, beliefs, lifestyle assumptions, adornment styles and dance styles and in most cases, each with its own gender-specific sub-sub-culture.[12] These 'tribes', like any of the traditional tribal or peasant social systems we have discussed previously, achieve a cultural reality primarily and most fundamentally through the medium of style – physical cultural style as embodied in dress, adornment and dance.

For while the modern age may have provided us with communication media which can instantly broadcast and internationalise our dress and dance styles, even we have not succeeded in finding an alternative to stylistic expression as an embodiment of culture. In this regard we are, as our most distant ancestors were, dependent upon style – in our dress and dance – as the definitive means by which we can crystallise our social experiences into cultural realities. Whether our cultures are traditional or modern, male, female or (hypothetically) unisex, they would cease to exist if we did not wear them and dance them. At the most fundamental and significant level, to be a punk, as to be a Masai, is to dress and move as one. Words fail us in such metaphysical territory and while Wittgenstein may well be right that 'What we cannot speak about we must pass over in silence'[13] that has never stopped human beings from achieving some bottom-line, schematic cultural reality in their dress and dance. For even in a disco in Benidorm the movement of sweaty bodies in time and space can sketch out the schematic outlines of some much-longed-for utopian society.

Notes and References

1. See J. Kristeva (1978) for a fuller discussion of the power of the word in the Judaeo-Christian tradition of thought.
2. The work of Alan Lomax and his choreometrics team (1968), which is also of interest here, will be discussed later in the paper.
3. For a more detailed discussion of this from a variety of perspectives see T. Polhemus, ed. (1978).
4. See A. Lomax, ed. (1968), p. 223.
5. This development became increasingly necessary as the realisation grew that song could be best defined as 'danced speech'.
6. Ibid., p. 223.
7. Ibid., p. 234.
8. However, for critical assessments of these see A. P. Royce (1980), chapter 6, and S. Youngerman (1974).
9. Durkheim sets out his view of society as a 'reality sui generis' in the Preface of the second edition to *The Rules of the Sociological Method* (1982).
10. It is perhaps useful to note that sex refers to biological maleness or femaleness whereas gender refers to features that are associated with being male or female which are socially constructed and defined.
11. One is reminded, here, of a famous quote by Ginger Rogers who, when asked if she considered herself to be as good a dancer as Fred Astaire, replied: 'Let's put it this way, I did everything he did but in high heels and backwards.'

12. It is important to state that no qualitative distinction is being made here between traditional and modern in terms of a unilineal evolutionary framework.
13. L. Wittgenstein (1961), p. 74.

Bibliography

G. Bateson and M. Mead, *Balinese Character* (Special Publications of the New York Academy of Sciences, Vol. II, 1942).

R. Birdwhistell, *Kinesics and Context* (London: Allen Lane, 1971).

M. Douglas, *Natural Symbols* (London: Barrie & Rockliff, 1970).

E. Durkheim, *The Rules of Sociological Method*, ed. S. Lukes (London: Macmillan, 1982).

R. Hertz, 'The Pre-eminence of the Right Hand: A Study in Religious Polarity', in R. Hertz, *Death and the Right Hand* (Aberdeen: Cohen & West, 1960).

J. Kristeva, 'Gesture: Practice or Communication?' in T. Polhemus (ed.), *Social Aspects of the Human Body* (Harmondsworth: Penguin, 1978).

A. Lomax (ed.), *Folk Song Style and Culture* (Washington, DC, American Association for the Advancement of Science, Publication No. 88, 1968).

M. Mauss, 'Techniques of the Body', *Economy and Society*, Vol. II, No. 1 (1973), pp. 70–88.

M. Mead and F. C. Macgregor, *Growth and Culture* (New York: Putnam, 1951).

T. Polhemus, 'Social Bodies', in J. Benthall and T. Polhemus, (eds), *The Body as a Medium of Expression* (London: Allen Lane, 1975).

T. Polhemus and L. Procter, *Fashion and Anti-Fashion* (London: Thames & Hudson, 1978).

T. Polhemus (ed.), *Social Aspects of the Human Body* (Harmondsworth: Penguin, 1978).

T. Polhemus, *Body Styles*, (Luton: Lennard, 1988).

A. P. Royce, *The Anthropology of Dance* (Bloomington: Indiana University Press, 1980).

L. Wittgenstein, *Tractatus Logico-Philosophicus* (London: Routledge & Kegan Paul, 1961).

S. Youngerman, 'Curt Sachs and his Heritage: A Critical Review of World History of the Dance with a Survey of Recent Studies that Perpetuate his Ideas', *Cord News*, Vol. 6, No. 2 (1974), pp. 6–17.

2 Dancing in the Dark:
Rationalism and the Neglect of Social Dance

ANDREW H. WARD

This essay is concerned with dance as an activity of everyday life and, more specifically, with how dance has been represented within particular kinds of sociological literature. The paper is premised upon three related and, I think, uncontentious assumptions. These are that dance is generally a neglected topic for analysis; that it is inherently social; and that, as a non-verbal form of communication, dance is categorised as being non-rational. (This latter assumption has particular consequences for the study of dance that – as we shall see – are highly significant.)

Of course, establishing that any field of study has been ignored is a standard way of justifying the occurrence of new work in that area, but the paucity of scholarship on dance is remarkable. Experts may disagree over which form of dance activity is the *most* ignored[1] but practitioners in – for example – anthropology,[2] aesthetics,[3] and sociology[4] have all bemoaned the lack of '. . . substantial written material to guide [an] interest in dance'.[5]

But is dance really ignored? Perhaps the facts, for instance that dance is not a part of the National Curriculum and that there are only 11 higher education dance courses in the UK,[6] simply indicate that dance is no longer a significant phenomenon in Britain, and that the coverage it receives accurately reflects its general importance in society? Apart from the self-fulfilling prophecy inherent in this as an argument, empirically such a view cannot be sustained. Standard statistical surveys indicate the prominent part dance continues to play in British cultural life. For example, the 1989 edition of *Social Trends*[7] reports that after 'going out for a meal or drink' dancing is the most popular 'social and cultural activity' in Britain. Similarly, the 1986 *Gallup Survey of Britain*[8] reveals dancing to be significantly the most frequently practised 'cultural activity'; whereas the Department of Education and Science's massive survey *Young People in the 80s*[9] shows that 54 per cent of boys and 59 per cent of girls attend discos and 22 per cent of young people identified 'going to the disco' as their favoured activity. (More than for any other pursuit.)

Such data indicate not merely that dance is a regularly practised activity but that for many people in this society it is *the* most popular cultural activity. And this is borne out by other types of indicator. As an example, *Come Dancing* is the longest running TV programme in the UK (and the longest running music-based programme in the world[10]). Despite the programme's kitsch image (and the derision it provokes), its longevity cannot be summarily dismissed. Some explanation of this lasting appeal is required. And that this may seem to be an unlikely piece of evidence is itself suggestive of the point at issue here. Another indicator points to something even more basic: the tacit knowledge we all possess that in the pleasure hierarchy of social events those that cater for dancing (or at which dancing occurs) score more highly than those that do not (and that this seems to hold regardless of class, race or region). Obviously, this is not to say that whenever dancing takes place pleasure is automatically maximised for everyone; rather, social events where dancing takes place are generally understood as having a particular potential for pleasure maximisation. Commonsensically, then, dance both produces and indicates pleasure.

Given these pointers to the social significance of dance, the question must be addressed as to why dance is ignored? Reasons for this neglect are much more readily found for performance than for social dance. For example, dance scholars such as Thomas and Redfern offer the explanation that other arts are '. . . more accessible to study than dance by virtue of the fact that a researcher can consult a text or score'.[11] Because there is no 'universally accepted system' for recording dance its identity and traditions are difficult to 'fix' and 'grasp'. This is obviously a persuasive argument but it is not wholly sufficient. Take the extensive variety of analysis of music in a number of disciplines that do not depend at all upon notational literacy.[12] Not knowing the notes has never been a bar to interpreting music.

A more fundamental argument (and one that covers both performance and social dance) questions whether dance can ever be successfully examined by a sociologist. Blacking, for example, states that dance 'eludes straightforward sociological explanation because its structures are conceived non verbally';[13] whilst McRobbie tells us that 'dance seems to retain at its centre a solid resistance to analysis'.[14] Although these are slightly different points (one referring to the nature of sociology, the other to dance) at their heart is the same issue: the essential non-rationality of dance. They can be seen to feed into the thesis that because sociology – the Logos of the Socius – comprises modes of discourse steeped in and wedded to particular forms of rationality that are by definition literate the discipline is unable to cope with dance.[15] In a sense this reverses the Thomas/Redfern point. They explained that there was no formal or standardised language through which dance could be recorded. Here the formal and standardised forms of language which constitute sociology apparently do not allow for a discursive treatment of dance.

What is interesting here is that there is a synchronicity between this perception of sociology's response to dance and a more general conception of the place social dance is deemed to have in society. Developed into an argument,[16] this conception holds that, as a non-verbal form of communication, dance is non-rational and thus more important within pre-literate than other social structures. From which it follows that within rational, industrial/post-industrial societies dance will be peripheral to the main forms of activity and social relations. Where dance does appear as a central life interest this appearance is culturally anachronistic and dislocated. And those groups for whom dance does play this role are definitionally marginal and almost always suspect. The exception here is young people for whom dance is an acceptable (if tiresome) central life interest because they can grow out of it. For them, an enthusiasm for dance indicates a transitional rather than an absolute marginality.

The postulate here is that this view comprises a dominant perception of dance within this society.[17] It contains a number of hypotheses upon which its overall predictive value depends. These are that:

1. dance is a marginal phenomenon in this society and therefore could receive little rigorous attention;
2. those groups for whom dance is a central activity will be socially marginalised;
3. if dance is considered it is most likely to be young people who are the focus of study, and

4. the tendency will be to link dance practices with mainstream activities.

The substance of this paper attempts to demonstrate that this postulate is correct and that these hypotheses hold. Dance is ignored because it is an activity outside the rationalist auspices of modern society. There is no standardised notational system or language to represent dance whilst the forms of language of sociology have generally proved to be unable systematically to address dance or to take it seriously. Given the importance actors themselves attribute to it,[18] the neglect of dance by the discipline glosses actors' interpretations of their own activity in a way that has been widely denounced as epistemologically unsound.[19]

Yet, as this paper's concern is with the treatment of dance in particular kinds of sociological literature, the discipline's avoidance of dance cannot be complete. And certainly within ethnographic and community studies dance is discussed but virtually always with reference to young people. This very modest 'tradition' of dance references makes even more surprising those community and youth studies' texts which make no mention of dance whatsoever.[20] The references that there are have three key features in common: their slightness – usually just a few lines, and even in more sustained treatments[21] the attention is never solely on dance; the absence of any reference to dance or movement scholarship; and the tendency to talk around dance (about dance venues,[22] its social functions[23] and political significance[24]). As Mungham says in one of the fullest treatments there is within the literature 'this study is not of dancing as such . . .'.[25]

Obviously any sociological address of dance must presume its sociality. And there are a number of different senses in which the sociality of dance is conceived. One is that relationships within dance might be seen as reflecting or re-establishing relations outside the dance arena, so Chambers speaks of dancing that 'involved ground rules that had been persuasively laid down elsewhere, outside the walls of the dance hall or youth club';[26] whilst Mungham tells us (in the study mentioned earlier) that 'it was typical for working class youth not to venture far away from their own patch'. This means that dancing and local dance halls were characterised by an 'effective ghettoization' which 'both reflected and reinforced the tightness and solidarity of working class community'.[27] The occasion of dance here, then, is seen to 'reflect' and 'reinforce' other social relations.

Alternatively, dance activity can be seen as serving some function for the wider social context (i.e. society). So that within the literature there are, for example, many references to dance as providing a 'meeting place' for marriage partners.[28] Here dance is institutionally functional.

Other writers have chosen to catalogue what dance can achieve socially. Brinson (primarily a dance scholar but also a sociologist) provides the following list. As well as being a shared experience, dance acts to fortify the sense of community, to regulate behaviour, as an organ of social control, as a constraint, and as an educator. Dance also transmits taboos and conditions youthful enthusiasm![29]

These senses of dance's sociality are complimented by a range of depictions of the character of dance found in the literature. Brake, for example, speaks of dance in black popular culture as providing a means of *resistance*.[30] Chambers[31] and Frith[32] tell us of dance as *escapism*; McRobbie of dance as the 'purveyor of fantasy'.[33] Willis, in his study of a motor-bike culture, talks of dance as being *homological*: 'a direct extension of the motor-bike boy's attitudes and style in general life'.[34] Similarly, Hebdige[35] indicates that punk dancing comprises part of a cultural *bricolage*.

These references are concerned with young people and/or socially marginal groups and, certainly, their tendency is to link dance practices with mainstream activities. Indeed, what might be surprising to those who do not know the field is the functionalist tenor of these views of dance. Dance reinforces community; it regulates, controls, constrains and conditions behaviour. Dance facilitates marriage. Even the roles of dance as escapism and as fantasy are open to functionalist interpretation. For society to continue operating effectively (it can be argued) it is necessary for individuals to have some release from their daily routines and pressures.

These releases – in this case dance – act as safety valves which enable the defusing of frustrations which would otherwise accumulate to threaten the social order. This is a classic line of argument[36] offered both by traditional functionalists and by their Marxist counterparts. The contention here is *not* that any of these writers are functionalists (indeed, we shall see how some of them provide clear anti-functionalist views of dance). It is that what they say of dance implies more or less strongly a functionalist logic and that it is notable how readily these views fit with a catalogue of similar views that have appeared through history and across disciplines which depict dance in explicitly functionalist terms.[37]

If this paper's central tenet regarding the perception of dance in this society is correct this affinity to functionalism should not be unexpected. Functionalist analyses are archetypically rationalist. They perform the alchemy of making rational what at first sight is unreasonable. They direct attention away from both individual actors and the specificity of acts (for example, dancers and dance events) to focus on some broader rationale. In other words, the different depictions of dance recorded here have the heavy scent of the rationalist postulate about them. They explain what otherwise within the rationalist hegemony would be inexplicable.

To pursue this a little further: a corollary of the idea that dance facilitates the finding of marriage partners is that dance is 'a convention of courtship, dating and sexual bargaining'.[38] So in Mungham's memorable phrase, dance represents 'the Meccanization of the sexual impulse',[39] where 'chatting up a girl becomes the centrepiece, the core-drama of the evening's play'.[40] This view of dance as 'an unfortunate prerequisite to courting'[41] for 'packs of males moving in predatory pursuit of female victims'[42] finds echoes throughout the literature. Given what was said earlier, its frequency suggests that dance comes to be discussed because as dance is a means of obtaining sex it is not necessary to discuss dance in its own terms at all. Dance becomes important only for what it can enable to be achieved. This apparent inability to appreciate that dancing is an end in itself says as much about the male, intellectual writers who express this view, as it does about the practices they seek to depict and analyse.[43]

What is missing in views of this kind is the realisation that dance itself is not just a means to sex (although of course it may well be such) but that it is or can be a form of sexual expression in itself. Frith understands this well: 'the most obvious feature of dancing as an activity is its sexuality – institutionalised dancing . . . is redolent with sexual tensions and possibilities, as private desires get public display, as repressed needs are proudly shared . . .'.[44] And Chambers extends the point: dance permits 'a deeper, internalised moment where a serious self-realisation – sexual and social, private and public – is being pursued'.[45] These authors speak directly, if not about dance, at least about what is happening when people dance. Here attention is not brought to dance to be immediately deflected elsewhere. And their focus on needs, desires and self-realisation is clearly different from the mechanistic view of dance as a 'routine and joyless affair' carried out in pursuit of sex by boys whose emotional responses are merely 'stereotypical'.[46] Rather than the implication of the hidden hand of society determining unconscious behaviour patterns the emphasis here is on individuals coming to terms with their circumstances with dance providing the moment in which 'commonsense is often taunted, teased and twisted apart'.[47]

A similarly focused (but more sustained) approach to dance comes in McRobbie's 'Dance and Social Fantasy';[48] a paper which certainly advances serious discussion of dance. Central to McRobbie's argument is the refusal to accept the reduction of dance to the promise or provision of sex. In support of this, she describes a fundamental change in the relationship between males and dance. She tells us that 'men can now demonstrate sophisticated dancing skills with expertise and pleasure without inviting criticism or disdain from their male peers'.[49] But in asserting this I believe McRobbie to be caught up in a myth about masculinity and dance which, although common, perishes with historical scrutiny. The contention that dance has been 'an ordeal or something faintly ridiculous for men' reflects rather less the empirical reality of dance activities than it does the pervasive marginalisation and neglect of dance that even sensitive writers cannot entirely shake off. This is not to say that for some (even many) men dance has not been an ordeal or faintly ridiculous, but it is to reject this as a *categorical* assertion. What has never been explained is why, in a patriarchal society, if men were so uneasy about dance did it persist? Why did men allow it to? Why did it not become only a female pursuit?

Post-war cultural history reveals quite a different picture from one that depicts decades of reluctantly dancing males. From the tap-dancing craze which broke out immediately after the war to acid-house today, boys have been dancing and doing so not just in 'desultory fugs and clinches'[50] but with conviction and frequently great skill. When Frith remarks that 'whatever else happened to mass music in the 50s and 60s there were many people . . . who never stopped dancing'[51] he is obviously not saying that only girls were dancing or that they were always accompanied by boys 'uncomfortably, shuffling around the floor . . .'.[52] With the advent of Rock 'n' Roll in 1956, Teddy boys took to the floor, and very shortly rock 'n' roll dancing became 'a sort of art form'.[53] A writer of the period indicated the centrality of dance to these boys when he declared that for the Ted 'the point where he [felt] most at one with the culture of contemporary society' was when 'he was incited to movement' by 'manufactured voices bawling'.[54] As different dance moves became fashionable – such as the Twist, Stomp and Shake – boys were there, not marginally but centrally. And by the time the Mods arrived dancing had become an epidemic amongst the young. 'It was practically all they ever did' and 'the guys were the focus of attention and girls took a back seat'.[55] Moreover, not only was it no longer necessary to have partners; if you did, likely as not they would have been of the same sex.

After the Mods this pattern of same-sex dancing was frequently repeated. In 1979 Taylor wrote 'Skinheads are great dancers . . . but never with a girl, always either alone or with other Skins'.[56] The male, heavy metal 'idiot dancers' always danced together. Punk dances – the Pogo, the Pose and the Robot – could only 'allow for a minimum of sociability, i.e. it could involve two people. The "couple" were generally of the same sex, physical contact was ruled out and the relationship depicted in the dance was a "professional" one'.[57] Boys danced alone, together, with girls and in groups. For Willis's motor-bike boys dancing was almost as important as the bikes themselves.[58] '"Northern Soul" was largely a male dominated, dance culture.'[59] For the principally male and narcissistic Glamrockers, New Romantics and Casuals dance and performance was absolutely central. Reggae spawned a particular variety of male-only dancing,[60] and there are very few female Hip Hop exponents.[61] But even more significant than these examples was the Disco explosion. In the 1970s 'disco music had become the dance music par excellence'.[62] Disco departed from the Mecca dance halls and even the Mod cellar parties and indeed from everything that had gone before in one simple but vital respect: its continuity. Again Frith describes this well: 'disco pleasure is not closed off, bound by the song structures, musical beginnings and ends, but is expressed, rather, through an open-ended series of repetitions, a shifting *intensity* of involvement'.[63] As the concept of continuous sound took hold, not just in the sense of playing one track immediately after another which had been standard practice for years, but in the sense of continuity between tracks, the idea of the dancing 'partner' suffered another blow. Dance activities and relations were as diffuse as the music. Because the clear interchanges between tracks that are essential for the rituals of finding, selecting and enjoining with partners do not occur in Disco, the role of partner cannot be enacted. To quote Frith once more, Disco is 'an experience in which the dancer is, simultaneously, completely self-centred and quite selfless, completely sexualised and, in gender terms, quite sexless'.[64] But Disco also revived the idea of the validity and necessity of formal dancing instruction. Boys wanted to be taught how to dance. As one male ex-disco devotee recalls: 'it really caught on . . . everybody was going to dancing lessons'.[65]

Disco was a remarkable moment in an extraordinary cultural history. Obviously within this history not every boy was a Ted, Mod, Punk, etc. but there were very few young people who did not feel the influence of these movements and whose actions did not in some part reflect this influence. Apart from challenging the view that boys have been traditionally or categorically absent or reluctant dancers, this discussion points to another important issue. Each of these youth cultures represents and constitutes the structural realities of race, class and gender. And this raises the question of the relationship between particular dance activities and their social contexts. Two approaches suggest themselves here. Firstly, one which holds that this dance activity *happens* to be performed by these people in this place at this time but others in the same place or elsewhere at different times could carry it out. Or, secondly, the view that a given dance activity *can only* take place within its originating subculture with its particular social conditions. It cannot transfer, or if it does, it is only to appear as pastiche or mimicry.

This second approach has many echoes within dance scholarship and the sociological literature. For example, when the dance historian Martin tells us that in the nineteenth century 'ballet could not have been established in America because it was a foreign art form that had its origins in the hierarchical social order of Europe',[66] he is effectively endorsing this approach. And when Brake points out that in modern urban Britain particular dance activities are best carried out by black youths ('white kids cannot do them or do them as well'[67]) he too gives weight to this position. But then the idea of some essential connection between a dance activity and the dancers' social context would seem to be implied within all subcultural analysis. For the project of recognising and analysing subcultures makes little sense unless it is assumed that there is some boundary which distinguishes any one grouping from other cultural formations. It would therefore be explanatorily enigmatic if dance practices in one sphere spilled over to, or were taken up by, others.

The discussion here is not hypothetical. Cultural analysts *do* become puzzled! Frith, albeit in a piece of criticism republished in an academic text, expresses exactly this confusion. At an Aswad concert (black, reggae and hip), Frith rubs shoulders with 'public schoolboys home for the holidays'. The experience appears to disturb Frith acutely. He tells us:

> Aswad's appearance at the Venue was a sell out, but the audience was decidedly uncool. Tall (public school) boys blocked my view. . . , passed each other self-conscious joints, and jogged on the spot with a sort of loose-limbed foppishness. "Fantastic!" they kept agreeing, and I got distracted from whatever was actually happening on stage. My sense was that Aswad hovered around but rarely hit the perfect pitch of their records. However, I brooded more about what was happening on the dance floor, shuffling to the beat as Aswad sang imperviously about African children, mused in their odd, sweet cloudy way about inner city concrete, the dingy white tenement setting of the Afro-Caribbean diaspora. "Fantastic!" exclaimed the boy next to me.[68]

Public school boys are an obviously easy target but to imply either that these boys were being disingenuously enthusiastic about what was from the viewpoint of Frith, the expert rock critic, a low-key performance, or that it was a low-key performance because of the 'uncool, self-conscious, foppish' audience hardly seems a serious response to what is a genuine dilemma: 'the relationship between black performance and white pleasure'.[69]

Of course, if the first approach was followed there would be no problem here. Dance activities can be transferred directly from one social setting to the next because there is only an arbitrary attachment of any dance to its social setting. This approach would seem to depend upon a view of dance as a universal response to and of the human condition. Dance is bound to appear in every society with a common, basic grammar of movement because dance like language, is an innate human capacity.[70] This implies that the central concern here would be the taxonomy of physical movements. Such a concern begs the question of meaning and there are at least two directions in which this question might be pursued. The first is where movements themselves are seen to generate meaning.[71] This is to recognise the 'grammar' of movement as being autonomous within the particular contexts in which it appears and creates semantic textures. The way this view has been developed indicates that it has tremendous predictive powers. For once we had uncovered the deep structural rules of the grammar not only could we predict all human movements but we could go on to prefigure a vocabulary of human meanings. This is possible because the grammar is limited by the body's anatomical structure – 'the laws of hierarchical motility'[72] – and these laws and the meanings that ensue from them are potentially fully knowable. This view indicates that a transferred dance activity will have the same meaning for whoever dances it even though other (perhaps all other) social conditions vary between the originary and secondary dancers.

Alternatively, there is the view that the reality of any dance activity cannot be reduced only to its particular physical movements. Rather these movements obtain their reality from the meaning context from which they emerge: '. . . it is [the dance's] social context that gives it meaning'.[73] And this applies for both the generation and the interpretation of dance. Thus 'although the meanings of different dance styles are . . . ultimately associated with social and cultural systems the act of performing the movements can generate somatic experiences that are detached from specific meanings and can be reinterpreted in a variety of ways'.[74] So the same movements can generate a variety of meanings depending on the particular context in which it takes place, where the context includes the socio-economic background of the dancers.

Few people versed in the social sciences in recent times could support the first view here. Its behaviourism runs counter to the idealism and the materialism that have characterised social scientific thinking since the Second World War. More specifically, the ontology of this view in which the primary reality for humans is their physical behaviour would now be seen as untenable, not least because the very identification of what a movement is requires a prior 'cognitive framework. Moreover, dance movements do not arbitrarily appear as unconscious motor impulses: they are learnt, deliberately and selectively.

Obviously, Frith would not endorse the anti-sociological tenets of this first approach. What he seems to want to do in the Aswad concert review is to convey that the meaning his public school boys derived was degraded compared to the true meaning that he paradoxically is able to uncover. Clearly, a song about the black experience in Britain is going to have a different semantic impact on a black than a white audience, but it will also make a different impression on a black audience who feel their repression than those who do not or who have never done so. To indicate that public school boys could never know the black experience is one thing and is probably unarguable, but to imply that the meaning they derive from a black band's performance is phoney, unreal or patronising is something quite different and highly contentious.

What is curious about Frith's attitude here is that he, along with many other writers,[75] has recorded how each major British music fashion can be traced back to some prior black form. Indeed, he tells us that 'black musical forms and styles have been aspects of Western popular culture since at least the middle of the nineteenth century',[76] and would undoubtedly concur with Gilroy that 'black styles, music, dress, dance fashion and languages became a determining force shaping the styles, music, dress, fashion and language of urban Britain as a whole'.[77] So the idea of cultural transfer *per se* is not a concern for Frith, it must be the *distance* of this transfer that troubles him so.

But this too is somewhat strange given, for example, Frith's sensitive account of Disco[78] which (as he acknowledges) has undergone remarkable geocultural transferences. Beginning is black clubs in Detroit and New York, becoming a youth fashion across the Western world, and being entrenched now as a virtually universal currency amongst urban gays,[79] Disco has shown a striking lack of cultural specificity. Other dance movements are equally mobile. Acid House may have its roots in Chicago but its home is now the English home counties where its exponents defy traditional subcultural classification. The 'moral panic'[80] that Acid House or, rather, the drug Ecstasy has engendered masks what the craze is about. Yes, it is based on a particular synthesised sound. Yes, hallucinogenics are part of the scene. But both these are artefacts to what is ultimately a *dance* movement. Reading the popular press in 1988 and '89 would hardly have made this clear. Apparently even here the rationalist postulate is in operation: that people should want to travel many miles in secret to *dance* in fields or warehouses is beyond the grasp of reason.

Frith's perplexity stems from his vestigial commitment to subcultural analysis. The view of society as a stack of subcultural lockers makes it problematic to understand aspects of social reality through positing an overly static and totalised view of the world. As Gilroy explains, 'culture is not a fixed and imperme-able feature of social relations. Its forms change, develop, combine and are dispersed in historical practices.'[81] Indeed, 'the defensive walls around each subculture gradually crumble and new forms . . . are created in the synthesis and transcendence of previous styles'.[82] So on the one hand we can see how black British cultures 'cannot be contained neatly with the structures of the nation-state' because 'Black Britain defines itself crucially as part of a diaspora' which draws inspiration from cultural forms 'developed by black populations elsewhere'[83] On the other hand we can note how 'the cultural resources of the Afro-Caribbean communities provide a space in which whites are able to discover meaning in black histories, style and language . . .'.[84] This opens up the possibility of a cultural phenomenon – dance, for example – not only being understood 'as a feature of the socio-cultural context of its creation' but approached in terms of how it also 'constitutes reflexively a significant resource for understanding that context itself'.[85]

The particular forms of rationalism that have until very recently characterised cultural analysis and given so little room for the address of dance are now being challenged. Attention is turning to modes of analysis in which 'the relation between groups and classes' are identified as 'continually shifting'; where 'complex ideological formations' 'structure' 'lived relations' and are 'composed of elements derived from diverse sources [that] have to be actively combined, dismantled, bricolaged'; and 'new politically effective alliances can be secured between different factional groupings' which can no longer be related to 'static, homogenous classes'.[86] This new analytic direction refuses to 'subsume' the social's '. . . . contradictory dynamics underneath the impossible quest for universal validity claims'.[87]

The recent developments in cultural analysis map out a conceptual and theoretical terrain that make more likely a rigorous appreciation of dance. The move away from the ultra-rationalist obsession with ultimate causes; the withering away of the utopian practice of evaluating phenomena as leading to or standing in the way of some final solution; the opening up of the categories of race and gender; the recognition of erotic possibilities beyond phallocentric limits; the focus on the Subject and Desire; the development of conceptual frameworks that can sustain 'contradictions' (rather than see them as epistemic faults); the abandoning of the assumption that the interconnectedness of phenomena always follow predictable pathways. All these developments run counter to that rationalism which has ensured dance's neglect. With them rests the possibility of bringing dancing out of the dark.[88]

Notes and References

1. Thomas tells us that 'when sociologists and cultural analysts do display an interest in dance, their attention is drawn towards consideration of "popular" dancing as opposed to "art" or performance dance', H. Thomas (1986), pp. 8–9; whilst Brinson speaks of the need 'to correct the balance between excessive attention to stage dance, so noticeable in Western dance studies, and the broader issues that need consideration for any full understanding of dance is present-day society', P. Brinson (1985), p. 206.
2. P. Spencer (1985), pp. ix, 1.
3. B. Redfern (1988), p. 3.
4. G. Mungham (1976), p. 84.
5. A. McRobbie (1984), p. 131.
6. B. Heap (1989), p. 139.
7. HMSO 'Social Trends', No. 19 (HMSO, 1989), Table 10.3.
8. G. Heald and R. Wybrow (1986), p. 260.
9. DES 'Young People in the 80s' (HMSO, 1983), pp. 74, 32.
10. *Radio Times*, 19–25 August 1989.
11. H. Thomas, (1986), pp. 12–13; see also B. Redfern, op. cit., pp. 15–18.
12. See, for example, T. Adorno (1949), and, for popular music, S. Frith (1983).
13. J. Blacking (1975), p. 89.
14. A. McRobbie (1984), p. 143.
15. For a discussion of these themes see M. Phillipson (1976).
16. H. Thomas, op. cit. pp. 9–10.
17. Dominant in formal or academic rather than in normative terms.

18. See notes 7–9 above.

19. D. Walsh, et al. (1972), passim.

20. To take just one example of each: B. Williamson (1982) and K. Roberts (1983).

21. For example, A. McRobbie, op. cit., also focuses on a range of other cultural artefacts (films, magazines, TV programmes).

22. G. Mungham, op. cit.; D. Robins and P. Cohen (1978), pp. 47–57.

23. See the discussion on the functionalist implications of many of the key descriptions of dance that follows later in the paper.

24. M. Brake (1985), pp. 126–7.

25. G. Mungham, op. cit. p. 82.

26. I. Chambers (1985), p. 41.

27. G. Mungham, op. cit. p. 90.

28. Ibid., p. 99. But also see N. Dennis et al. (1956), p. 126; M. Kerr (1958), p. 32; R. Roberts (1973), p. 233 and Brake, op. cit., p. 170; Frith, op. cit., p. 245; and Chambers, op. cit. p. 235. For an interesting historical perspective of dance (that focuses on a different class location), see L. Davidoff (1986), pp. 49–50.

29. P. Brinson, op. cit. p. 207.

30. M. Brake, op. cit. p. 126.

31. I. Chambers (1986), p. 135.

32. S. Frith, 1983, p. 245.

33. A. McRobbie, op. cit. p. 134.

34. P. Willis (1975), pp. 246–7.

35. D. Hebdige (1979), pp. 107–9.

36. For a useful overview of the classic functionalist positions see W. Moore (1978).

37. Examples of this approach to dance are discussed and to be found in P. Spencer, ed., op. cit. and R. Copeland and M. Cohen, eds (1983).

38. G. Mungham, in Mungham and Pearson, op. cit. p. 85.

39. G. Mungham, op. cit. p. 92.

40. G. Mungham, op. cit. p. 93.

41. A. McRobbie, op. cit. p. 143.

42. J. Clarke and C. Critcher (1975), p. 162.

43. *Re* C. Wittman (1987): 'There is some risk in saying that dance forms "celebrate" or "represent" something else, anything else. The dancing is intact and self-sufficient – and all the struggling to find proper meaning is only necessary because we have been so brainwashed by our social and sexual conditioning. I believe that these dances are not sacred in some symbolic way – they are not representational of some greater truth. They *are* that truth, pure and simple.' p. 85.

44. S. Frith, 1983, p. 19.

45. I. Chambers, 1985, p. 17.

46. G. Mungham, op. cit. p. 92.

47. I. Chambers, op. cit. p. 210.

48. In A. McRobbie and M. Nava (1984).

49. A. McRobbie, op. cit. p. 143.

50. D. Hebdige, op. cit. p. 108.

51. S. Frith, 1983, p. 245.

52. G. Mungham, op. cit. p. 94.

53. P. Everett (1986), p. 33.
54. T. Fyrel (1963), p. 78.
55. P. Everett, op. cit. p. 56.
56. I. Walker (1982), p. 8.
57. Hebdige, op. cit. p. 108.
58. P. Willis, op. cit.
59. I. Chambers, 1985, p. 146.
60. S. Jones (1988), chapter 2.
61. S. Hager (1985).
62. M. Brake, op. cit. p. 125.
63. S. Frith, 1983, p. 246.
64. Ibid.
65. R. Everett, op. cit. p. 140.
66. *Re* H. Thomas, op. cit., p. 92; J. Martin (1967).
67. M. Brake, op. cit. p. 127.
68. S. Frith (1988), p. 186.
69. Ibid., p. 188. Frith also pursues this theme in his 1983, pp. 15–23.
70. The echoes of de Saussure and Chomsky are clear here. See also P. Spencer, ed., op. cit. pp. 35–8.
71. D. Williams (1978), pp. 211–30. I am grateful to Helen Thomas for bringing Williams' work to my attention.
72. D. Williams, op. cit.
73. J. Middleton (1985), p. 165.
74. J. Blacking, op. cit. p. 68.
75. *Re* M. Blake, op. cit. and D. Hebdige, op. cit.
76. S. Frith (1983), p. 15.
77. P. Gilroy (1987), p. 155.
78. S. Frith (1983), pp. 243–8.
79. R. Dyer has discussed the affinity of gays to discos in his influential 'In Defence of Disco', *Gay Left*, 8, 1978.
80. *Re* S. Cosgrove, 'Forbidden Fruits', *New Statesman and Society*, 2 September 1988.
81. P. Gilroy, op. cit. p. 217.
82. Ibid., p. 217.
83. Ibid., p. 154.
84. Ibid., p. 217.
85. H. Thomas, op. cit. p. 4.
86. D. Hebdige (1988), chapter 8, p. 205.
87. Ibid., p. 205.
88. Copious thanks are due to Helen Thomas for sharing so many dance performances with me, for introducing me to dance scholarship and for demonstrating that sociologists can meaningfully discuss dance.

Bibliography

T. Adorno, *Philosophy of Modern Music*, trans. A. Mitchell and W. Bloomster, (London: Sheed & Ward, 1949).
J. Blacking, 'Movement, Dance, Music and the Venda Girls' Initiation Cycle'

in P. Spencer (ed.), *Society and the Dance*, (Cambridge University Press, 1975).

M. Brake, *Comparative Youth Cultures*, (London: Routledge & Kegan Paul, 1985).

P. Brinson, 'Epilogue: Anthropology and the Study of Dance' in P. Spencer (ed.), *Society and the Dance*, (Cambridge University Press, 1985).

I. Chambers, *Urban Rhythms – Pop Music and Popular Culture*, (London: Macmillan, 1985).

I. Chambers, *Popular Culture*, (London: Methuen, 1986).

J. Clarke and C. Critcher, *The Devil Makes Work*, (London: Macmillan, 1975).

R. Copeland and M. Cohen (eds), *What is Dance?*, (Oxford University Press, 1983).

S. Cosgrove, 'Forbidden Fruits', *New Statesman and Society*, 2 September 1988.

L. Davidoff, *The Best Circles*, (London: Century Hutchinson, 1986).

N. Dennis, F. Henriques and C. Slaughter, *Coal is our Life*, (London: Eyre & Spottiswoode, 1956).

DES, *Young People in the 80s*, (London: HMSO, 1983).

R. Dyer, 'In Defence of Disco', *Gay Left*, 8, (1978).

P. Everett, *You'll Never Be 16 Again*, (London: BBC Publications, 1986).

S. Frith, *Sound Effects*, (London, Constable, 1983).

S. Frith, *Music For Pleasure*, (Cambridge: Polity, 1988).

F. Fyrel, *The Insecure Offenders*, (Harmondsworth: Penguin, 1963).

P. Gilroy, *There Ain't No Black in the Union Jack*, (London: Hutchinson, 1987).

S. Hager, *Hip Hop*, (New York: St. Martin's Press, 1985).

G. Heald and R. Wybrow, *The Gallup Survey of Britain*, (London: Croom Helm, 1986).

B. Heap, *The Complete Degree Course Offers*, (London: Trotman, 1989).

D. Hebdige, *Subculture: The Meaning of Style*, (London: Methuen, 1979).

D. Hebdige, *Hiding in the Light*, (London: Comedia/Routledge & Kegan Paul, 1988).

HMSO, *Social Trends*, No. 19, (London, 1989).

S. Jones, *Black Culture, White Youth*, (London: Macmillan, 1988).

M. Kerr, *The People of Ship Street*, (London: Routledge & Kegan Paul, 1958).

J. Martin, *America Dancing*, (New York: Dance Horizons, 1967).

A. McRobbie, 'Dance and Social Fantasy' in A. McRobbie and M. Nava (eds) *Gender and Generation*, (London: Macmillan, 1984).

J. Middleton, 'The Dance Among the Lugbara of Uganda' in P. Spencer (ed.), *Society and the Dance*, (Cambridge University Press, 1985).

W. Moore, 'Functionalism' in T. Bottomore and R. Nisbet (eds), *A History of Sociological Analysis*, (London: Heinemann, 1978).

G. Mungham, 'Youth in Pursuit of Itself' in G. Mungham and G. Pearson (eds), *Working Class Youth Cultures*, (London: Routledge & Kegan Paul, 1976).

M. Phillipson, 'Sociology, Metaphorically Speaking', *Writing Sociology*, No. 1, (1976).

Radio Times, London, BBC Magazines (1989).

B. Redfern, *Dance, Art and Aesthetics*, (London: Dance Books, 1988).

K. Roberts, *Youth and Leisure*, (London: George Allen & Unwin, 1983).

R. Roberts, *The Classic Slum*, (Harmondsworth: Penguin, 1973).

D. Robins and P. Cohen, *Knuckle Sandwich*, (Harmondsworth: Penguin, 1978).

P. Spencer (ed.), *Society and the Dance*, (Cambridge University Press, 1985).

H. Thomas, *Movement, Modernism and Contemporary Culture: Issues for a Critical Sociology of Dance*, PhD Thesis, University of London Goldsmiths' College (1986).

D. Walsh, in P. Filmer, M. Phillipson, D. Silverman and D. Walsh, *New Directions in Sociological Theory*, (London: Collier-Macmillan, 1972).

I. Walker, 'Skinheads: The Cult of Trouble' in P. Barker (ed.), *The Other Britain*, (London: Routledge & Kegan Paul, 1982).

D. Williams, 'Deep Structures of the Dance', *Yearbook of Symbolic Anthropology*, 1, (1978).

B. Williamson, *Class, Culture and Community*, (London: Routledge & Kegan Paul, 1982).

P. Willis, 'The Expressive Style of a Motor Bike Culture' in J. Benthall and T. Polhemus (eds), *The Body as a Medium of Expression*, (London: Allen Lane, 1975).

C. Wittman, 'Loving Dance' in F. Abbott (ed.), *New Men, New Minds*, (California: The Crossing Press/Freedom, 1987).

3 Ballet, Gender and Cultural Power

CYNTHIA J. NOVACK

People know and understand ballet because they watch it or study how to do it or perform it. In more formal terms, they participate in widespread social and cultural structures through which they learn about ballet, thus perpetuating and sometimes altering it. These structures are both institutional (ballet classes, dance schools, companies, performances, film presentations, producing organisations and government agencies) and ideological (beliefs about art, dance, choreography, the body and gender). These structures also exist through time, so that the ways people have created ballet historically affect the present.

In this essay, I would like to talk about gender in ballet. I take 'gender' to mean sets of characteristics and practices attributed to a male or female person as distinguished from either the biological sex or the sexuality/sexual preferences of a person. In order to look at these characteristics and practices, I must consider numerous situations in ballet which define gender, often in conjunction with the definition of other major themes or issues.

I am an anthropologist, but I am also a dancer and I begin my investigation of gender in ballet by using my dance experiences as a case study. The method I employ falls under the category of processual analysis in anthropology,[1] an approach which seeks to show 'how ideas, events, and institutions interact and change through time', often by focusing on a case study.[2] This focus assumes that an individual's particular institutional and ideological experiences necessarily raise issues which are shared and which can serve as the basis for a larger commentary. While an anthropological analysis of this sort cannot typify everybody's encounter with ballet (for, in fact, no 'typical' encounter exists), it can help illuminate the themes and constraints that constitute 'gender in ballet'.

To choose my own experiences with ballet as my case study may seem somewhat unorthodox, though it is not unprecedented.[3] I adopt this approach because it allows me to shift between my memories and comments as a dancer and my analyses as an anthropologist, in a sense using autobiography as fieldwork data.[4]

I will also look at the relationship between my case study and discussion and several other commentaries on ballet and gender in ballet. Accounts by people close to the professional sector of ballet, in particular dancers Toni Bentley and Gelsey Kirkland, provide another perspective. Then, commentaries about gender by several viewers of ballet offer further evidence of the interaction of ideas, events and institutions in the definition of gender.

One of my earliest memories: watching my sister, Linda, take her ballet class. Eight years older than I, Linda epitomised everything I wanted to be when I grew up. She danced with grace and authority; observing her, I was amazed that my own sister, who often took care of me and was like a second mother, could transform into a magical presence. I couldn't wait to begin lessons, and at age three, I started my study of dance in the only ballet school in South Charleston, West Virginia. My enthusiastic, though ill-informed, teacher allowed me to dance in pointe shoes at the age of four. Luckily, I sustained no injuries from this highly risky training. My primary recollection is the exalted, thrilling, physical sensation of walking around on my toes.

My early experience with ballet had little to do with seeing ballet performance, although I must have seen some dancing on film and television. But my most immediate contact with ballet came in the dance class, where learning the techniques satisfied my identification with an important role model and my appetite for moving. The vocabulary of the ballet began to pervade my body, effecting its development and shaping my understanding and perception of movement. I experienced potentially harmful techniques as fun.

Continuing my studies at a dance studio in St Louis, Missouri, at age six, I also learned tap dance 'routines'. Tap delighted me with its rhythmic movements and challenging foot coordinations. However, the pervasive attitude of teachers and parents in the dance studio assigned far greater prestige to the study of ballet – according to this view, ballet was more difficult and it was art, whereas anyone could tap and it was entertainment. I knew these things by what people said and by the structure and content of the classes. More time, care and energy were given to ballet, whereas the tap routines were taught for very short periods at the beginning or end of a class. In the annual school recitals in which I performed, those who did ballet counted as the most serious, accomplished dancers.

I rarely saw dancing of any sort on stage, live. Television and movies showed ballet, tap and varieties of Broadway/Hollywood dancing (a hybrid of ballet, tap, and vernacular jazz forms), as either short acts in TV variety shows or as danced interludes in musical comedies. The St Louis Municipal Opera presented eight or ten musical comedies in the park every summer, with one yearly concert appearance by ballet stars from New York. Also, every few years, the American Ballet Theatre came to town, and I could then watch a professional company perform complete ballets.

The men in ballet were total oddities to my (girl) child's eyes. No boys studied in my ballet classes, and I had never seen men dancing in a live performance who wore tights. My girlfriends and I giggled at their costumes and briefly admired their leaping excursions around the stage, but we saved most of our attention for the prima ballerinas' overwhelming skill and beauty. I idolised Melissa Hayden and Maria Tallchief.

What ballet did I experience as a white, lower middle class, midwestern, female American child in the 1950s? Ballet was dance for girls, in my mind and it was an art form – a bit rarified and not frequently performed, something to be studied seriously and treated with respect as well as applause and admiration. Because of the highly technical content of my ballet classes, I saw ballet as an individual's craft, and I attuned myself to the skills of the performers.

The fact that I learned to dance by studying ballet meant that I practised a particular set of exercises and movement combinations for fifteen years, and this kinesthetic reference has remained with me through time. Anyone who watches dance may feel kinesthetic identification, simply because all people move their bodies; years of dancing intensify this kinesthetic imprint. For the children who study ballet, an orientation to the technical content of the ballet performance has been inculcated.

As a child watching the prima ballerina on stage, her evocative power for me resided only minimally in the role she played (the Firebird or the Swan Queen) – I never even got the stories straight until I studied dance history as an adult. The ballerina was an admired female (like my sister), a public figure who had achieved technical perfection, a woman of great accomplishment and agency.

Anyone may interpret my response to ballet as a child – I'm sure that I absorbed complex messages about movement, behaviour and society. Whatever other kinds of analysis one might make, however, my own conscious, positive identification with the female dancer resonates throughout my dance-viewing experience. I have no doubt that it was a major feature of my attraction to ballet as a child. How many other little girls study ballet and form this cultural identification? Even those who dislike practising ballet, or quit their studies, may still feel awe and admiration for the ballerina. Or, in fact, even girls who never study ballet but who see images of the ballet dancer as an admired woman, may identify positively with the ballerina.

Finally, I understood that ballet was classical dance with a long tradition, something I knew years before I formally studied any dance history. It was counterposed to other kinds of dance which were consequently thought of as less serious, less artful, less worthy of respect. For my family, ballet was a means of giving 'culture' to granddaughters of immigrants living in an area of the country with limited cultural opportunities.[5] Implicitly, in segregated St Louis/America, ballet was a dance for a white audience of social status and different from (superior to) the dance associated with black people and show business. It was some years later that I recognised the truncated way in which I had first learned tap dance, devoid of improvisation, technical intricacy, and historical content.

As a college student in the late 1960s, my dance world transformed. I enrolled in some modern dance classes, initially because they fulfilled a physical education requirement, and any kind of dance seemed preferable to athletics. I quickly realised that modern dance had its own technique(s) which were different from ballet – I first studied in a Wigman-based class, then in a Humphrey-Weidman class, and then in a Graham class – but were challenging, rigorous, and exciting, nonetheless.

My gradual conversion to modern dance had other sources. In adolescence, I had realised that I did not possess a 'ballet body' (very slender and long limbed) and never would, whereas the range of acceptable bodies in modern dance seemed to include mine. Also, the choreographic ideas of modern dance fascinated me and seemed more in accord with contemporary art, more vital and immediate. Finally, the breadth of representation of gender in modern dance attracted me. The movement vocabularies for individual women and men and for dancers interacting varied far more in modern dance than ballet. The experience of moving in new ways changed my perception and changed *me*.

As I became involved in the feminist movement, I felt angry and embarrassed by the stereotyping of women in ballet as frail, delicate, beautiful objects, displayed and controlled by men. I perceived the discrepancy between the egalitarian technique of the non-professional ballet classroom, in which women and men practise the same exercises and the predictably differentiated movement vocabularies in most ballet choreography (for which professionals train in special adagio classes, pointe classes, men's classes and so forth). As issues of gender intertwined with my new technical and choreographic interests, I rapidly distanced myself from ballet.

During my career as a modern dancer and improvisational performer, I have occasionally returned to ballet classes, and have even taught several college courses in ballet. My own investigations of movement, choreography and improvisation, however, have largely involved other styles and conventions. I have found that people who do not dance usually assume that I study ballet, in part because they perceive its influence on my movement, but also because they assume that all dancers must study ballet in order to acquire technical proficiency. When I tell people I meet that I am a dancer, 'Are you a ballet dancer?' is the most common question they ask. After that, they often ask if I dance like the performers on the American television show, 'Solid Gold' – Hollywood/jazz style accompanying the latest pop hits. And although I have experienced my ballet training as both asset and liability in trying to perform other kinds of dance, it has carried considerable positive weight in my quest for teaching jobs.

The small, collaborative modern dance group with which I work periodically applies for government grants. The New York State Council on the Arts, one of the agencies to which we have applied, gives away over two-thirds of its budget to three ballet companies, considered as, in the language of government, granting 'primary cultural institutions'. My experience makes it clear that generally within the professional world, as well as popularly, ballet holds a position of cultural and institutional dominance.

What social and ideological processes have been at work in the ballet I have participated in and seen over the last thirty-odd years? Stereotypes of gender which perpetuate representations of women as fragile creatures supported by powerful men are connected to a training system which is extremely technical and rigorous, and is offered to large numbers of children, mostly girls. Furthermore, ballet allows for great achievement in a physical art by female performers, for which they receive public acclaim. These circumstances link female virtuosity and public female role models to a physical practice at once highly technical and highly gendered.

As a performance form, ballet's aesthetic stems from a long and by now respected artistic tradition. It is also simultaneously associated with both a bourgeois, white audience and, through television and film, with a more general popular audience. Since the founding of the Dance Theatre of Harlem, ballet can claim at least some availability to dancers of colour and the admission of modern dance choreographers into ballet companies suggests a contemporary flexibility. Thus, ballet seems both an élite artform connoting bourgeois respectability and an art accessible to large numbers of people. The 'purely technical' emphasis of its teaching contributes to an image of ballet as an art transcending cultural boundaries, a dance that is not 'ethnic'.

Systems of ballet training and performance have gained greater institutional support than any other dance form in numerous countries, support which involves schools, companies, producing organisations, the media and government agencies. Ballet is considered the premier art dance form by governments of Europe, North America, Australia, and the former Soviet Union, and enjoys popularity in many other parts of the world. This institutional support means that ballet's ideas and practices gain cultural power, a power which attaches to the concepts of gender it defines.

Moving from my own history to some accounts of and by ballet dancers presents a clearer picture of ballet's professional practice. I begin with the publication in the early 1980s of books criticising professional ballet from a social perspective, an event which marked a sudden turn in the dance literature. Until then, biographies and autobiographies of ballet figures tended toward anecdote and romantic adulation of choreographers, other dancers, and the world of ballet in general. Works by L. M. Vincent (1981), Joan Brady (1982) and Suzanne Gordon (1983), however, took the ballet world to task for abuses of dancers, particularly women.

Vincent and Gordon, not dancers themselves but a physician and journalist respectively whose professions have involved them with ballet, criticised the encouragement of what they saw as excessive thinness among female ballet dancers, and claimed a relatively high frequency of anorexia nervosa. Gordon also criticised the infantilisation of dancers, particularly the women; she felt that their training left them susceptible to compliance with the needs of the (male) choreographer even when they were injured or psychologically troubled. Brady's bitter account of her failed career as a dancer offered her own version of many of the same circumstances which Vincent and Gordon addressed.

Toni Bentley (1982) and Gelsey Kirkland (1986), both successful professional dancers, published personal stories which more acutely exposed the complex position of the female dancer. Bentley, a member of the *corps de ballet* of the New York City Ballet, described a season with the company, her short departure from performing and her subsequent return. She both loved and hated the demands of her profession, for ballet seemed simultaneously a way to realise herself as a woman and an artist and a way to deny herself as a woman and a person in the world. Yet to be a dancer, Bentley finally accepted what seemed oppressive and returned to the closed world of the ballet company.

Bentley's book contained a defence of anorexia; 'The anorexic has absorbed a great knowledge. She has control – some control – over her destiny and has taken responsibility for that destiny'.[6] Bentley also argued against a dancers' union; 'Those who loved themselves more than [George] Balanchine have made their stand and demonstrated their lack of faith in him . . . What would have happened if Van Gogh's brushes one day had refused to be manipulated because they wanted better living conditions?'[7] Moreover, she portrayed George Balanchine as a kind of human god; 'We are all his children, but his adult children – his working, dancing, performing children . . . As an apprentice one hears that he needs to see only one demi-plie, and he knows how you dance, how you live, who you are and what your future is'.[8]

While the books by Vincent, Brady and Gordon suggested that more public attention might be paid to the sexism of ballet and that some of the abusive conditions in ballet training and production might be reformed, Bentley's book presented a different reality. Women's near-starvation and submission to a male choreographer evidently constituted part of Bentley's training and outlook, inseparable from artistry and devotion to great performance. Just as asceticism and obedience to spiritual leaders can be an integral part of religious life, so too can such practices be part of dancing.

Gelsey Kirkland's autobiography, *Dancing on My Grave* (1986), revealed as extreme an outlook as Bentley's. Kirkland had been an exceptionally gifted young dancer with proclivities toward self-destructive behaviour in the service of self-discipline. As her career developed, she also cultivated an intense desire to choose her own teachers and coaches and to define her own roles, engendering clashes with male choreographers (notably Balanchine and Baryshnikov) and managers. Serious bouts with drug addiction which, she claimed, were tolerated by producing organisations because she was still capable of performing and drawing large audiences, interrupted her career, which she then resumed in London in 1986 after her recovery.

The professional American ballet community's angry reception of Kirkland's exposé would seem to confirm Bentley's portrayal of that community's sectarian closeness. For example, Kirkland was among those honoured by the National Rehabilitation Hospital at a benefit in 1987 in recognition of people who overcame handicaps or life-threatening accidents or setbacks. A story about the benefit in the *New York Times*, headlined '[Edward] Villella Asks Forgiveness for Kirkland', stated that the organiser of the benefit 'had asked many dancers, choreographers and ballet masters to appear with Miss Kirkland and that Mr. Villella was the only one who accepted'. Villella was quoted as saying that colleagues 'should forgive Miss Kirkland despite having been offended'. Later, he commented that she 'drew attention to our world that normally is looked at through

rose-colored glasses'. According to the article, Villella also revealed that 'he was not taking sides' and that, in fact, he 'purposely had not read Miss Kirkland's book'![9]

For those inside the ballet world, it seems that Kirkland's sins
of indiscretion lay as much in her sharing her criticisms with
outsiders as it did in the criticisms themselves. Whatever the
validity or distortion of Kirkland's accusations, Kirkland
seriously violated the rules of a closed society, stepping out of her
place as a dancer, a female and an acclaimed insider. Edward
Villella could only sympathise with her difficulties by avoiding
her book, thereby remaining uncontaminated.

Most spokespeople for ballet seem committed to portraying it
as a self-contained world. In a sense, they present it as an
organism, a whole whose pieces all fit together. Part of the
dominance of ballet as a cultural form rests not only in its
historical longevity and institutional entrenchment, but in its
professional ideology of exclusivity and completeness. I understand now why I felt at one point that I must totally abandon
ballet – one is either in the ballet world or out of the ballet world.
Consequently, professional ballet dancers who write about ballet
tend toward extremes of abject loyalty or bitter attack.

Furthermore, ballet's ideology of completeness mitigates
against 'reform' of gender representation, because gender makes
up one part of a larger fabric. Despite many experiments with
gender representation in ballet in the twentieth century, the
importance of tradition reinforces the primacy of a nineteenth-
century image of gender. Theoretically, one might imagine ballet
companies which presented classical works as historical docu-
ments, in conjunction with selected modernist and contemporary works which contain radically different and wide-ranging
representations of male and female. As currently produced and
performed on a professional level, this does not seem to characterise the dominant direction of ballet.

Now to move on to some viewers of ballet, and to analyses of
gender which have appeared recently.[10] These analyses have
been made in the context of a feminist movement by authors
concerned with the relationship between the sociological features
and the aesthetic properties of ballet. In a number of instances,
the authors have examined the dancing in order to interpret its

representation and evocation of gender. This important enter-
prise constitutes a kind of textual analysis; it stresses the pervasive, long-lasting social symbols which are embedded in the
narrative, movement techniques and choreography of ballet.

To summarise briefly, ballet has been seen to stress sexual
dimorphism, i.e. difference in the relative sizes of women and
men; men virtually always lift and manoeuvre women, embody-
ing strength and exhibiting control over the more fragile ballerina. One of ballet's central choreographic structures, the *pas de
deux*, evokes romantic, heterosexual love on both a literal and
metaphoric level, emphasising opposing characteristics and distinctions between male and female. Contrast in movement vocabularies, narrative roles and costuming for men and women further
reinforce these oppositions and distinctions and, as Ann Daly
(1987/88) persuasively argues, perpetuate nineteenth-century gender stereotypes of 'female difference/male dominance'.

The innovations in gender representation that have occurred,
particularly in the ballets of the past half-century, remain marginal in the ballet repertory.

An obvious question arises: if ballet is so sexist, why do so
many people enjoy it? One obvious answer would be that ballet
reflects and reinforces the pervasive sexism of the society in
which it exists. While this statement has some truth, it seems
unsatisfactory in its sociological reductionism. To what else are
they responding? Or, as sociologist Janet Wolff asks, how can
work 'pronounced ideologically incorrect or unsound' be found
'enjoyable, technically excellent, or in some other way "aesthetically good"'?[11]

Wolff looks to classical ballet as one of her examples of art with
ideologically troublesome content, since many of the major
works of the ballet repertory, she says, 'are based on reactionary
and sexist (not to say silly) stories'. In fact, Wolff confesses, her
own 'critical "reading" of those ballets does interfere with [her]
enjoyment of their performance, though it is still possible to
appreciate skill, design and choreography of parts of the
works'.[12] Here Wolff implicitly suggests that one can watch a
ballet and separate different aspects of its performance. If one
rejects or ignores the representation of gender in ballet, one may
still enjoy the choreographer's craft and the dancer's skills.

To shift back to autobiography for a moment, I have certainly
experienced such moments at the ballet. For example, last

spring, a friend visiting from out of town invited me to attend the New York City Ballet. One of the ballets on the programme, *Tchaikovsky's Piano Concerto Number 2*, featured Merrill Ashley. A short time into the dance, I found myself gasping audibly at Ashley's particularly subtle phrasing. Inexorably, it seemed, Ashley brought me into the ballet with her simultaneous appearance of natural ease and deliberate control. The uniqueness of her presence, her awkward, Amazonian grace, invited my attention to the particular qualities of other dancers on stage as well, while the clarity of her movement repeatedly illuminated the choreography. All the performers seemed to me inspired, intelligent and very human.

However, an argument that 'art transcends social content' (which might be deduced from the comments just made) cannot completely satisfy. For at this same performance, I was uncomfortably aware of the expensive perfume that wafted through the theatre and of the virtually all-white audience, a startling contrast to the ethnic and racial mixture of riders on the subway I took to Lincoln Center to see the ballet. I had to shake off these thoughts and make an effort to focus my attention on the stage as the performance began. Then, during the first ballet, a sudden image struck me – that the women's feet were bound, compressed into the stubby ends of their pointe shoes – and I could not help but be distracted every time the ballerinas clip-clopped their way across the stage, their hardened toes striking the ground (like reverse high heels) at every step. Eventually, I gave in to the bizarre image and amused myself with it for some time.

Evan Alderson, in an article entitled 'Ballet as Ideology: *Giselle*, Act II' (1987) describes yet another viewing experience at the ballet. He discusses being 'seized by beauty' at a crucial moment during a performance. Alderson analyses his response in some detail by investigating the confluence of aesthetic qualities with social values. 'Thinking back on my response,' he writes, 'I realized that I had been hooked on the point of my own desire: I had been "let in" through Albrecht's longing for the absolutely faithful, absolutely unattainable woman whose death he had occasioned, because I share with much of nineteenth-century culture an attraction to what is sexually charged yet somehow pristine.'[13]

Alderson suggests that a conjunction of technical innovations in nineteenth-century ballet, the narrative of *Giselle* and bourgeois values create the image of the female body of Giselle as ethereal and chaste and at the same time, erotic. Alderson perceives that his own admiration of beauty subtly but powerfully evokes loyalty to a social order. For him, representation of gender and appreciation of craft are linked for and by the viewer.

None of these viewers is 'wrong' from an anthropological standpoint. Natives think and act as natives, which is what Wolff, Alderson and I (a British, Canadian, and American native, respectively) are all doing. Our responses are not merely personal idiosyncrasies or preferences; they engage both the ballet we watch *and* the ideological and institutional experiences of our lives.

Wolff follows an aesthetic theory about viewing art which allows her to dislike ballet's ideology of gender but appreciate the choreographer's craft and the performers' skills. This theory matches the structure of the ballet itself, which often presents 'pure' virtuosity and can shift its focus among, for example, character, dramatic encounter, musical artistry and athletic display.

Alderson (1987) finds himself responding most strongly to a moment in which techniques and character within the ballet unite to evoke his emotional reaction. His attraction to what is 'sexually charged but somehow pristine' connects the definition of gender in the ballet to Alderson's social experience of gender.

As a viewer, I seem to focus most strongly on the ballerina. Because of my childhood familiarity with ballet technique, as well as my ongoing preoccupation with movement, I am attuned to technical and choreographic artistry and oriented to the agency of the dancers. Because of my distaste for the oppressive representation and evocation of gender, as well as my discomfort with associations of social class, race and aesthetic categorisation that seem embedded in ballet, I often feel disturbed and alienated. Because of my interest in other kinds of movement, I sometimes become bored with the limitations of ballet. My state as a viewer may change many times during a performance.

Do I enjoy the ballet only in those moments which are 'politically correct' and feel distanced from it when partnering or sexist narratives occur? Probably not always. Am I able to separate ideology from craft? Sometimes. At other times, the profusion of thoughts, sensations and associations I have when I watch dance flood over one another. Beauty, distortion, brilliance, silliness, intelligence, stupidity, power, weakness – the ballerina can embody them all. Positive and negative implications in my own life history are paradoxically linked; I am caught in contradiction (perhaps even perversely attracted by it – art gives licence not always available in other realms of life). As Evan Alderson felt complicity with the desire of Albrecht, I, too, have feelings of complicity with the ballerina, with her dual embodiment of the powerful and the ineffable.

In conclusion, I have tried to illustrate that definitions of gender in ballet pervade not only ballet choreography and performance but many other ideas, events and institutions. I have suggested what some of these might be: the values associated with dance, conceptions of art, the structure of children's and non-professional dance classes, perpetuation of female role models, the nature of ballet technique, the social organisation of ballet audiences, the financial/organisational support of ballet and the hierarchical nature of ballet production.

I have also suggested that these forces come together in particular ways. The technical prowess of the ballerina is often linked to stereotyped practices of gender, uniting images of power to images of being manipulated and controlled. At the same time, the emphasis placed on virtuosity allows one to view ballet on a technical level and ignore or dismiss ideological content. Stereotyped practices of gender are connected simultaneously to acclaimed public figures, an honoured artistic tradition and bourgeois respectability. Ballet appears in so many different kinds of institutions that it may be seen as both popular and élite art. Yet at its professional level, ballet is conceived and organised as a closed and unified tradition, making it resistant to change.

I am in complete agreement with those who urge a social analysis of dance performance which does not dismiss the dance's aesthetic values. In this essay, however, I have chosen to emphasise the point that social content, such as the representation of gender, resides not only within the dance itself but also in the dance's connections to the (aesthetic-social) life experiences of the audience. The anthropological commonplace that dance and life are inextricably related gets easily applied to the people of Bali or Ghana or Morocco; it applies as well to the people who perpetuate ballet. Only through understanding something about those relationships can we understand ballet's cultural power and the problematic nature of gender in ballet.

Notes and References

1. See V. Turner (1957) and C. Geertz (1973).
2. Quoted from R. Rosaldo (1989), pp. 92–3.
3. See, for example, the following: E. S. Bowen (1964), J. Briggs (1970), J. Chernoff (1979), J. Clifford and G. E. Marcus, eds (1986), G. Obeyeskere (1981), and R. Rosaldo (op. cit.).
4. Often, of course, I wear both hats at once . . . When is one a participant and when is one an observer in one's own life?
5. I use the word cultural in this case to mean 'high art', a normative judgement, rather than an anthropological term.
6. T. Bentley (1982), p. 56.
7. Ibid., p. 89.
8. Ibid., p. 58.
9. I. Molotsky (1987).
10. See, for example, the work of E. Alderson (1987), pp. 290–304, L. Garafola (Fall 1985/Spring 1986), pp. 35–40, A. Daly (1987/88), pp. 57–66, C. J. Novack (1986), (1990), and M. Goldberg (1987/88), pp. 7–31.
11. J. Woolf (1983), p. 23.
12. Ibid., p. 24.
13. E. Alderson, op. cit. p. 293.

Many of the ideas for this article grew out of conversations with Evan Alderson, Richard Bull, Ann Daly, Susan Foster, Mark Franko, Susan Manning and George Russell. I thank them for our on-going discussions and in particular Richard Bull and Susan Manning, who read drafts of this article and made valuable suggestions.

Bibliography

E. Alderson, 'Ballet as Ideology: *Giselle*, Act II', *Dance Chronicle*, Vol. 10 (3) (1987) 290–304.
T. Bentley, *Winter Season*, (New York: Vintage Books, 1982).
E. S. Bowen, *Return to Laughter*, (New York: Doubleday, 1964).
J. Brady, *The Unmaking of a Dancer: An Unconventional Life*, (New York: Harper & Row, 1982).
J. Briggs, *Never in Anger: Portrait of an Eskimo Family*, (Cambridge, Mass: Harvard University Press, 1970).
J. Chernoff, *African Rhythm and African Sensibility: Aesthetics and Social Action in African Musical Idioms*, (University of Chicago Press, 1979).
J. Clifford and G. E. Marcus (eds), *Writing Culture: The Poetics and the Politics of Ethnography*, (Berkeley: University of California Press, 1986).

A. Daly, 'Classical Ballet: A Discourse of Difference', *Women & Performance*, Vol. 3(2) (1987/88) 57–66.

A. Daly, 'The Balanchine Woman: Of Hummingbirds and Channel Swimmers', *The Drama Review*, Vol. 31 (1) (Spring 1987) 8–21.

L. Garafola, 'The Travesty Dancer in Nineteenth-Century Ballet', *Dance Research Journal*, 17/2 and 18/1 (Fall 1985/Spring 1986) 35–40.

C. Geertz, *The Interpretation of Cultures*, (New York: Basic Books, 1973).

M. Goldberg, 'Ballerinas and Ball Passing', *Women & Performance*, Vol. 3 (2) (1987/88) 7–31.

S. Gordon, *Off Balance: The Real World of Ballet* (New York: Pantheon, 1983).

G. Kirkland with G. Lawrence, *Dancing on My Grave*, (Garden City, NY: Doubleday, 1986).

I. Molotsky, 'Villella Asks Forgiveness for Kirkland', *New York Times* (28 October 1987).

C. J. Novack, *Sharing the Dance: Contact Improvisation and American Culture*, (Madison, Wis.: University of Wisconsin Press, 1990).

C. J. Novack, 'Sharing the Dance: An Ethnography of Contact Improvisation', PhD Dissertation, (New York: Columbia University, 1986).

G. Obeyesekere, *Medusa's Hair: An Essay on Personal Symbols and Religious Experience*, (University of Chicago Press, 1981).

R. Rosaldo, *Culture and Truth, The Remaking of Social Analysis*, (Boston: Beacon Press, 1989).

V. Turner, *Schism and Continuity in an African Society*, (Manchester University Press, 1957).

L. M. Vincent, *Competing With the Sylph: Dancers and the Pursuit of the Ideal Body Form*, (New York: Berkeley, 1981).

J. Wolff, *Aesthetics and the Sociology of Art*, (London: George Allen & Unwin, 1983).

4 'I seem to find the happiness I seek'

Heterosexuality and Dance in the Musical

RICHARD DYER

Fred and Ginger meet. He fancies her and she's quite taken with him, but he pesters her too much, or she's got her own career to get on with, or she thinks he's married, or he's promised never to marry. Whatever the reason something keeps them apart, except that when they start to dance . . . Well, what? It's heaven, they're in heaven, but just what is it that makes it so, what notion of happiness is embodied in their dancing?

The impulse of most musicals is towards just such moments of heaven, of grand and glorious feeling. In the unsung, undanced narrative, the characters have all sorts of problems, from raising money for a show to winning strikes (*The Pajama Game*) and escaping from the Nazis (*The Sound of Music*); in the numbers they either resolve or get away from these problems. Heterosexuality is at the heart of this. The heterosexual couple are usually the main characters and either the problems are what prevent their getting together (misunderstandings between them, obstacles in their way, like parents, class or nationality) or else their love is the way they escape from problems external to the relationship (intrigues at court, the show going badly, social conflicts). What interests me here is how that heavenly relationship, that heterosexual ideal, is imagined, incarnated in the couples' dances together.

Our culture seems to have two prevalent models of heterosexuality and its attractions. One might be labelled the Jane Austen model, the idea of complementarity within equality. What makes a heterosexual relationship agreeable is the blending of opposites, the balance of, say, his pride against her prejudice, both sides making up the deficiencies of the other, either through learning from one another or through the creation in the state of

49

coupledom of a fuller human entity than either partner alone can represent. At the moral level, these personal qualities need not be gender-specific (women can be proud, men prejudiced) but the notion of heterosexual complementarity generally implies that masculinity and femininity are themselves tantalisingly incomplete opposites which can be rapturously fused in an equal, loving relationship. The alternative model we might label the Barbara Cartland model. Here the spice is inequality as well as difference; the intoxications are having power over, surrendering to a greater power, manipulating the powerful to your own ends, ceding power before the charms of the less powerful. Here there is no question of the possibility of these roles being freely spread among women and men. The Cartland version of heterosexual heaven insists on the correlation between gender and power, men relishing having power, women luxuriating in surrender.

There is a third, much less common model of the appeal of heterosexuality, which suggests that qualities of sameness and identity, of finding what you have in common, might also be delightful. It was the ideal of the 'new woman', meeting your intellectual match or discovering perfect intuitive sympathy across the superficial divide of gender (although as Ruth Brandon (1990) has suggested, it proved difficult to realise with the male raw material available). Sameness is an ideal often derided ('how boring it would be!'), although research shows that on the whole heterosexuals marry people from their own social background who look rather like them.

In couple-dances in musicals, all three of these ideals figure but with increasing emphasis (in the course of a given film, in the development of the genre) on the Cartland model. In his book *The American Film Musical*, Rick Altman proposes a paradigm for the musical of simple underlying oppositions, embodied in the persons of the central heterosexual couple, which are finally resolved by their coming together, both in numbers and in narrative closure (marriage or the assumption of it). He points to the pattern of the numbers in musicals: one for him, one for her, each expressing their personal qualities (complementary à la Austen) and very often their yearning (for each other or simply for a mate as yet unknown); then more numbers for him and for her until, or interspersed with, numbers in which they sing and/or dance together. Altman suggests that this structure represents a way of handling contradictions in general social values:

Society is defined by a fundamental paradox: both terms of the oppositions on which it is built (order/liberty, progress/ stability, work/entertainment, and so forth) are seen as desirable, yet the terms are perceived as mutually exclusive. Every society possesses texts which obscure this paradox, prevent it from appearing threatening, and thus assure the society's stability. The musical is one of the most important types of text to serve this function in American society. By reconciling terms previously seen as mutually exclusive, the musical succeeds in reducing an unsatisfactory paradox to a more workable configuration, a concordance of opposites. Traditionally, this is the function which society assigns to myth. . . . the musical fashions a myth out of the American courtship ritual. (1987:27)

This is all very nice, all very Austen (without the bite). What remain unproblematic though are the terms of the courtship ritual itself. If what happens in the numbers is sameness or complementarity within equality, this is a pleasant fantasy of social resolution within personal relationships, and none the worse for being idealisation, since it is important to have ideals to live by. But not all ideals are equally fine. If the numbers have at least as much to do with power imbalance, then someone is paying a price, and being asked to believe they love it, for this 'concordance of opposites'. (Still others, those excluded from the charmed circle of heterosexual privilege, have no place in this supposedly general social idealism.) While the overall impulse of the musical is towards the utopia of the heterosexually embodied reconciliation of opposites, there are also intimations of other, perhaps more dubious utopias, and these become clearest when, as in dance, the body, the elemental ground of the self, is in question.

I'm going to be looking at the construction of heterosexual happiness in couple-dances principally in two groups of musicals: the Astaire-Rogers films of the thirties (and especially *Top Hat*) and the MGM musicals of the forties and fifties (in particular *On the Town*, *The Band Wagon* and *Brigadoon*). This may seem to aficionados of the genre an unadventurous selection, but in fact couple-dances are far less common than one might expect. Rogers and Astaire are the only durable dancing couple in the genre's history, and if one moves away from Astaire and Gene Kelly, both of whom did couple dances with many different partners, such *pas de deux* become really quite rare. This is especially true since the fifties, where sung duets have remained strong but not danced ones. I will touch briefly on this towards the end and on the occasional couple-dances in seventies and eighties films that can be thought of as musicals, such as *Saturday Night Fever* and *Dirty Dancing*.

I want to examine the dancing in these numbers in relation to the notions of heterosexual happiness that I have sketched above. To do this I'll take into account the number's function in the narrative, the kind of dance used and its formal qualities. I want here to say something more about one aspect of the dancing itself that is particularly germane to my theme, the arrangement of the two bodies in relation to each other. I use below four terms to describe different kinds of arrangement, claiming no notational breakthrough for these, merely convenience, a way of shortening discussion later. Bodies in a couple-dance may be *side by side, mirroring, mutually holding* or in *relations of dependency*.

In *side by side* both dancers face in the same direction. Most commonly they do exactly the same thing; occasionally they may do aesthetically complementary things (one puts their right hand up, another their left hand down, both holding their arm in a curved shape); more rarely, they do radically dissimilar things. I count here the common pattern of one dancer behind another, side on and slightly turned towards the camera. This is the common form in vaudeville routines, often explicitly referenced in musicals (e.g. Betty Grable and June Haver in *The Dolly Sisters*, 1946, Gene Kelly and Donald O'Connor in 'Fit as a Fiddle' in *Singin' in the Rain* 1952). It is most common in single-sex duos, the most sublime exception being Judy Garland and Fred Astaire's 'A Couple of Swells' in *Easter Parade*, 1948, where, all the same, both are dressed as (male) tramps.

In *mirroring*, the partners face each other and either do exactly the same thing or the inverse. (If both kick their left leg up, then one kicks, say, towards the camera, the other away from it; whereas if both kick towards the camera while facing each other, they are using different legs.) Either suggests aesthetically the sense of each dancer reflecting the other's movement. Though rehearsed to within an inch of its life, the effect of mirroring is the same as that of the musical genre itself, as discussed by Jane Feuer (1982), namely, to give the impression of spontaneity, of just doing what feels right at the moment. Side by side and mirroring both suggest the thrill of instinctive rapport, but the former suggests the experience of it with someone who already is like oneself, whereas mirroring conveys the pleasure of becoming like someone else.

In 'perfect' mirroring, it is impossible to say that one dancer is the mirror of the other, that one is the reality giving rise to the reflection. Sometimes however one partner will, barely perceptibly, initiate a movement which is then mirrored by the other, suggesting the matter of 'who leads' common to couple-dancing. This is clearer with *mutual holding*. Here the couple may be side by side or face to face but touching, most commonly by the hand. Simple hand in hand has no gender dimension, but I include here the standard ballroom dance arrangement (her right hand in his left, her left at his shoulder, his right at her waist) and the arm in arm strolling arrangement, which is in fact her arm through his. As one watches a dance, it may be a bit heavy to insist too much on such gender differences, though there are occasions when his leading pressure can be quite marked. Mutual holding may thus stress the pleasures of mutuality or intimate the intoxications of power play.

Finally, *relations of dependency* obtain when one dancer is in a position that she or he (but nearly always she) could not maintain without the support of the other. Here there is a distinction to be made, between those relations where one dancer's support *enables* the other to do something thrilling of their own (as in the supported arabesques and *fouettés* of classical ballet) and those where the support becomes *disabling*, though not necessarily any less thrilling (as in the way women are twirled, thrown and wrapped around men's bodies in jitterbugging).

These arrangements are found to varying degrees in couple-dances in most musicals, though the first two are more common in Astaire-Rogers than in MGM musicals and almost absent in seventies and eighties dance films. The most usual pattern is for side by side and mirroring to predominate early on in a dance, sometimes entirely structuring a first dance together, while holding and dependency predominate in later numbers. What this pattern suggests is the difference between the promise of happiness at the moment of courtship/dating and the form it takes at the point of consummation.

'Isn't This a Lovely Day?' and 'Cheek to Cheek' in *Top Hat* represent to perfection the model of a couple-dance early in a film consisting largely of side by side and mirroring and one later with more emphasis on mutual holding and female-on-male dependency. Both dances start off from a position in the story where Ginger does not want to dance with Fred – in the first case, because he is a nuisance (he woke her the night before by tap dancing on the floor above her, now he won't leave her alone, even tracking her down to the bandstand in the park where the dance takes place) and in the second, because, mistakenly, she thinks he is the husband of her best friend, Madge. By the end of each number they are rapt in mutual love, but the nature of what has so deliciously triumphed over narrative adversity differs between one dance and the other.

In both cases, Fred initiates, by being the one to sing the song through to her and then by leading off the dance. With 'Isn't This a Lovely Day?', the latter takes the form of him standing up and strolling/dancing a few paces across the bandstand away from her, then back to her, then turning to start off away from her again. At this point she stands up and strolls/dances behind him. Throughout the dance, she does what he does. He puts his hand in his pocket, so does she; he introduces a staccato tap pattern, so does she. Initially this is sequential, her after him, but then, in a glorious moment, it becomes simultaneous; they just know what to do, the same side by side. There is some mirroring, notably in a section near the middle, where first he makes a single tap move which she 'reflects', and then she does one for him to ' reflect'. This initiates a faster final section, which begins with them in mutual holding position for a few quick twirls round the bandstand before two astonishing moments: he sends her spinning out and then she does the same for him; he holds both her hands and she leaps up round him, and then she does the same for him. Both these movements involve the dependence of one dancer upon the other and are not in themselves remarkable, but usually it is the man who spins out and throws round the woman. Here they both do both, in turn.

The basic pattern of the dance then is for him to initiate

movements but for them both to do the same thing, usually sequentially, occasionally simultaneously, mainly side by side but even when involving dependencies, not exclusively female-on-male. The sense of sameness as the core design principle of the dance is reinforced by dress. She wears jodphurs and riding jacket, he a grey lounge suit. They look alike because she is dressed more like a man and because there is no great tonal contrast in their clothes (compare the high contrast of Fred's black tail coat and trousers and Ginger's all white feathers dress in 'Cheek to Cheek'). The significance of the sameness is increased by characterisation and star images. He has already been established as a professional dancer within the plot of the film and we have seen him do the virtuoso tap number 'No Strings'; she is fashion model, has not been seen dancing and has even brought 'No Strings' to a halt by complaining about the noise. Her character is thus less associated with dancing ability and inclination than him, and this was true of Rogers herself. By *Top Hat*, their fourth film together, no one doubted she was a good dancer, but she had originally come to prominence as a wise-cracking show girl, standing and moving about scantily clad, but not really dancing. She never has solo dance numbers in the films, whereas he always does; and his early fame was based entirely on his dancing, most notably in the theatre with his sister Adele. Thus in 'Isn't This a Lovely Day?', Rogers, as both character and star, by doing the same thing as Astaire, is showing that she can do it and as well.

Dances like this are common in Astaire-Rogers films (other include 'Let Yourself Go' in *Follow the Fleet*, 'Pick Yourself Up' in *Swing Time* and 'The Yam' in *Carefree*). Arlene Croce in her book on the pair calls these 'challenge dances' and much of the fun is both the sporty sparring and the demonstration of equality in their ability, a demonstration with clear 'new woman', feminist implications (a woman can do everything a man can and as well). Best of all is the suggestion, in many of Astaire's facial reactions and the numbers' narrative function of effecting their love as well as in Roger's evident élan, that this version of feminism is not incompatable with heterosexual delight. It's a lesson that is seldom found in later films, and in any case has been forgotten by the time we get to the romantic numbers like 'Cheek to Cheek'.

As in 'Isn't This a Lovely Day?', Fred leads 'Cheek to Cheek',

serenading Ginger as they foxtrot among other couples on a café
dance-floor before moving her off across a bridge into a pavilion,
the separate, unwatched space characteristic of true romance. In
ballroom dancing the man leads, but this is not stressed here
beyond the fact that he has moved her away from the public
space and she is more reluctant than ever to dance with him, her
best friend's husband. Rather his dominance is attained through
the gradual introduction of movements in which he puts her into
a position of dependence on him. Three times, at the end of a
musical phrase, he swings her back from the waist, with her
going lower to the floor each time. A little later, he drags her
backwards and then in the final section repeatedly holds her as
she leans back in his arms, him bending over her, each time
closer to the ground, until at the climax she is all but on the
ground and the music stills and they don't move for a pause until
he very gently pulls her up and they move slowly to the back of
the pavilion. As Jim Collins (1981:144) argues, the sense of a
sexual climax is very strongly suggested and the whole dance
could be seen as the consummation of what remained at the level
of courtship in 'Isn't This a Lovely Day?'. But what seems a
promise of equality and mutuality in the early dance has become
a realisation of ecstatic dependency, her on him, in the later one.

Couple-dances in the MGM musicals of the forties and fifties
play variations on the construction of heterosexuality, but with a
greater emphasis, compared to Rogers and Astaire, on both
difference and female-on-male dependency. Here I look at three
examples. 'Main Street' and its partial reprise in the 'Day in
New York' dream ballet in *On the Town* complicate the notion of
sameness, by moving from a dance based on identical movements to one based on similarity and equivalence within difference; 'Dancing in the Dark' from *The Band Wagon* suggests an
idea of a fusion of difference within heterosexuality, which then
leads to a sense of enabling dependancy; 'The Heather on the
Hill' and its reprise in *Brigadoon* are both based on female-to-
male dependencies, but with a strong sense of enablement in the
former and disablement in the latter.
     'Main Street' in *On the Town* is virtually entirely side by side,
and strongly suggests the notion of sameness. Although he (Gene
Kelly) thinks that she (Vera-Ellen) is a sophisticated New Yor-

ker, she knows, as we do, that they both come from the same small town, Meadowville. When he sings to her of the Main Street in that town and then dances with her as if dancing along that street, she knows it just as well as he. Apart from a very brief section in which he mimes proposing and she mimes accepting, their movements are identical, either sequentially or simultaneously. There is some mutual holding where difference is conventionally apparent (her arm through his, for instance, in a strolling movement) but only lightly suggested. The main difference from the Astaire-Rogers challenge dances is that there is no sense of conflict or competition. Indeed, the conflict has been resolved before the dance starts (he has been a show-off, she has been dismissive, he has climbed down, she has begun to take an interest), and although her character is a dancer (a ballet student paying for classes through burlesque dancing) and Kelly was the better known dancing star, the movements throughout are so apparently artless and easy, giving no impression of difficulty or strenuousness, that the idea of one showing s/he is as good as the other is irrelevant. Never was getting on such open hearted, simple bliss as in this number.

The setting (a ballet studio) of 'Main Street', though not the melody, is used for Kelly and Vera-Ellen's dance in the *Day in New York* ballet, which is a daydream by the Kelly character recapitulating the events of the day he and his two shipmates have spent in the city. As befits a dream sequence in a culture informed by a vague Freudianism, the tone of the reprise is more passionate and sexual and yet only at the end introducing any dependency. The barre (not placed against a wall) is used as a basic element in the choreography. Sometimes Vera-Ellen and Kelly mirror each other, standing on opposite sides and both holding onto it. More often, they are arranged in separate and contrasting positions around it, positions which are organised, however, into sequences whereby each dancer repeats what the other has just done, not exactly but in ways suggesting similarity or equivalence. For instance, at one point, on the left of the screen, she holds onto the barre with both hands above her, crouched on one bent knee, the other leg held straight out, and in this position moves sharply from side to side under the barre; meanwhile, screen right, he extends himself along it, raising his torso slightly from the crotch. Moments later, there is a reversal, to similar but by no means identical positions. Now he is screen

left, below the barre, holding both hands to it, spinning on one
foot with the other leg bent up tight towards him, while she,
centre screen, sits on the barre and opens her bent legs in a
crab-like movement from the crotch. There is no suggestion of
dependency or relative power here and all the movements signify
pleasure, but the elements of dissimilarity suggest equivalent
rather than identical pleasure, most obviously (and most explicitly sexually) in the contrast of his crotch to the barre, her
opening her legs out from the crotch. (In terms of sexual imagery, this implies equivalence between phallic and vaginal,
rather than clitoral, pleasure, and this is what is to be expected
from a forties or fifties movie.) Only at the end does he picks her
up and move her round him several times, lowering her to the
floor to which he sinks with her, a movement involving her
dependence on him but also connoting the ebbing away, for both
of them, of passion and, perhaps, orgasm.

If Vera-Ellen and Kelly reach this different-but-equal (but
passingly dependent) arrangement through an initial experience
of identity, Fred Astaire and Cyd Charisse, entirely within the
one number, 'Dancing in the Dark' from *The Band Wagon*, reach
it through a sense of the fusion of differences, achieved through
both an accommodation to each other's (dance) style and a use
of (dance) ground uncommon to both.

This number and its function in the film could not exemplify
the Altman paradigm better. The dancers, as characters and
stars, represent two different sets of values explicitly embodied in
their dancing styles. He is the old Hollywood musical, his dance
based on vaudeville, his idea of the purpose of the thing 'pure
entertainment'; she, with her background in ballet, represents
the new Hollywood musical of the forties, with its infusion of
American Ballet Theatre and its aspiration to be meaningful as
well as entertaining. The film is very deliberate in its use of
Astaire and Charisse and poses them the question of whether
they can dance together (with all that implies). 'Dancing in the
Dark' is the demonstration that they can. It follows a series of
disastrous and quarrelsome rehearsals for the show they are both
to appear in; having at last discussed the fact that they both feel
inadequate in relation to the other, they go at his suggestion to
Central Park to see if they are capable of dancing together. They
walk through a public dance-floor of couples and into a clear
space. The setting is important. It is not the theatre, it is not

professional dance of any kind, it is the recreational space and dance of 'ordinary people'. This both provides neutral territory for these two professional dancers and also suggests the idea of doing what they feel like, rather than what, as in rehearsal, they are being required to do. The joy, naturally, is that they discover that when they are themselves and ordinary, they can indeed dance together.

To achieve this the dance has to give the impression of spontaneity and intuition. She initiates the idea of dancing by idly sketching an expansive, balletic movement out into the area, establishing it as a space to dance in. He initiates the idea of dancing together by then doing a nimble turn which ends up with him posed facing her. As characters, both are spontaneously trying out the possibility of dancing. There then follows a longish sequence of mirroring, moving from side to side facing each other, looking into each other eyes. There is no sense of one being the reflection of the other: one does not start a movement a moment before the other, neither looks at the other's body. It is perfect intuition, pure transparency of understanding between them. The steps here and throughout are a combination of ballet and hoofing, equally shared, practically impossible to disentangle. In other words, the perfect fusion, through spontaneity, intuition and transparency, of difference.

As the number develops, there is an increase in mutual holding and her-on-him dependency positions. Out of the fusion of what they really are/want develops a new awareness of difference and dependency. The instances of the latter are enabling; he spins her out or pulls her up in ways that allow her to flourish, to extend exhilaratingly upwards or outwards, with an energy and expansiveness at odds with the contained and inward movement associated with pretty femininity in showbiz dance. This is not to say that her movements connote masculinity, they are far too graceful for that; rather they suggest the ideal of womanhood confidently flowering in the ground of male support.

'Dancing in the Dark' accomplishes the movement from courtship (getting to know one another) to consummation (reaching a peak of passion) within one number. *Brigadoon* follows the more common pattern of two separate dances for these two phases, with the latter being melodically a reprise of the former, 'The Heather on the Hill'. The difference in tone between the two is strongly signalled in her costume (the glimpse of red petticoat beneath an oatmeal dress becomes a vivid all-red dress in the reprise), the setting (on a hill-top in full daylight as compared to down in a forest clearing by a ruined chapel at night) and of course dance.

Both versions are far more fully within the vocabulary of classical ballet than any other numbers considered in this essay and both involve the woman (Cyd Charisse) being held by and thus dependent on the man (Gene Kelly), but there are still considerable differences. In the first version, the melody is orchestrated with a tiny pause at the end of each phrase, and there are points at which the dancers momentarily freeze. At these points, he is generally in a taut, 'yearning' pose, knees and elbows bent, but limbs straight, reaching forward yet held back, straining and strained, tumescent. She is given much more to do. Sometimes she freezes in a turn away from him or else holds on to him in a balletic position, leaning against him with one leg raised laterally or adopting an arabesque on pointe. At one instant she is held at the waist and swings her torso backwards in a lolling movement; at another, she twines herself round him with her knees held together and bent towards her chest; towards the end there are several moments at which she leaps up and is held by him with her arms in the air. Although all these movements require his presence to hold her, he remains a mere support; he doesn't spin her out or throw her, it is she who twines round him, goes into an arabesque, leaps up. It is her large, expansive movements that are most noticeable, not his smaller, tighter ones. Only very briefly do they dance side by side and in unison. Difference predominates, suggesting contrasting contructions of sexuality, his taut straining, her lively release.

The setting suggests something further. The fact that it is on the ridge of a hill connotes both freedom and privacy (the dance starts with them running up to the ridge, away from the constrictions of the valley and beyond that, the restrictions of the village where she lives); but as a dancing space it is extremely limiting. The dance is choreographed laterally, along the ridge, across the screen, an effect reinforced by the use of wide-screen (emphasising breadth over depth), a mainly laterally tracking camera, and bare ash tress, which provide support for the dancers but also act as barriers between them. All of these elements put a limit on how far the dancers can go, a choreographic limitation analogous to the social/moral sexual preoccupations of the day, and this is made explicit at the end of the dance, where she is held aloft facing him, is lowered as if about to kiss him, but breaks away and instead gives him a sprig of heather. (Ending on a unconsummated kiss is a common feature of Kelly *pas de deux*, especially those near the beginning of a film.) However, whereas for him, this then translates as straining, yearning, unfulfilled movements, for her it provides the security for big, energetic, liberated movements. She no longer has these by the time we get to the reprise.

Here there are few ecstatic lifts. She is carried by him, first leaning against him with her arms around his neck and her feet lifted clear of the ground, then curled up against his chest; she is dragged backwards, the point of one foot just barely touching the ground; she is held in an arabesque *penchée*, an insecure position with no outward and upward exhilaration to it; she is held virtually to the ground and finally supine across his knees as he kisses her (the kiss denied in the earlier version). There is no contrast between his frustration and her release – her supine surrender now responds to his taut mastery. Throughout the dance, she frequently uses gestures (stroking his face, leaning her head against his shoulder) suggesting her desire for him. In other words, she enjoys being overpowered.

In the earlier version, we have of sense of both radical difference (reinforced by the fact that his character is twentieth-century American, hers eighteenth-century Scottish) and a restraint, that is experienced as frustration by him (though one he accepts as proper for this stage of the relationship) and a basis for release for her. This cannot continue into the reprise/consummation. He must be fulfilled too; but the insistence on radical difference does not permit his discovery of the pleasures of identity and similarity found in other numbers discussed here. The only possibility is for her to accommodate to his sexuality, to be receptive to his urge.

Many have argued, following Molly Haskell's 1974 lead, that film images of women within heterosexuality lay much greater stress on independence and equality with men in the thirties and early forties than since. Though I have not done a full survey, couple-dances in musicals seem to support this view. In the thirties and forties, the dances were prepared to go some way to exploring heterosexuality in terms of identity, mutuality and equality, but in the late forties and fifties, despite the actual growth of female independence (taking going out to work, control over conception and spread of educational opportunity as indices), there is a renewed insistence on the differences between women and men, sometimes pushed to the point of a virtual incompatability. The utopia of heterosexual happiness can no longer be the cracking sport of Astaire and Rogers or the lilting easiness of 'Main Street'; it becomes the initial promise that women will realise their womanliness in male support giving way to her fullest fulfilment in abjection to him.

Apart from its consistency with other cinematic trends, this development may have a more specific explanation. The impulse on the part of the genre's dominant figures (notably Stanley Donen, Arthur Freed, Gene Kelly and Vincente Minnelli) to make it more serious led them to look for dance forms with more lofty, aka male-centred, credentials than ballroom dancing and stiptease/burlesque (the heart of Astaire-Rogers and Busby Berkeley respectively). There were three broad contenders: modern dance (above all, Graham), ballet and folk. The first ruled itself out, despite its ultra-high seriousness, for left-wing associations unlikely to go down well in the McCarthy era, female-centredness and being a bit too serious to fit into Hollywood (it is lampooned in several musicals including *White Christmas*, 1954, and *Funny Face*, 1956). Ballet had no such associations and offered artistic respectability in the form of a dance vocabulary drenched in dependency. As for folk, it turned out to mean tap and rodeo dancing, by tradition male forms. A dance-style developed which gave more prominence to men, permitted them to dance things other than love, free of the slur of effeminacy and worse; within couple dances it also meant a renewed sense of gender polarity (to make the men look more like men) and female dependency.

None of this should take away from the fact that musicals have always given strong roles to women. Betty Garrett, Ann Miller and even winsome Vera-Ellen in *On the Town* have more about them in every way – energy, intelligence, nous – than the men they fall for (Frank Sinatra, Jules Munshin and Gene Kelly, respectively). Since the mid-fifties the genre (in its showbiz rather than rock form), though in decline, has been dominated by such spirited stars as Julie Andrews, Doris Day, Liza Minnelli and Barbra Streisand. However, none of these are dancing stars; indeed, apart from Minnelli, they can hardly dance at all. Consequently there are no couple-dances in this period. The subordination within heterosexuality which had become so insistent within couple-dance choreography sat ill with women whose stock in trade was guts, wit and self-assertion. It was as if it was no longer possible to imagine in bodily terms a heterosexual happiness for which the star woman did not have to pay too high a price in terms of subordination. Interestingly, their men often can't sing much either: the equation is her sung emotionality traded for his social power, as for instance, his aristocratic position (*The Sound of Music*), monied charm (*Funny Girl*) or British snottiness (*Cabaret*). This is a familiar heterosexual division of labour: he earns the money and social position, she does the emotional work for the pair of them, without challenging him bodily. If, like Shirley MacLaine in *Sweet Charity* and Liza Minnelli in *Cabaret*, she is a pretty good mover, she ends up alone.

It seems that with heterosexuality in dance, the nearer you get to sex the less sameness and equality can be tolerated. While it is still courtship and having fun together, dancers can still do the same thing, simultaneously or sequentially; differences can be sunk in finding common ground or be the source of complementarity. But once you really get down to It, once the dark secret world of 'laying' is clearly on the agenda, then the woman has to know her place, her difference and her subordination. In rock-oriented dance films of the seventies and eighties, such as *Saturday Night Fever*, *Staying Alive* and *Dirty Dancing*, where the sexuality of the dance is infinitely more explicit, the sexual subordination of the woman in dance is even more insisted upon. The dance sequences tend visually to favour the macho strutting and flexing of John Travolta and Paytrick Swayze over the girations of whoever it is (in fact Karen Gorney, Finola Hughes and Jennifer Grey). *Staying Alive* does have sections where Hughes and Travolta writhe and leap side by side but their climactic dance consists mainly of his throwing her perilously about, making her dynamic and spectacular but apparently entirely at his mercy (under the circumstances, she must have thanked God for editing). Gorney and Grey do not even get this: they are flung about, held to the ground and borne aloft, but do very little themselves.

Yet the Altman paradigm, of the coming together within heterosexuality of opposing value systems, certainly applies to *Saturday Night Fever* and *Dirty Dancing*, only not at the level of the dance. Rather, she represents social and moral values that he has to learn to aspire to and take on: Gorney is the culturally ambitious one who has learnt to speak nicely and begun to make it in Manhattan, while Travolta is still stuck in a paint shop in Brooklyn; Grey is the nice middle-class girl staying with her parents at the holiday club where Swayze works as an exhibition dancer and gigolo on the side. Both men initially reject and ridicule the women and then come to respect their values, Travolta moving in with Gorney 'just as a friend', Swayze giving up prostitution and gaining acceptance from Grey's family. Yet none of this has anything to do with dancing, where it is the women who have to make all the changes, Gorney fitting in with Travolta's ideas of disco dancing (against her inclination to learn ballet), Grey learning to do Swayze's repellently crude sexual idea of Latin American dance (as contrasted to the dreary, stiff dancing her parents expect her to do). These films are positively Victorian in their construction of heterosexuality: the man embodies sexuality, dangerous, low, exciting; the woman embodies morality, social position, niceness. A perfect human unity is achieved by their coming together.

My original assumption in writing this article was that I would argue that there was a contradiction between the utopian narrative function of couple-dances, the moment of pure understanding and love between a man and a woman in the face of plot vicissitudes, and what actually happened choreographically, the gradual assertion of male domination. I assumed it was a contradiction because it seemed self-evident to me that women lost out in the process and it was pretty much a strain on men too. I wonder now, however, how naive I was. These are utopian numbers, expressions of what being happy within heterosexuality would feel like, yet they move from the pleasures of mutuality to a construction of heterosexuality as, in Sheila Jeffrey's phrase, 'eroticised power difference'. Surely no one as it were 'really' wants this? But then I realise we're still rather early on in making sense of heterosexuality, still stuck with the question Freud never thought to ask: what, after all, do heterosexuals want?

Credits

The Band Wagon
   1953 MGM; director Vincente Minnelli; choreographer Michael Kidd
Brigadoon
   1955 MGM; director Vincente Minnelli; choreographer Gene Kelly
Dirty Dancing
   1987 Vestron Pictures; director Emile Ardolino; choreographer Kenny Ortega
On the Town
   1949 MGM; director/choreographer Stanley Donen, Gene Kelly
Saturday Night Fever
   1978 Paramount; director John Badham; choreographer Lester Wilson
Staying Alive
   1983 Paramount; director Sylvester Stallone; choreographer Dennon Rawles, Sayhber Rawles
Top Hat
   1935 RKO; director Mark Sandrich; choreographer Hermes Pan, Fred Astaire

Bibliography

R. Altman, (ed.), *Genre: the Musical* (London: Routledge & Kegan Paul, 1981).

R. Altman, *The American Film Musical* (Bloomington: Indiana University Press, 1987).

R. Brandon, *New Women and Old Men* (London: Secker & Warburg, 1990).

J. Collins, 'Towards Defining a Matrix of the Musical Comedy: The Place of the Spectator within the Textual Mechanisms', in Altman, pp. 134–46.

A. Croce, *The Fred Astaire and Ginger Rogers Book* (New York: Dutton, 1972).

R. Dyer, 'Entertainment and Utopia', *Movie*, 24 (1977) 2–13; reprinted in Altman, pp. 175–89.

J. Feuer, *The Hollywood Musical* (London: Macmillan, 1982).

M. Haskell, *From Reverence to Rape* (New York: Holt, Rinehart & Winston, 1974).

S. Jeffreys, *Anti-Climax* (London: Women's Press, 1990).

Part Two
Ethnography

5 An-Other Voice:
Young Women Dancing and Talking

HELEN THOMAS

This paper is divided into two sections. The first section sets out the grounds for doing sociological research in the area of dance and gender. The second section explores some aspects of the relation between dance and gender which emerged from a nine months' study of a local community dance project in London which holds open dance classes and maintains a dance group. This research involved sitting-in on classes, filming and interviewing members of the dance class and Group. Particular emphasis in this study was given to interviewing a number of young women between the ages of 16 and 19 years. Because of the composition of the classes and the group and indeed, the character of the project, I was able to draw on young women with varied experience and interest in dance.

I should indicate at the outset that I do not consider the study of men in dance is unimportant; it is simply that my particular interest, as discussed below, is in exploring the role that dance plays in women's lives. However, during the course of the research I found it necessary to look at some of the issues surrounding men in dance because, clearly, any discussion which focuses on one gender has implications for the other. The word gender is used here rather than sex because, although the terms are often used interchangeably, I want to maintain a distinction between them. The sex of a person refers to the 'fixed' or biologically-given characteristics of a male or female. The concept of gender, on the other hand, the formulation of which stems largely from the past two decades of feminist research, entails much more than biological 'maleness' or 'femaleness'. Rather it refers to features that are acquired and developed within cultures. Gender here, in other words, is viewed as a social characteristic.

My own interest in exploring the relationship between dance and gender came from several related sources. Through researching into the development of American modern dance for my PhD thesis, I became fascinated with assessing why and how women played such an important role in the development of American modern dance at both an institutional and a practical level. This fascination was reinforced by my growing interest in feminist analyses of representations of women.[1] A further impetus came from two interrelated sources: my students at art school and my own obsession with maintenance of (light) body weight, which I had long suspected had some connection with my first training in dance.[2]

The students referred to above had little or no experience of dancing prior to working with me. In discussions after showing different kinds of dances from the Western theatrical tradition, the students would continually compare the bodily 'look' of the dancers before them with their own physicality and movement expression. Moreover, they would often link the dancer's grace or strength to ideas about femininity and masculinity. The women in particular, were inclined to compare the elegance of the female dancers with what they perceived to be their own lack of these features. What was of interest to me there, was that this was something that I related to also, it was something that we shared in common.

It was almost as if underneath the surface of this talk there lay an idea of an 'ideal' female body, which dancers, at least to the eye of the (female) beholder, appeared to be more likely to reach than most ordinary mortals. Contrary to our commonsense perceptions, ideas about the body are not purely founded on the body as a thing in nature. Rather, as writers such as Douglas (1970), Turner (1984), Haug (1987) and Szekely (1988) demonstrate, ideas about the body are mediated through society. The body, as Szekely (ibid.) argues, 'is always in society' which means that it 'must be understood in its concrete existence socially and historically'. From this perspective it can be argued that the student's responses which evoked a recognition in me, were not purely individual, rather they were grounded in ideas that we share in common, and as such, they become worthy of sociological investigation.

Sociologists, for a number of reasons, as I have indicated elsewhere, have been extremely reluctant to focus on dance as a

topic and a resource for sociological inquiry.[3] Usually, performance dance is seen as an activity which is marginal in complex
industrial societies and therefore is not deemed worthy of
sociological research. But the paucity of sociological research on
dance is not restricted to performance dance. Although sociologists and cultural analysts[4] indicate and in some instances discuss at some length, the significant role that dancing plays in
working-class youth sub-cultures which are transitory in character, their insights have not generated much systematic research,
that is until recently.[5] As Ward stresses in his paper in this
volume, notwithstanding the fact that several major statistical
surveys show that dancing continues to play an important role in
British cultural life, there has been a real neglect by sociologists
to examine seriously the *activity* of dancing.

But if we turn our attention to the related discipline of anthropology, there is evidence to suggest that dancing not only plays
an important role in the life of a number of pre-industrial
societies, but it also performs a significant function in the process
of gender construction and identification.[6] Although dance
anthropologists such as Royce (1978) and Spencer (1985) often
bemoan the fact that anthropology has neglected dance, there is
more research in this area. Elsewhere I have argued that, in
part, the reason for this lies in the way in which dance has been
treated and to some extent is still viewed, as a form that exists
outside of and prior to language.[7] Because dance's primary
means of expression (at least in the West) is the body, it is seen
as being nearer to nature and as anthropology started out by
studying 'exotic' peoples who were seen as being less rational
and less advanced than Western industrial cultures, dance as an
activity of the body has received more attention from anthropologists than sociologists, whose prime concern was and is still
with understanding the processes and the major features of
modernity.

However, if we turn the telescope round and redirect our
attention back towards our own society, it can be argued that
dance not only plays a significant role in youth cultures, but as
McRobbie (1984) and Frith (1978) have revealed, it also plays a
role in the processes of gender identification. This view has been
advanced and substantiated by more recent studies from North
America that draw on the insights of British cultural studies.[8]
Given this, we might reasonably expect to find that feminist

social scientists have given dance more than a passing glance over the course of the past twenty years or so of the second wave of feminism. But, unfortunately, this has not been the case, except perhaps for the tentative treatments of dance in popular culture by writers like McRobbie (1984).

But feminist social research in dance need not have been restricted to popular culture. From the history of art dance in Europe, it is clear that dance was one of the few areas in public life that provided women with the opportunity for self-expression and for some social advancement. The evidence further suggests that dance offered a means for some, albeit minimal, social mobility and self-expression for working-class girls.[9] Moreover, the relatively recent emergence and successes of black dance companies like Alvin Ailey and Dance Theater of Harlem in America and black British companies like Phoenix, indicate that dance is also beginning to provide opportunities for young black women (and men) from traditionally disadvantaged ethno-cultural minority groups, and that individuals from these groups are perceiving it thus.[10]

It is somewhat surprising then, that this 'women's realm' of activity has not been viewed worthy of serious consideration by feminist social researchers, particularly in the initial stages of the movement where the concern was to 'add women' to historical and sociological accounts in order to undercut the androcentric bias inherent in the tradition and hence to generate a more accurate picture of socio-historical processes.[11] Greer (1970), however, simply dismisses the art of ballet in which the female dancer rose to predominance in the nineteenth century, as little more than the 'favourite spectacle of middle-class women' and ballerinas as the archetypes of the 'eternally feminine.' Even if this were wholly the case, it would be interesting to explore and examine how these archetypes were constructed through the dance and how they were promoted and sustained. Of course this would be seeing the relationship between dance and (the female) gender solely in negative terms, as something which simply contributed to the exploitation of women in society. There would be little room here for considering the possibility of the pleasure of dancing or indeed that it might have a positive or liberating function. Yet, often these ballet dancers whom Greer dismisses, through their expansive use of space and their dress, challenged the established codes of appropriate female bodily expression which placed severe strictures on women's mobility, both literally and symbolically. This was also the case with 'modern' dancers like Duncan, St. Denis, Graham and Humphrey, who not only performed but also created and controlled the production of their own dance images.[12] But perhaps matters are improving because, despite the fact that feminism has not considered dance worthy of inquiry, dance scholars like Daly (1987) and Foster (1988) have added a further dimension to dance analyses by drawing on the insights of feminism and cultural studies.

The community dance project which I chose as the site of the research in question is at present funded by a local authority and a major dance institution provides the dance space. The project has been running for about six years. There are two open classes per week, one mid-week in the evening and the other on a Sunday morning, for young people between the ages of 14 and 25 years. The classes are led by one teacher who is white and male, and are provided free of charge. From these classes the teacher invites individuals to join the dance Group. The Group rehearsals and the staging of new work takes place on a Sunday afternoon after the morning class. Some of the dancers taking the classes and a number of the Group go on to or indeed are students in more formal dance training courses. In general they wish to go on to become professional dancers. Others come to classes because they enjoy the experience and because the classes are free of charge.

The primary aim of the classes is not to develop a specific set of technical skills, but rather to provide a space for young people living in an inner-city, multi-cultural environment to experience the pleasures of theatrical or performance-based dance who might not otherwise be able to do so. The style of the classes can be seen as loosely jazz-based and most of the musical accompaniment is contemporary popular music. Although the teacher seldom corrects the 'technique' as such, principally because there are too many people in the class, the class is quite fast and the dancers have to develop a good movement memory in order to keep up. Despite the fact that the atmosphere in the classes is lively and not quite as serious or perhaps studious as a 'formal' dance class, the dancers work very hard. Indeed the semi-formal atmosphere gives an air of democracy about the classes and the new members do not seem to feel inhibited by their lack of dance experience *vis à vis* some of the more technically competent dancers. The climate of the classes further reinforces the aim to promote the notion of dancing as a pleasureful experience.

The Dance Group has around twenty members at any one time, some of whom will be more experienced than others. New dancers are brought into the Group as others leave or stop attending regularly. Sometimes those dancers who have left the Group because of the demands of their formal dance-training courses rejoin after they have completed their courses. Others stay with the Group throughout their training because they find the work different and less pressurised than that at their colleges or schools.

The Group performs regularly throughout the year in the local area and to larger audiences outside the locality. The Group has a programme of dances that lasts about one and a half hours. As new dances are brought in, so old ones disappear. Some dances stay in the repertoire for longer than others depending on their popularity with the audiences, the dancers and the teacher who choreographs most of the work. Some dances, however, are choreographed by individual members of the Group.

In part, this project was chosen as the site for doing the research because of its location. Ballet is often viewed as a pursuit of the middle classes and this project is somewhat unique in that it deliberately tries to draw upon young working-class people who live in an inner-city multi-cultural environment. The dance classes and the Group attract a large number of young black people who come largely through 'word of mouth'. The value of choosing a social setting such as this lies in the fact that other factors apart from gender such as race or class would have to be brought into the analytic frame. However, although these factors cannot be separated out, the discussion below focuses primarily on gender issues that emerged from the interviews.

The methodological approach used here is *qualitative* in character as opposed to *quantitative*. It is broadly situated within the framework of the *interpretive* tradition of sociology. The concern is to draw out layers of meaning – the structures of signification – concerning some aspects of dance and society; to operate on the basis of what Geertz (1975) calls 'thick description'. It is important to stress that the research methods that social scientists use are not simply neutral or disinterested sets of techniques or procedures which somehow give accurate accounts or pictures of the social world. Whilst 'qualitative' methods such as partici-

pant observation, unstructured interviews, etc., have been used
for this study of dance and gender, it is crucial to emphasise that
they do not exist outside the analytic frame. I am using the term
'method' here, in a wider sense than is often proposed by the
normative tradition of sociology, which sees that sociological
method is composed of objective techniques that exist apart from
and as a check on the vagaries of theory and/or the biases of the
researcher.

Over the past twenty years, feminist research has provided
various challenges to the 'neutrality' of method.[13] It has shown
that questions of method involve asking methodological and
epistemological questions and indeed, often contain ontological
assumptions. In exposing the myth of ethical neutrality, feminists have systematically demonstrated that the topics and
methods of research in social science display an androcentric
bias. They have shown that sociology has largely been sex-blind
but that it has been written by men under the banner of value
freedom. Moreover, feminist research has put the issue of gender
into the central arena of the social sciences. Although feminism
has not taken dance very seriously, it has addressed in some
depth the issue of the hitherto invisible woman in sociological
analyses and pointed to the androcentric character of the discipline. Any study of the relation between dance and gender can
learn much from the best that feminist research has to offer in
this light.[14]

One of the important factors of feminist research is that it is
generated from and through the perspectives of *women's* experiences. This means that the subjects of study, their ideas and their
concerns, must be taken very seriously. That is, there is a concern that those who are being studied should be given a voice or
voices. Women, from this standpoint, are seen as agents of
knowledge, in contrast to mainstream sociology where their
presence is almost made visible by their consistent absence as
knowing subjects.

But, as Harding (1987) points out, the best of feminist research goes further than this in that the aim is to locate the
observer in the same critical framework as the observed. That is,
it seeks to operate on the basis of a reflexive practice. It proposes
that those who have traditionally done the analysis should themselves be placed under the microscope. Thus, the aim becomes to
examine critically the social sources and the discourses of power

and knowledge. The researcher, in other words, should question and reveal his/her grounds as he/she proceeds, and his/her role as a social actor in the research. Feminist research, then, sees that the attitudes and beliefs of feminist researchers shape the research and the analyses as much as androcentric research models. The researcher, as Stanley and Wise argue, is an essential component of all research.

> One's self cannot be left behind, it can only be omitted from discussions and written accounts of the research process. But it is an omission, a failure to discuss something which has been present within the research process itself.[15]

It is important to take account of the fact that I (the researcher/interviewer) was an active agent in the research setting, attempting to make sense of and contributing to the dancers' discussions about an activity that is not bound by verbal language. I would contend that my intervention in the interview process was enabling rather than, as an objectivist approach would argue, a hindrance to the research. Because of my dance background and my understanding of the difficulties of bringing ideas about the experience of dancing into the domain of the verbal, I was able to empathise with the dancers' attempts to search for the appropriate words, to ask other questions, or to participate in the discussions in such a way as to facilitate their talk. Along with writers like Finch (1983) and Smith (1989) I would seek to maintain that interviewers are substantive people in the interview setting and the research process. Thus, the idea inherent in an objectivist framework that the researcher is an invisible being who drops into and reveals the practices and ways of others (the researched) becomes redundant, in favour of a reflexivity of accounts. As Harding (1986) points out, this does not mean that the project should be full of 'soul searching' or 'navel gazing'. It entails, rather, that the researcher reveal or uncover his/her grounds for speaking; that he/she should be reflexive on the context, methods and procedures adopted and at the same time, enable the voices of the researched to speak.

In light of the above, it is a major concern in the second section of this paper to treat seriously the views of the young men and women I have been talking with, to try and understand and analyse their perceptions and feelings about dance. That, however, does not mean that the discussion should be directed only at an individualist level, precisely for the reason given above, that the body is always in society and that our perceptions of it are mediated by social processes. Moreover, as Mauss (1973), Douglas (1970) and Garfinkel (1987) demonstrate, this is particularly so in the area of gender. So that at the same time as attempting to treat the subjects of the discussion as knowing subjects, the concern is also to locate their individual speech within a wider socio-cultural frame.

As I stated at the beginning of this paper, the research took place over a period of nine months. During this time I sat in on classes and talked with dancers, filmed rehearsals and performances and conducted in-depth interviews with nine of the participants. The interviews took place on a one-to-one basis in a room away from the dance class, usually during the lunch break. Although all the interviewees were asked the same set of basic questions (see Appendix 5.1) the interviews were open-ended in as much as if a dancer said something that evoked a response in me, or led me to ask her/him to elaborate or explain a point, or indeed to ask other questions, then the interview would take on a different shape, and of course would last much longer than if s/he simply answered the questions. Some interviews lasted twenty minutes, others forty-five minutes.

From an examination of the tapes and the transcripts it was noticeable that certain topics were raised and discussed at some length by all or most of the dancers interviewed. These were grouped together under separate headings. The dominant categories that emerged were Dancing, Body Shape, Diet and Food, with performance and technique as subcategories of Dancing.[16] The discussion that follows centres on the talk that was subsumed under these three major categories.

When I asked the women dancers what they liked about dancing their responses pointed to the fact that it performs a positive function for them; it makes them feel good, it enables them to express themselves in a particular way, it takes them to another world, it helps them to relax.

For example, Dawn (16 years), who has been dancing for about two years, and who is a student on a dance foundation course, said:

Well, I find it expressive for me because I find it hard to express myself in words.

When I asked what kind of feeling did she get from dancing, Dawn replied:

You can't actually explain it . . . I can't see anything . . . You just *feel really different* and I don't know, you're *floating about.*

Trisha (17 years) has been dancing since she was three. She is in the second year of her foundation course and hopes to go on to become a ballet dancer. Trisha also spoke of the difficulty of explaining what she liked about dancing.

I don't know. It just seems natural to me because like I said I've been doing it for so long, it's just natural. I don't know.

Asked how she felt when she danced, Trisha said:

It depends really. It's just a matter of letting the music – I don't know – I sometimes *let the music just take control* . . . sometimes I just *black out.*

Trisha went on to say that it was difficult to explain how she felt and when I asked her why this was so she responded, like Dawn, that 'You have to experience it', i.e. I would need to experience it to understand it and if I had, then there would be no need for words. What Trisha was pointing to here, is the problem of bringing feelings about an activity like dancing, which engages both the mind and the body in a corporeal manner, into the domain of verbal language. In part, what these young dancers are referring to is dance's difference to language, its constitution as an-other voice.

Michelle (17 years) is still at school studying for her A-levels. She does not want to pursue a career in dance, although, like Trisha, she has been dancing since she was small. For Michelle, dancing is a form of relaxation.

It *relaxes* you – I mean if I'm at school and I've had a really hard day, I feel fed up at school and I go dancing. I come here, I *feel completely different.* It just relaxes you.

When I asked Michelle how dancing relaxes her she said:

I think it's because in dancing you have certain rhythms that make you – you've got to stretch, and there's others that you've got to relax and it helps you to relax your muscles and *just release tension.*

Monique (17 years) who has been to different dance classes over the years but like Michelle, does not wish to take it further, said that dancing took her out of herself:

> Well, it makes you, you know, *take out your emotions*; if you're feeling down or something like that, you can just kind of *dance it off* and it makes you feel better.

I asked Monique how dancing does that and she replied:

> ... it's just like your body's doing something completely different. You're *forgetting what happened before* or something like that, or if you're in a really good mood you *just let go, just relax* yourself.

Nessa (19 years) has also been dancing since she was small and is now in her second year of a dance theatre course. Like Trisha, she found it difficult to explain exactly what she likes about dancing.

> What I like about dance is that I'm moving, I'm not just sitting around being in an office or something I don't want to do . . . I don't know, *it's something I get from it*, I get such a buzz out of doing it.

Sharon (17 years) has been dancing 'off and on' as she put it, since she was four. Her mum would like her to be a dancer, but Sharon sees it as a hobby only which enables her to relax and which gives her a different feeling. When I asked Sharon what dancing made her feel, she said:

> Well, I don't know. I think it's to do with your mind: it *relaxes my mind*, I think sort of *lets everything go free and easy* . . . it make me think a bit and then . . . I don't know, it's *just another feeling* I suppose.

In all of these young women's talk, dance emerges as a source of pleasure. For some such as Dawn, Nessa and Trisha, it enables them to express themselves in a way that they cannot with words. For Michelle and Sharon and Monique, dance helps them to relax and feel differently. Furthermore, in all of the talk there is a notion of transcending reality or, as Dawn put it, of 'disappearing' or 'going to a different place'. The sense of dance as a feeling of otherness was brought out most strongly in the discussions on performance and performers. For example, when

I asked Dawn, 'How do you get taken over [by dance] and at the same time perform [to an audience]?' she replied:

> Well, the main thing is, when you're doing a performance and you get nervous . . . just forget the audience is there. And that's the best thing to do. But don't forget the dance you're doing, and you probably won't because you've been rehearsing for ages and it's *just right inside you.*

When I asked Trisha what she meant by 'blacking out', she replied:

> When we were in Germany we did one of the performances at a college and it was like, I went so full out that I couldn't remember . . . *I just forgot about what had happened* . . . It's weird, I sometimes *just get blackouts* with a dance if I do it really well.

Although Vanessa said initially she could not talk very well about how dancing and performing made her feel but that she could 'show me in movement', she went on to say that:

> Just before a performance I get very nervous. I think I'm going to forget something, I try and *block it out* . . . there's *something different about being on the stage* than in class, it just like brings you in . . . I don't know whether you sparkle or what it is, it's just the atmosphere.

When I asked them if they had a favourite dancer I found that Baryshnikov and Nureyev were mentioned most frequently, although only Trisha expressed a preference and a love of classical ballet. However, it is not so surprising that these names should emerge because both these dancers have star status and have been given high profiles in the mass media perhaps because, in addition to the fact that they are virtuoso performers, they stand out in what is generally thought of as a women's realm of activity, at least in our culture. But it could also be that women dancers are not as visible for these young women. Nessa, whose favourite dancer is Baryshnikov, was aware of this:

> There aren't many women that I look up to in dance . . . There aren't many because they're not given a chance . . . there are hundreds of women doing auditions and going on cabaret things but – they don't stand out, you just don't see them, they're just like background.

Helen Thomas

1.   Keith O'Brien, teacher of the Youth Dance Group, leading the class

Helen Thomas

2.   Members of the Sunday class demonstrating sections of a new dance to other class members

3. *(left)* Michelle, an interviewed member of the Group, in rehearsal

Helen Thomas

4. *(below)* The end of a Group rehearsal

Helen Thomas

5. *(above)* Dawn, an interviewed member of the Group, in rehearsal

Tiwi Dance

6. *(left)* Roberta Mungatopi dances in the women's style

7. *(left)* Alan Papajua
   performing in the
   men's style

Dominique Bernard

8. *(right)* Big Don
   Mwalamini
   demonstrates the
   women's style

Dominique Bernard

9. *(right)* Leo Morton performing the Wunantawi/pulanga dance

Dominique Bernard

Dominique Bernard

10. Denise, Joan, Jovita and Helen Puruntatameri perform the Wunantawi/ pulanga dance

11. Big Don Mwalamini dances the Wunantawi/pularti dance

Dominique Bernard

12. Anita Pangarimini and Nora Cook performing the Wunantawi/pularti dance

Dominique Bernard

Dominique Bernard

13.   Francis Mukwangkimi does the Kiakiae dance

Jacob Ross

14.　Bolaji Adeola with the Adzido Pan African Ensemble

Jacob Ross

15.　Master drummers of Burundi on tour in London

When I asked Dawn why her favoured dancers were male she said:

> I don't know, I just do. It's not that I don't like women . . . I
> don't think I've seen as much on video perhaps of women and
> women talking, most of the time [it's the] men choreographers
> talking about the dance they've made up and things like that.

Later on in the conversation Dawn mentioned that she liked
Graham because 'she made a flexed foot look good' and Makarova because 'she's just magic really . . . she *seems to disappear to
someplace else*'. I then asked Dawn if she wanted to go to her
(Makarova's) place but she said, 'no, not hers'. That is, she went
to her own space.

> I suppose it can be really selfish, because you just say to
> yourself, *forget everything*, and *everything pours out of you* whatever
> you're doing.

To begin with I thought that this notion of being able to express
themselves through dance, to 'disappear', 'black out', 'freak out',
'pour out', 'relax', etc. was gender-specific. After all, as discussed
above, dance has provided women with at least the possibility of
self-expression in public spaces in a culture where women traditionally have been confined to the private sphere. In the tradition of Western cultural thought, the body is treated as a thing in
nature as opposed to culture, which, like other aspects of nature
needs to be controlled.[17] Women are located on the nature side of
the culture/nature dichotomy through their perceived nearness
to their bodies, to nature.[18] Dance, which is characterised by its
attention to the body, primarily by its *non-verbal* mode of expression, could provide a prime site or a gap for women to voice their
difference(s), their otherness, to break through the dominant
(public, male) discourses, to which they have been denied access
and through which they have been silenced. In order to explore
this further I decided it was necessary to interview at least one of
the men in the Group.

Mark (21 years) has only been dancing for about two years.
He had a little dance experience at school which he enjoyed.
Several years after leaving school Mark decided to start going to
dance classes. He came to Keith's class and was asked to join the
group after a short period. Mark then decided to give up his job
and take up dancing seriously. He is now on the same dance
foundation course as Trisha and Dawn.

During my conversation with Mark he said that different types of dancing brought out 'different things' in him. When I asked him to elaborate on this he responded in a similar vein to the women.

> I can't . . . I can't put it into words. It's for the person who knows.

I asked him what he felt like when he was dancing and he replied:

> it puts me in a *different world* in that sometimes I can *forget that I'm actually there* in front of people, especially in performing; or if I get really stuck into it and *it takes me over*, and I *can't control it*. That's what it feels like . . . I'm learning how to fly, that's the way I would put it, so I want to fly higher, faster.

Clearly, Mark's comments were so similar in tone to those of the women interviewed that I thought it would be prudent to interview another male dancer in order to see if his comments also coincided with the others.

Errol (21 years) has been dancing for three years and is in his second year of the same foundation course as Mark. Like most of the others Errol said it was almost impossible to talk about how dancing made him feel and again as with the others, he spoke very clearly about it.

> It makes me feel like – I feel there are *no boundaries to me* at all . . . It makes me feel *more than I am*, than I am now in a sense . . . It makes me feel *really expressive* . . . it makes me feel great.

I then asked Errol if he could relate to the idea of 'disappearing' or 'blacking out'. His reply seemed to articulate clearly how he saw the difference between dance and everyday life, i.e. dance's otherness. Errol was aware that to a certain extent dancing offers him a means of escape from the 'reality' of the world out there. It takes him to a different space.

> it's like I *cross a porthole into a different dimension* because I mean society's not perfect and sometimes dancing and – dancing for a reason – makes you feel really good . . . Sometimes I just feel fed up with sitting on a bus that's really packed and then listening that somebody else got killed in the news, and I just

want to get to Keith's – or get to class and just *sort of escape for a while.*

For Errol dancing 'is the exact opposite to what society is in a sense'.

It [dancing] makes you know the differences between what feels good and what isn't.

Thus, the feelings experienced through dancing, the pleasure of moving, of releasing tension, of transcendence, were present in the talk of both the young men and the young women interviewed. It appears to cut across the specificity of gender, at least in this instance. It may be that this desire to 'black out', to go to 'a different dimension' could be related to other factors such as race or class. All of the dancers interviewed are black and are from a predominantly working-class area. The project itself was set up to attract young people like the above who otherwise would be unlikely to experience performance dance on a regular basis. Both the class and Group are overwhelmingly participated in by young black men and women. New people are brought into the class by 'word of mouth'. They like the atmosphere, the movement style, the music and the teacher who is white and male.

Before I sat in on the classes I had expected to find some young black people there because of the multi-cultural character of the area, but I was quite surprised to find that the majority of the participants were black. I was not alone in this, because Errol said:

That's exactly what I thought when I first came . . . and I saw so many black dancers and I just said Keith must be some kind of superman . . . I came here and he had a certain attitude, I could completely relate to him without even knowing him, and like his movements as well, I could actually relate to them.

Mark, on the other hand, thought there was no simple answer as to why so many young black people liked to come to the class and be in the Group. He said it was 'too vast to pinpoint it' and that you had 'to look at the spectrum'. Like Nessa, Trisha and Monique, Mark thought that the use of contemporary music and the jazz-like dance style were important factors. He added that the class wouldn't work if it were a ballet class because it would present a 'sort of upper-class Royal Ballet sort of picture'. His remarks seem to be pointing to a relationship between race and class and dancing, but at the same time he recognised that male dancers were not taken very seriously in the culture in general. Errol added weight to Mark's first point by saying that when he went to a ballet audition, he stood out because he was black, although he felt he had the same poise and aptitude for ballet as the others. He said that the [white] others in the audition were looking at him in a curious manner, but not necessarily in a bad way, although, as he said, 'a lot of actual dancers don't immediately relate ballet to black people'. However, Errol thought that this attitude was changing slowly.[19]

Although the feelings of otherness, of difference, that were experienced through the activity of dancing and performing did not seem to be gender-specific, there were other elements of the dancers' talk that appeared to be more so. These centred around discussions that were subsumed under the categories of Body Shape and Diet and Food. Although there was no fixed direct question on shape, it emerged as a topic for discussion around questions seven and eight.[20] For the most part I brought it up directly as a result of something that the dancers had said which indicated that this might be worth pursuing. Once again, however, it should be remembered that I have long been concerned with my own shape and weight and it could be that my notion that this was indeed something most women shared in common, could have helped me to manoeuvre the discussion in this direction. At the same time, it should be pointed out that there appeared to be nothing in the men's talk that indicated an overriding concern about a sort of ideal dancing body shape and the steps that men took to attain it, in the way that it almost seemed to emerge 'naturally' out of my discussions with the women. I brought these topics into the discussions with the men in a much more interventionist manner.

When I asked Tricia if, in the light of what she had been saying about dancing and performing, she thought that there was a particular body shape or look that a dancer should have, she replied:

No, I mean I would like to think I was about *5'7" with long legs* but sometimes it's a disadvantage – you know, it's *better to be short*, but I *don't think you can be too skinny* . . . you *can't be too fat*, to be a dancer . . . *if you're too fat you're clumsy*, but in between.

Although Monique thought it did not matter if you were fat, 'as long as you were trying hard', she also said that 'it [dancing] looks better if you have a slender body'. When I asked her if she had a version of an ideal dancer, like Trisha she responded that:

> Well, *not too fat*, *not too slim* or anything; always keep your hair out of your face.

Dawn also felt that 'it helps to be slim' and that clothing and dress can make a dancer look better: 'it [clothes] changes your appearance'. While Nessa recognised that worrying about shape or weight was not restricted to dancers, 'it's everywhere': women in general are 'worried about their weight'. Like the others, however, Nessa did have a concept of an ideal dancer which, she thought, other people also held and that there was pressure to conform to this image.

> There's an *ideal* of a dancer as *slim, long-legged, perfect,* and everybody wants to be like that. That's the image, the *ultimate image* and wherever you go, whatever type of dance, that is what everyone wants to aim for. You *want to look good* and that's what it is. And if you've got people telling you you don't, or you're rubbish, you start to think oh, maybe it's my shape, maybe it's restricting me from doing such and such a movement.

Sharon too, considered dancers should be a certain shape, otherwise the look of the dance was affected adversely:

> they [dancers] *can't be too overbuilt* or *under-weight or too skinny* but there has to be something about them . . . *a slim build but not anorexic* or anything . . . but I don't think it looks good *if they're overweight*, it just *doesn't look attractive or appealing* to the dance . . . it spoils it.

However, when I asked Mark if he thought there was a preferable male body shape for dancing, he replied in the negative:

> Oh no, no. So long as your limbs are stretched and you haven't got short, stocky muscles.

Although the detail of the image is not as clear as the women's, nevertheless there is a broad notion of a male dancer. Errol also spoke in these terms. He did have a version of an ideal body shape but he felt that his training would enable him to achieve this by 'stretching' and 'strengthening' particular muscles.

Thus, despite the fact that all the interviewees did have some version of an ideal dancing shape, there is a difference in detail and in attitude between the men and the women. Mark and Errol discussed it in terms of strength and action: 'I've got to lift the girls and if I'm not strong enough to lift them then you can't progress any further', said Mark. For the women, on the other hand, it is about how they look or appear – 'the slim', 'not-too-thin', 'not-too-fat', 'long-legged' image, 'the ultimate image', which has to do with 'how you dress as well as the shape of your body'. For the women, then, it is about looking good, for the men it has to do with building strong muscles. Their talk, in many respects, reinforces stereotypical notions of women as passive beings who 'are' and men as active agents who 'do'.

This difference in talk was reinforced when the discussions focused on Food and Diet. It became clear, for example, that the more involved the women were with dance, the more they were aware of diet and its possible dangers. Neither Sharon, Monique or Michelle seemed particularly bothered about diet. I say 'seemed' because Michelle told me after she had read this article that indeed she was very concerned about diet and that she wanted me to say so in the final version. Neither were Mark or Errol worried, they just 'sweated it off'. Dawn, Trisha and Nessa were acutely aware of diet but only Nessa saw it as an issue for herself. Trisha, for example, noted that *other* people worried about their weight, particularly those on her course:

> They [the other students] *worry about their weight all the time*, it really annoys me. But then I annoy other people because I've got a very high metabolism, *I can stuff my face* and not put on any weight if I need it, it isn't a problem . . . They [the others] think *they have to be a certain weight*.

However, Trisha did go on to say that if she did put on weight then 'it would probably bother' her. She was also aware that it was to do with how people 'saw you'.

Dawn, like Trisha, noted that some of her friends at college had problems with weight and food, particularly the sweet variety, but that she did not; she did not taste it any more. Dawn tries not to think about weight. However, she is very conscious of what she puts into her mouth on a daily basis, and this does not appear to be very much, given the amount of physical exercise she does most days.

> I *try not to think about it* and just to wake up in the morning and say I'm going to have *something at the break* and then *nothing else and then have my dinner* when I get home and then do that, but instead they [the foodies] *bring in healthy food* and question everybody else.

Dawn went on to say that with the foodies in her group it was not so much that they looked fat but that the problem lay in their attitude towards the forbidden or calorific foods which they liked so much.

> It can get so that someone saying *oh I'm fat and they're not* at all, because *they've eaten a chocolate bar*, but now *I eat chocolate now* to give me energy. *I don't taste it* anymore really but I eat a lot of chocolate. I don't really taste it. It *doesn't taste good* anymore really but I eat a lot of chocolate to give me energy.

While Dawn and Trisha displaced a concern about weight and diet onto others, Nessa saw it as a problem for herself as well as her co-dancers. She has dieted and binged on 'custard creams' before class.

> I start going on *short diets* and they *don't work* for me at all . . . I eat out of boredom and I might *eat a bar of chocolate* or something just to pick my energy up . . . *I start* [dieting] and *I give in.* I don't know, I do worry, I still worry.

For Nessa, the concern about food and the need to eat sweet things worked at a collective level:

> *Everybody did it* – well, like the group: you had your own selected friends, we all did it, and then it was *digestives and ice cream before class* to work it off. I think that *everyone has binges,* you all do, you just can't help it.

Mark and Errol, on the other hand, did not see weight and diet as a problem for themselves or for the other male dancers. They were more interested in keeping up their strength. According to Mark:

It *doesn't really matter*, as long as you *keep yourself in good condition*, that's all you really need.

Errol, like Mark, felt he could eat what he liked because:

We're doing the sort of *exercises that need strength*, so *I do eat*.

They both thought that they did not need to think about their weight because they 'sweated' so much during and after class that any weight that they would have gained through eating would automatically be lost through perspiration. Errol and Mark considered that in their experience women dancers were much more concerned with the weight–diet syndrome than men were. And certainly the women, as discussed above, were aware of other women's obsessions, if not always their own and they also felt that the men didn't have to worry too much about their weight. Moreover, it was easier to get quite long and detailed discussions going with the women about issues of shape and weight and diet in particular. Of course a concern with one's own body shape and weight is not restricted to female dancers, rather it pervades the consciousness of most women, as the studies of the pursuit of slenderness demonstrate.[21] All you have to do is raise the issue in the company of women and long and detailed conversations evolve about how they feel about their shape, what they ought to do to lose weight, how many diets they've been on and so forth.

When I asked Nessa why women in general seemed to be more concerned than men with their shape she responded:

It's – maybe that *they want to attract* people *by the way they look*, not necessarily men but make other people aware of how they look, like *look at me – I'm a size whatever*, I *look pretty good* and I'm *in shape*. I mean they just *want to attract attention* by *the way they look* . . .

Nessa also pointed to how feeling good or bad about herself (in terms of her shape) had consequences for how she looked at herself in the mirror. If she was feeling bad, she could only look at certain parts of her body in the mirror because seeing the reflection of her whole body would make her feel even worse. This notion of the 'look' and the 'mirror' also cropped up in Dawn's and Trisha's discussions. Again, a number of feminist writers have argued that the idea of the mirror, of looking at oneself as if one were being looked at, the sense of surveillance, the relationship of how one looks to one's sense of identity or self-worth, for the most part, is gender-specific.[22] As Mulvey has argued:

> In a world ordered by sexual imbalance, pleasure in looking has been split between active/male and passive/female . . . In their traditional exhibitionist role women are simultaneously looked at and displayed, with their appearance coded for strong visual and erotic impact so that they can be said to connote to-be-looked-at-ness.[23]

Whilst I do not want to suggest that this study is representative of all young dancers, the language which these young people use to describe their feelings about dancing and their own body shape is so strikingly similar that their talk cannot be reduced simply to individual manifestations. It is clear that, for example, the body in dance, for both the men and the women, is an active doing body. However, there is a disjuncture between the active doing female body and the appearing body in the women's talk. The active doing female body is countered by a more passive image of the body as one which is looked at and which is surveyed and perceived in terms of its 'to-be-looked-at-ness'.[24] I do not wish to push Mulvey's argument concerning the 'male gaze' or the passivity of female looking too far because it was generated out of analysing the structure of narrative cinema and clearly one medium does not translate exactly into another because they involve different specificities. Moreover, in her later work Mulvey argues that other 'active' and not necessarily masculine elements can come into play apart from the male gaze when the female protagonist is placed centre stage in the narrative.[25] That having been said, this asymmetrical relation between the active doing body and the passive appearing body of the women does not seem to come through in the case of men. Rather, their ideas of both the dancing body and the appearing body are located in terms of activity and strength. In order to understand the role of dance in the process of feminine gender identification, the play between the asymmetrical elements needs to be explored and examined in a more detailed manner.[26]

Notes and References

1. See for example R. Betterton (ed.) (1987), R. Parker and G. Pollock (eds) (1987), L. Mulvey (1989) and L. Gammon and M. Marshment (eds) (1988).
2. This view has been supported by studies on the pursuit of slenderness such as L. M. Vincent (1979) and J. Buckroyd (1989).
3. See H. Thomas (1986), (1992).
4. See the work by S. Frith (1978), D. Hebdige (1978), F. Rust (1969), A. McRobbie (1984) and P. Gilroy (1987).
5. Clearly, this book is evidence of at least the beginnings of such systematic study.
6. See, for example, A. R. Radcliffe-Brown (1964), M. Mead (1943), C. Geertz (1975) and J. L. Hanna (1980), (1988).
7. H. Thomas, op. cit.
8. For examples of these see L. Gotfrit (1988), S. Stinson (1988) and J. Boyce et al. in *The Drama Review*, Vol. 32 (Winter 1988), pp. 82–102.
9. See E. Kendall (1979), Prologue, and W. Sorrell (1981), *Fin de Siècle: A New Beginning*.
10. The numbers of young black men and women entering into dance training in this country have risen in recent years. From my discussions with the members of the community dance group who wish to go on to take up a career in dancing, it was clear that they saw dance as a vehicle for 'getting on' in the world or for enabling them to express themselves in ways that they could not do otherwise, with speech for example.
11. For a discussion of this phase see J. Kelly-Godel in S. Harding (ed.) (1987) pp. 15–28.
12. See E. Kendall, op. cit., Part I, and N. Ruyter (1979) on this.
13. This has been well documented in S. Harding (ed.) (1987), S. Harding (1986), H. Roberts (ed.) (1981), L. Stanley and S. Wise (1983), and D. Smith (1989).
14. See S. Harding (1987), Introduction.
15. L. Stanley and S. Wise, op. cit. p. 163.
16. Clearly, these were not the only categories that could have been used. For example, categories such as The Family, Mother, Pedagogy and so on could have generated further discussion.
17. See B. Easlea (1981), chapters 1 and 2, and J. Rutherford in R. Chapman and J. Rutherford (eds) (1988), pp. 9–20 on the relationship between nature and culture in patriarchal systems of thought.
18. For a discussion of the perceived relationship of women to nature, see R. Sydie (1987), S. Griffin (1978) and F. Haug (ed.) (1987).
19. A number of the dancers were aware that they were viewed differently because they were black. In one of the filmed group interviews Juliet pointed out that it was even more difficult for a black woman than a black man to get 'serious' dance work. She felt that the men were treated more seriously and that black women were often seen as 'exotic' (sexual) dancing bodies and that this limited their career prospects more than black male dancers. Again, it would seem crucial to develop this area of research further to consider the inter-relationship between dance, gender and race in a more systematic manner.

20. The questionnaire follows (Appendix 5.1).
21. See for example K. Chernin (1982), (1986), E. Szekely (1988), S. Orbach (1978).
22. See R. Betterton (ed.), op. cit. Section One, for a variety of papers on the way women look. Also see J. Berger's early discussion of this (1972), chapters 2 and 3. However, perhaps the most influential discussion on what has now come to be termed the 'male gaze', stems from the analysis by L. Mulvey, op. cit., of the representation of women in the narrative cinema.
23. Mulvey, op. cit., p. 19.
24. I am grateful to Janet Ransom for pointing this out to me. Moreover, I would like to thank Janet for reading the first draft of this paper, and for making a number of valuable suggestions.
25. See L. Mulvey, op. cit., chapter 4, where she discusses her afterthoughts on the earlier paper on Visual Pleasure and Narrative Cinema which was written in 1973.
26. I would like to thank Keith and the members of the community dance class and Group for allowing me to conduct the research.

Appendix 5.1

Questionnaire

1. How long have you been dancing?
2. Why did you come to South-East London Youth Dance?
3. Would you like to go on with dance?
4. What do you like about dancing? – How does it make you feel?
5. What kind of dance do you prefer – and why?
6. Who is your favourite dancer?
7. What is it you like about the dancer?
8. Do you compare yourself to other dancers? – If so, how?
9. What do your family and friends think about your dancing?

Bibliography

J. Berger, *Ways of Seeing*, (London: BBC, and Harmondsworth: Penguin 1972).
R. Betterton (ed.), *Looking On*, (London: Pandora Press, 1987).
J. Boyce, A. Daly, B. T. Jones and C. Martin, 'Movement and Gender: A Roundtable Discussion', *The Drama Review*, Vol. 32, No. 4 (Winter 1988), pp. 82–102.
J. Buckroyd, *Eating Your Heart Out*, (London: Macdonald, 1989).
K. Chernin, *The Hungry Self*, (London: Virago, 1986).
K. Chernin, *The Obsession*, (New York: Harper & Row 1982)
A. Daly, 'The Balanchine Women: Of Humming Birds and Channel Swimmers', *The Drama Review*, Vol. 31, No. 1 (Spring 1987), pp. 8–21.

M. Douglas, *Natural Symbols*, (London: Barrie & Rockliff, 1970).

B. Easlea, *Science and Sexual Oppression*, (London: Weidenfeld & Nicolson, 1981).

J. Finch, *Married to the Job*, (London: Allen & Unwin, 1983).

S. L. Foster, *Reading Dancing*, (Berkeley: University of California Press, 1988).

S. Frith, *The Sociology of Rock*, (London: Constable, 1978).

L. Gamman and M. Marshment (eds), *The Female Gaze*, (London: Women's Press, 1988).

H. Garfinkel, *Studies in Ethnomethodology*, (Cambridge: Polity Press, 1987).

C. Geertz, *The Interpretation of Cultures*, (London: Hutchinson, 1975).

P. Gilroy, *There Ain't No Black in the Union Jack*, (London: Hutchinson, 1987).

L. Gotfrit, *Dancing and Disruption: The Paradoxes of Women Dancing Back*, (Unpublished research paper: Ontario Institute for Studies in Education, 1988).

G. Greer, *The Female Eunuch*, (London: MacGibbon & Kee, 1970).

S. Griffin, *Woman and Nature*, (New York: Harper Colophon Books, 1978).

J. L. Hanna, *To Dance is Human*, (Austin: University of Texas Press, 1980).

J. L. Hanna, *Dance, Sex and Gender*, (Chicago: University of Chicago Press, 1988).

S. Harding, *The Science Question in Feminism*, (Milton Keynes: Open University Press, 1986).

S. Harding (ed.), *Feminism and Methodology* (Bloomington: Indiana University Press, and Milton Keynes: Open University Press, 1987).

F. Haug, *Female Sexualization*, (London: Verso, 1987).

D. Hebdige, *Subculture: The Meaning of Style*, (London: Methuen, 1978).

J. Kelly-Godel, 'The Social Relation of the Sexes: Methodological Implications of Women's History' in S. Harding (ed.), *Feminism and Methodology* (Bloomington: Indiana University Press, and Milton Keynes: Open University Press, 1987)

E. Kendall, *Where She Danced*, (New York: Alfred A. Knopf, 1979).

M. Mauss, 'The Techniques of the Body', in *Economy and Society* (1973) 2:1, pp. 70–88.

A. McRobbie, 'Dance and Social Fantasy' in A. McRobbie and. M. Niva, *Gender and Generation* (London: Macmillan, 1984).

L. Mulvey, *Visual and Other Pleasures*, (London: Macmillan, 1989).

S. Orbach, *Fat is a Feminist Issue*, (London: Arrow Books, 1978).

R. Parker and G. Pollock (eds), *Framing Feminism* (London: Pandora Press, 1987).

R. Parker and G. Pollock, *Old Mistresses*, (London: Pandora Press, 1987).

A. R. Radcliffe-Brown, *The Andaman Islanders*, (New York: Free Press, 1964).

H. Roberts (ed.), *Doing Feminist Research*, (London: Routledge & Kegan Paul, 1981).

A. P. Royce, *The Anthropology of Dance*, (Bloomington: Indiana University Press, 1978).

F. Rust, *Dance in Society*, (London: Routledge & Kegan Paul, 1969).

N. L. C. Ruyter, *Reformers and Visionaries: The Americanization of the Art of Dance* (New York: Dance Horizons, 1979).

J. Rutherford, 'Who's That Man' in R. Chapman and J. Rutherford (eds), *Male Order* (London: Lawrence & Wishart, 1988).

D. E. Smith, 'Sociological Theory: Methods of Writing Patriarchy', in R. A. Wallace (ed.) *Feminism and Sociological Theory* (London: Sage, 1989).

W. Sorrell, *Dance in its Time*, (Garden City, NY: Anchor Press/Doubleday, 1981).

P. Spencer (ed.), *Society and the Dance*, (Cambridge University Press, 1985).

L. Stanley and S. Wise, *Breaking Out*, (London: Routledge & Kegan Paul, 1983).

S. W. Stinson, untitled paper from the Form Panel on *Dance, Gender and Culture*, (CORD Conference, 1988).

R. Sydic, *Natural Women, Cultured Men*, (Milton Keynes: Open University Press, 1987).

E. Szekely, *Never Too Thin*, (Toronto: Women's Press, 1988).

H. Thomas, 'Towards a Sociology of Dance: The Intrinsic/Extrinsic Approach' in H. Thomas (ed.), *New Directions in Dance Study* (London: Ethnographica, 1992).

H. Thomas, *Movement, Modernism and Contemporary Culture: Issues for a Critical Sociology of Dance*, (unpublished PhD thesis: London University, 1986).

B. S. Turner, *The Body in Society*, (Oxford: Blackwell, 1984).

L. M. Vincent, *Competing with the Sylph*, (New York: Andrews & McMeel, 1979).

6 Gender Interchangeability among the Tiwi

ANDRÉE GRAU

INTRODUCTION

Although in the West there is no lack of philosophies or ideologies viewing masculine and feminine qualities not as the exclusive attributes of women or men respectively, but as forces, archetypal principles existing in both women and men (cf. for example Jung's (1953) discussion of the *animus* and *anima*[1] or Rudolf Steiner's (1959) discussion of cosmic evolution and of the place and role of human beings), there does not seem to exist a sphere in practical life where these principles can be put into practice. Two decades or so of the 'women's movement' may have changed the consciousness of many people, especially in broadening job possibilities and easing rigidified role definitions; they have not however erased the polarity woman–man constantly found in everyday life.

It is interesting to contrast this attitude with that of the Tiwi, a group of Australian Aborigines from the islands of Melville and Bathurst in the Northern Territory of Australia, with whom I worked in 1980–4. The Tiwi, too, had clearly-defined feminine and masculine domains which had practical consequences in the life of individuals. There were, however, whole areas of life, expressed more clearly through the performing arts, in which individuals had the opportunity to experience social roles other than those they were born or brought up into. These included roles that were impossible, men being pregnant or breastfeeding, for example, or unacceptable, such as women finding Spirit Children.

Role reversal, behavioural inversion and/or transvesticism are often found in dance/ritual throughout the world.[2] However I believe that the Tiwi gender-interchangeability is of a different order. We are not dealing with 'rituals of rebellion', with the diffusion of tensions between men and women, with ritual homosexuality, or with the inappropriateness of either men or

94

women to perform in specific contexts. Rather, fundamental principles of the society's world view are expressed: although feminine and masculine domains are clearly defined, masculine and feminine qualities within an individual are recognised to the extent that one can be a 'mother' or a 'father' irrespective of gender.

I will first say a few words about the background of my research and about the Tiwi environment in order to give a frame of reference to the discussion. Then I will give an outline of the Tiwi world in its feminine and masculine elements and describe the major characteristics of Tiwi dance as performed by men and women. Finally I will look at how gender roles were viewed within the dance practice at the time of my fieldwork.

BACKGROUND TO THE RESEARCH

Between 1980 and 1984 my husband and I spent nineteen months at Pularumpi, on Melville Island, spread over three visits. The first two, lasting fourteen months and four and half months, could be loosely described as 'work', in that they were sponsored by the Australian Institute of Aboriginal Studies (AIAS), and one of the tangible consequences was the writing of my doctoral dissertation. The third, for two weeks, could be described as a 'social' visit in order to introduce our baby son to our Tiwi families. For readers unfamiliar with the situation of the Aboriginal Australians, an explanation may be needed: kinship is so important among them, regulating most, if not all, aspects of life, that one cannot exist outside it. All outsiders who have a social as well as a professional involvement are, after a variable length of time, 'attributed' to and/or 'chosen' by individuals who become their parents. This connection gives them a specific place within the society and a framework in which to learn socially appropriate behaviours.

As a grantee of the AIAS, I was employed to document Tiwi dance from an anthropological perspective. In my understanding, an anthropological approach is twofold:

1. It is assumed that the making of dances is not simply an exercise in the intentional organisation of movements, but that it is, in part, a symbolic expression of the values and the ways of life of the human beings who create them.

2. In addition, dance is seen as a special kind of social activity:
it can be seen as a metaphor for feeling, a catalyst which
transforms acquired knowledge into understanding, both
reflecting and generating a special kind of social experience.
As such it could have profound effects on individual consciousness, which in turn could affect people's imagination
and decision-making in other social contexts.[3]

Additionally an anthropological approach, to me, implies that
work and personal life are associated, and I do not pretend – nor
even try! – to achieve absolute objectivity, if such a state exists.
In fieldwork situations, as in other spheres of life, I find that
there are people whom I like dearly, those with whom I have no
particular emotional commitments and those with whom I do
not especially wish to associate. As in other spheres I try to find
some sort of balance in my attitude so as not to be unfair to
people. I am always committed to them on a personal basis and
I cannot conceive of myself as an 'objective researcher' relating
to 'informants'. Thus when I worked among the Tiwi, it was
always clear in my consciousness that I was not only a AIAS
researcher working towards a PhD, but also a person, a woman,
a wife, a dancer, a mother, or whatever, depending on the time
and context. How I felt about myself and my role influenced not
only what I perceived but also the way in which I was perceived
by the Tiwi; thus each perception influenced the other.[4] There is
no doubt, for example, that my personal questioning at the time
about the coming together and struggle for balance of feminine
and masculine qualities, both within myself and within my
society, made me very receptive to the Tiwi ideas of the feminine
and masculine.

With hindsight it is interesting to note *when* I received *what*
information: for example from the beginning I had been interested in questions dealing with the Spirit Children and the
kinds of relationship they had with human beings but somehow
people never answered my questions. This evasion was done in
such a subtle way that I did not really think that no one wanted
to tell me about it; after all they were telling me about all sorts of
other things just as 'private'. Then one day, because my face had
'changed', the first sign of pregnancy among the Tiwi, information came pouring out because the time was apparently right for
me to know about these things. In fact I was not pregnant but at

about that time a desire to become parents was growing within us. Although I did not become a mother then, somehow the Tiwi knew that we would have a child in the near future and this change in ourselves enabled them to talk to us about different things (unless it was they who planted this wish, through their discussions with us, wanting us to have children and become 'normal'!).

THE TIWI ENVIRONMENT

Melville and Bathurst Islands are the traditional homelands of the Tiwi. They lie about eighty kilometres due north of Darwin, in the Northern Territory of Australia. They are fairly large islands with a rich environment providing an abundance of food even today, when most Tiwi can shop daily in their local super-markets.

Pularumpi, like the other four settlements of the two islands, has an airstrip and access from the mainland is usually by plane which, during my fieldwork, came twice daily. At that time, there were about four hundred people living at Pularumpi of which slightly over a dozen were Europeans, mainly employed in the service industries and/or married to Tiwi women.

In 1980–4 the Tiwi did not have any real means of income and they were largely dependent economically on the Australian government and on mining royalties. Communities received grants and employed a number of people to run the place: the majority of young to middle-aged men, and a small proportion of women, had jobs with the council, school, hospital, bank, shop, police, housing association, or garage. The others received un-employment benefits or some sort of pensions. Western lifestyle was present everywhere: most people lived in houses and wore fashionable clothes. Young people had ghetto blasters playing the latest tunes and went fairly regularly to pop concerts in Darwin. Many teenagers attended high school in Darwin. Old people played cards and usually spent late afternoons in the pub drinking beer, and most people went to the movies up to four nights a week or watched videos.

Ritual life was often influenced by 'modern' life: many cer-emonies had to be held during lunchtimes, weekends or holidays, because people were working; and many final mortuary rituals were held up because the pension cheque had been delayed and there was not enough money to pay the workers 'employed' to carry out certain ritual tasks. Nevertheless this 'intrusion' of 'modern' life did not mean that ritual life was dying. On the contrary it was very active and over the nineteen months I spent among the Tiwi there were an average of two to three formal dance events a week. Dance was an activity fully integrated into daily life. It was seen as representing a whole way of life and every Tiwi man, woman and child took part in the dance at one time or another. The condition for taking part was usually social: each individual had certain duties to perform towards his/her relatives which included dancing on particular occasions.

As soon as a Tiwi baby was old enough to be aware of the surrounding world it was exposed to dance. Children did not have a separate dance repertoire but were involved in almost all the ritual activities that took place, occasionally as spectators, more often as participants, learning the dances appropriate for the specific moment as they went along. Consequently, by the time they reached adolescence, all Tiwi were capable of at least an acceptable dance performance and the notion of a non-dancer was completely alien to them. To be able to dance was seen as a prerequisite of being human, as essential to survival as the ability to breathe or walk.

THE TIWI UNIVERSE IN ITS FEMININE AND MASCULINE ELEMENTS

The Tiwi said that the world was made by Pukwi, the Sun. She came out of the sky and made the animals and trees. When she walked the creeks were formed behind her.

Pukwi or *Imunga* was also used to refer to a number of female creative beings who today sit at special localities (all 'watery', e.g. an island, near the sea, a creek) and whom the Tiwi see as their ancestresses. These women were said to have founded the Tiwi descent groups into which every Tiwi is born and assumes right of membership through his/her mother. These two words, *imunga* or *pukwi*, were used by the Tiwi to designate the sun, the Sun-Woman, the clan ancestresses, and the matrilineal clans. They were also used to designate the human breath and the part of the body, in the sternum, which the Tiwi said held life. Thus one can see *imunga* and *pukwi* as the principle of, or the essence of life.

At birth one received an *imunga/pukwi* through one's mother and an individual could say 'I belong to the people of X', naming the mother's *imunga/pukwi*. But one also 'came out' of an *imunga/pukwi* through one's father; the Tiwi used the term *irumwa* to refer to it. Thus an individual would say 'I belong to the people of X and I come out of the people of Y', naming the father's *imunga/pukwi*. The *irumwa* was directly connected to one's dreaming. The species, geographical features, and places associated with its *imunga* were one's dreamings. The Tiwi referred to their *imunga* as mothers, or occasionally mothers' mothers; and to their *irumwa* as fathers' sisters.

In addition, at birth an individual also received a 'country'.[5] In theory a country was where one's father's or father's father's grave was located, and because the *Moporruwi*, the Spirits of the Dead, stay in the vicinity of their grave, where one's father's or father's father's ghost roamed and hunted. Each country seemed to have a number of characteristics. In one place for example, there were a lot of dingoes, in another a lot of jungle fowls, in yet another there was a rich deposit of ochre. All these characteristics were additional dreamings that an individual received.

The Tiwi universe was divided into three worlds: 1. The world of the Putaputawi, the Unborn; 2. The world of the Tiwi, the Living; and 3. The world of the Moporruwi, the Dead. In everyday life these three worlds were kept separate and the Tiwi were adamant that Ghosts or Spirit Children had no right to interfere with their daily life. However they were never far. They often appeared in people's dreams and some perceptive individuals were sometimes in waking contact with them. At the time of rituals, the three worlds were brought together: by acting in prescribed ways in accordance with the rules laid down by the heroes of the Dreamtime (the formative or creative period when the foundations of human life were established), the Tiwi could keep in touch with the power inherent in the Dreaming.

While the Tiwi acknowledged that sexual intercourse was necessary to make a child, they did not consider it the essential factor. As with all Australian Aboriginal people, an individual could not be born into the human world without being first dreamt or found by his/her father and/or paternal grandfather and even occasionally paternal greatgrandfather.[6] Once men had found their unborn children in their dreams they sent them to their wives who then became pregnant.

The Tiwi divided their world linguistically into feminine and masculine. This is a grammatical feature, as in French for example, and by itself it is not particularly remarkable. Certain correlations, however, seemed to underly significant cultural assumptions which were reflected in social behaviour. Jane Goodale demonstrated, for example, the correlation between the Tiwi sexual division of labour and their gender division of the universe. She argued that:

> While most species and genera of flora and fauna – edible, useful, or neither – are to be found in forms both masculine and feminine, the domains of the universe in which they are located and from which they are extracted are distinctly either masculine or feminine as follows: ground, dirt, land, sand, beach, reef, and island are all masculine in gender, yet within them are those items considered exclusively appropriate for women to extract. Conversely, the sea, clear sky, wind, tidal sandbank, and mangrove swamp are feminine in gender, and are the regions where that which is hunted exclusively by males is to be found.[7]

Thus, women exploited the resources rooted in the ground, which is a masculine domain, while the men exploited the resources of the sea and the air, which are feminine domains. When women dug yams out of the ground, they always broke a small piece and replanted it so that 'the plant would grow again'. Thus women were seen as being responsible for the maintenance of the ground resources: they replanted resources of the ground into a masculine domain, which then incubated and transformed them into a new whole. The men, on the other hand, did not hunt food only in the feminine domains, for the sea and sandbanks are also the home of the Spirit Children who are exclusively found by men, not women. The Spirit Children were found by their fathers in a feminine domain and placed into female wombs to be nurtured and transformed into human beings, who then died and became ghosts in the air, another feminine domain.

Thus while women, through replanting, maintained the resources of the land, men maintained the human population. The major difference is that human beings, unlike food, cannot be recycled. Because of events in the Dreamtime, human beings lost their immortality when the hero Purukupali declared that all human beings would have to die. To counteract this verdict Tiwi men performed a yearly ritual called *Kulama*. Unlike ordinary yams, the *kulama* yams were dug exclusively by men, an occupation which, under other circumstances, was considered inappropriate for them to do. During the ritual the *kulama* yams were treated in such a way that, from being toxic in their raw state, they became edible. They were also transformed from being masculine, when the men dug them out of the ground, into being feminine once they had been cooked. During the *Kulama*, over a number of years, young men were also transformed into fully adult members of the society. Goodale noted the direct correlation between the *kulama* yams and the initiates. They were submitted to the same treatment and, at times, substituted each other. Thus the *kulama* yam can be seen to represent life itself.

> In both its toxic and non-toxic forms, the yam serves to combine into a coordinated whole the two parts of the Tiwi world and the two distinct but complementary responsibilities for that world held by men and women. It is a world in which one part is considered masculine, but exploited and maintained by women, and in which the yam represents all life-sustaining food, integrated with a part of the world which is considered feminine, but exploited and maintained by men, in which the *kulama* yam represents all human life itself.[8]

One can argue thus that the main focus of *Kulama* was, so to speak, the recycling of human beings.

The description of the Tiwi universe in its feminine and masculine elements shows unequivocally that, although men and women were seen to have distinctive, separate roles, these were so intertwined that it is difficult to say where one finishes and the other begins.

This contrasts with accounts of earlier writers, such as Spencer (1914) or Hart (1954) or Hart and Pilling (1960). Theirs is essentially a picture of a male-dominated society where women had very little power, whilst mine shows a society where men and women have different but complementary roles. The discrepancy is not so much the result of historical changes as of different perspectives and emphasis taken by the writers. Spencer and Hart were writing from periods of fieldwork respectively in 1911–12 and 1928–9 before feminist, symbolic or reflexive developments characterising more recent social-anthropology took place. Their accounts were essentially from male points of view. When a female anthropologist, Jane Goodale, did fieldwork among the Tiwi in the 1950s, she proposed another perspective and her book *Tiwi Wives* (1971) shows the Tiwi world from the female point of view.[9]

The analysis which follows emphasises the complementary aspect of female and male contributions to the Tiwi world. Furthermore it tries to go beyond the 'different but complementary' picture, by discussing how the Tiwi seemed to have the possibility in their lives, especially through the performing arts, of moving through the spectrum of feminine and masculine.

GENERAL CHARACTERISTICS OF TIWI WOMEN'S AND MEN'S DANCING

The Tiwi notion of what was dance, what was not dance, and what was music, was different from European concepts. They had songs which I would classify as 'music', but which they classified as 'dance', and they had movements which I might classify as 'dance' but which they classified as 'music'.[10]

The Tiwi generally translated the word *yoi* into English as 'dance'; but 'dance' is too narrow to encompass all the concepts included in *yoi*. *Yoi*, for the Tiwi, included the songs used for dance, the rhythm of these songs, and singing for dance. Thus *yoi* denoted the whole event, the act of dancing, the music associated with the dance, and the performance of that music.

Yoi music was essentially vocal. With the exception of hand clapping or slapping parts of the body and the occasional beating with sticks of corrugated iron sheets, cans, pieces of wood, or whatever was available at the time, there were no instruments. All *yoi* songs were essentially of one style, with a small melodic range. However their tempo differed according to whether they accompanied men's or women's dancing. If a song accompanied the dancing of a man it started at a fairly slow pace; then the tempo increased, sometimes until it was too fast for the singing to continue and only the clapping and beating went on. The dance reached a climax with an accent, when both music and dance stopped. If a *yoi* song accompanied the dance of a woman the tempo remained constant. Each song contained only one verse, which was repeated over and over as long as needed for the dance performance. Similarly each choreography consisted of a small number of movements repeated over and over.

The *yoi* songs and dances could in theory be composed by both men and women, but few women created any during the time of my fieldwork. Choreographies and the compositions of songs were mainly the prerogative of middle-aged men (with occasionally individuals in their early thirties presenting their first tentative creations) and of old women. These women were always very knowledgeable about ritual matters and their creations were as well received as the men's. Song texts and choreographies were the property of their creators and if passed down to the next generation they were transmitted patrilineally.

Tiwi dances were, essentially, differentiated one from another by the different usage of the arms; only a few variations of foot movements existed. Men and women shared the same dance repertoire and a few characteristics in their dancing: the body was always relaxed, the knees had a slightly bouncing action, the head never went up and down but always stayed at the same level. However there were two distinguishable dancing styles, one for the men, one for the women. Women danced with their feet parallel, head slightly bent down, or eyes looking towards the ground, and one foot completely flexed back away from the ground on the beat. They used a regular tempo throughout their dance performance (see Figure 6.1[11] and Plate 6). Men danced with their knees slightly turned out, head straight or slightly bent back, and both feet on the ground on the beat. They increased the tempo, almost doubling it towards the end of their performance (Figure 6.2 and Plate 7). The Tiwi recognised these two major types of *yoi*. They talked about the *alawini yoi arrimi* or slow dance (women's dance) and the *mirati yoi arrimi* or fast dance (men's dance).

In all dance performances there was also a 'main' dance and an 'accompanying' dance. The songs were composed by and for those who performed the main dance, solo or in small groups, in the centre of the dancing area. I shall refer to these dancers as the 'soloists'. When they performed in a small group and a dance was being choreographed, one dancer was usually in charge of the choreography, but the others occasionally added variations which were or were not taken up by the rest of the group depending on a number of factors. These soloists were 'helped' by their close relatives, especially spouses or potential spouses, who usually accompanied them with another type of dance performed at the side of the dancing area, starting a few beats later. Every Tiwi was sometimes a soloist and at other times an accompanist. Men tended to dance alone as well as in small groups; women tended to prefer to dance in small groups. Men tended to perform the accompanying dance only to support their spouses; women tended to help most of their relatives, especially children and siblings, as well as husbands.

It was in the solo performances that the slow dance was associated with the women and was considered a feminine style, whereas the fast dance was associated with the men and considered a masculine style. But in the accompanying dance women sometimes danced fast. If they were good dancers they adjusted their dance step to follow the fast rhythm of the men's dance (see Figure 6.3).

If they were not sufficiently experienced or if the music was 'too rough' (that is too fast) they danced to half-time, transferring the weight from one foot to the other, taking two beats instead of one. Similarly men occasionally danced slowly when accompanying their wives. Furthermore men almost always performed the 'accompanying' dance in the women's dancing style described earlier (cf. Figure 6.1 and Plate 6).

INTERCHANGEABILITY OF GENDER WITHIN THE PERFORMING ART

The Tiwi had the possibility of 'changing' their gender at specific times within both the context of *Kulama*, for men only, and the context of *Yoi*, for both men and women.

An interesting aspect of *Kulama* as an initiation process was that, maybe uniquely among Australian Aboriginal peoples, no physical operation, subincision or circumcision, was performed. Instead, over the years, the initiates had to learn to be poetically creative so that by the time they were fully initiated, they were able to create a song cycle each year, performed over three days. Usually the whole cycle consisted of between ten and twenty songs, varying in length from a few verses to a dozen or more, depending on the individuals. The melody and rhythm of the songs were prescribed, as well as the topic for a number of specific contexts but new texts had to be created every year. Women were present in these songs in a number of ways: 1. the wives, and occasionally the sisters and daughters of the performers helped them by 'following them up', singing after them in an echo-like fashion; 2. some wives directly helped with the composition of the songs. However, although this was by no means hidden, they never shared the 'copyright'; 3. some of the song topics dealt with women. For example, the men had to sing about their father's sisters and about their mothers-in-law at specified times; 4. if women had been unfaithful during the year it was likely that it would be mentioned, usually metaphorically, in the part of the ritual that dealt with grievances and directly concerned with the present discussion; 5. at a specified time the men pretended to be women, usually singing 'I am so and so', listing names of women, either dead or alive, who were in a specific socially very important kinship relationship, and saying what they were doing as these women.

Gender changes were more obvious within the dance. Within the Tiwi dance repertoire, there was a group of dances which could be labelled 'kinship dances', because they showed a specific kinship relationship between the dancer and the person for whom the dance was being performed. Most dance performances were dedicated to someone, dead in the context of mortuary rituals, alive in the modern contexts of wedding, birthday, graduation, or other celebrations.

The Tiwi saw themselves as being all related through kinship. This was not difficult since their society comprised only a few thousand people and was, until fairly recent years, isolated on their islands. Consequently everyone always had at least one kinship dance to perform at every dance event. Occasionally an individual had more than one dance because s/he was related in different ways depending whether the genealogical connection was made via the father, mother, or spouse.

Every time someone died, everybody in the society changed status from the time of death to the time of the final mortuary ritual. These changes of status in some instances involved a change of behaviour: certain individuals, for example, were not supposed to touch food or drink and had to be fed by others; others simply stated the fact that a specific relative had died, and the bereaved continued to live as before. The name of each kinship dance was first the name of the bereavement status of the dancers who may perform it, and then, by extension, it became the label for the dance. The modern contexts of parties for birthdays and so on were modelled on the mortuary rituals, and the same terminology for labelling the status of performers and the dances was used even though no bereavement was involved.

Altogether there were ten kinship dances. Each said something about the relationships between individuals, especially between women and men. However not all are directly relevant to the present discussion of the interchangeability of gender through the dance. Therefore I will only present three dances: the *Wunantawi/pulanga*, the *Wunantawi/pularti*, and the *Kiakiae*. The Tiwi kinship system, like most Australian Aboriginal systems, is extremely complex. As the present discussion is on gender rather than kinship issues, I will only present the main recipients of each dance, rather than all those who could receive it.[12]

1. Men and women did not perform the *Wunantawi/pulanga* dance for the same individuals: men danced it for their own children and for their brothers' children, whilst women performed it for their brothers' children only. The text of the songs accompanying the dance almost always dealt with the Spirit Children, who were seen as small human beings carrying a spear, and with their mischievous ways. However the dance itself emphasised the physical making of the child: the dancers held their *pulanga* (glands in the groin), and occasionally their genitals, with their hands, making the sexual connotation fairly obvious (Figure 6.4[13] and Plate 9). One could call this dance the 'father's dance'.

2. The *Wunantawi/pularti* dance can be said to 'correspond' to the *Wunantawi/pulanga*. Women performed this dance mainly for their own children and for their sisters' children, whilst men performed it mainly for their sisters' children only. The text of the accompanying songs usually dealt with being pregnant, a child being born, breastfed and so on, though occasionally there were references to heroes from the Dreamtime. The movements of the dance showed the performer being pregnant with the person for whom the dance was being performed, having labour pain, breastfeeding, or nursing him/her (Figures 6.5a, b, c, d). One could call this dance the 'mother's dance'.

BENESH MOVEMENT NOTATION

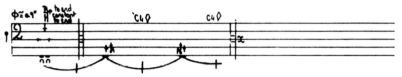

Figure 6.1 Women's dancing style

Figure 6.2 Men's dancing style

Figure 6.3 Women's fast dancing style

Notes on the Transcriptions in Benesh Movement Notation (BMN © 1954)

1. All transcriptions are prescriptive. They show the movements which must be performed in order for the dance to be recognised. In a performance situation, the dancer may add other movements.
   The approximate duration of a dance beat is given at the beginning of the transcription, for example '$\phi = 0.9'''$, one dance beat equals approximately 0.9''.
2. In transcriptions 4–6, the movements for the feet are not included as they vary if the dance is performed by a woman (Figure 6.1) or a man (Figure 6.2)

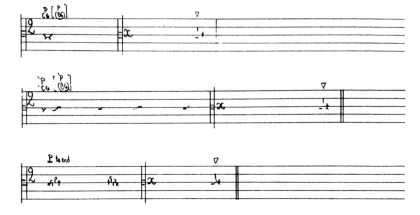

Figure 6.4 The 'fathers' dance'

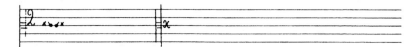

(a) showing the performer pregnant

(b) having labor pain

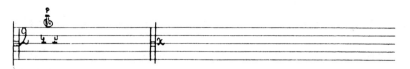

(c) breast feeding

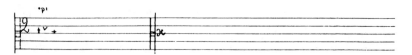

(d) nursing the baby

Figure 6.5 The 'mothers' dance'

Figure 6.6   The 'grandfathers' dance'

3. Men and women did not perform the *Kiakiae* dance for the same individuals. However it is slightly more complicated than in the previous examples. Men performed it mainly for their own grandchildren, for their brothers' grandchildren, and for their sisters' sons' children. Women performed the dance for the same people, with the exception of their own daughters' children. The texts of the accompanying songs also dealt with the Spirit Children. The movements of the dance showed how the small child was being carried on the dancers' shoulders (Figure 6.6 and Plate 13). One could call this dance the 'grandfather's dance'.

All three dances belonged to complementary units of two, that is: the dance of the father finding his child was related to a dance where the dancer was the Spirit Child being found; the dance of the mother giving birth and nurturing the baby was related to a dance where the dancer was given birth and nurtured; and finally the dance of the grandfather carrying the child was related to a dance where the child was being carried and looked after.

What is interesting in these three dances is that being a mother, a father, or a grandfather had nothing to do with the gender of the performer. Men and women both found Spirit Children even though in everyday life women were not supposed to know what the Spirit Children looked like and both men and women were pregnant, gave birth and nurtured the baby. Thus, not only did the Tiwi have a system where men and women had equal, complementary roles but they also had the opportunity somehow to 'become' the other, therefore experiencing the whole world rather than just the one limited by their gender.[14] Within the kinship dance-systems they also had the opportunity to experience other impossible roles such as being Spirit Children, or being parents to much older individuals for example; therefore they could explore through the dance all the social roles of their society and thus one could argue that they lived more balanced and fuller lives than they would have done, had the culture maintained more rigid gender divisions in all aspects of social life.

Notes and References

The use of the past tense in this essay is deliberate. The research was conducted ten years ago and I wish to emphasise that, contrary to unilineal evolutionary approaches, structurally simple societies, like the Tiwi, are not static but change over time.

1. On the topic of *animus* and *anima*, see also E. Jung (1957).
2. See Gluckman (1954), for examples in South East Africa, Mason (1975) in Libya, Buonaventura (1983) in the Middle East, Bateson (1958) in New Guinea or Chaki-Sircar and Sircar (1982) in India.
3. See A. Grau (1992) for a more detailed treatment.
4. This approach is by no means unique and has been quite common in anthropology for some decades.
5. Aboriginal people throughout Australia used this English term, rather than the possibly more appropriate term territory. For this reason I will use it and henceforth the inverted commas will be omitted.
6. I was told this has occurred with the two latter relatives especially in more recent times when fathers are much younger than in the past and not yet very knowledgeable in traditional matters.
7. J. Goodale (1982) pp. 202–3.
8. Ibid, pp. 207–8.
9. See also Hart, Pilling, and Goodale (1988) which shows clearly the complementary aspects of their respective analyses.
10. See A. Grau (1983) for a detailed discussion of this.
11. © 1954 Benesh Movement Notation. All transcriptions are prescriptive. They show the movements which must be performed in order for the dance to be recognised. In a performance situation, the dancer may add other movements. The approximate duration of a dance beat is given at the beginning of the transcription, e.g. $\phi = 0.9''$, one dance beat equals approximately $0.9''$.
12. A detailed discussion of all the kinship dances is in preparation, in A. Grau, *Do the Tiwi Dance their Kinship?*
13. In transcriptions 4–6, the movements for the feet are not included as they vary if the dance is performed by a woman (Figure 6.1) or a man (Figure 6.2).
14. It must be said that the men's ways were always more public and more 'glamorous' than the women's ways, although this does not necessarily have to imply inequality *per se.*

Bibliography

G. Bateson, *Naven: a survey of the problems suggested by a composite picture of the culture of a New Guinea tribe drawn from three points of view* (Stanford, Calif.: Stanford University Press, 1958).

W. Buonaventura, *Belly Dancing: the Serpent and the Sphinx* (London: Virago, 1983).

M. Chaki-Sircar and P. K. Sircar, 'Indian Dance: Classical Unity and Regional Variation', in A. G. Noble and A. K. Dutt (eds), *India Cultural Patterns and Processes* (Boulder, Colo.: Westview Press, 1982).

M. Gluckman, *Rituals of Rebellion in South-East Africa* (Manchester University Press, 1954).

J. Goodale, *Tiwi Wives: A Study of the Women of Melville Island, North Australia*, American Ethnological Society monograph No. 51 (Seattle and London: University of Washington Press, 1971).

J. Goodale, 'Production and Reproduction of Key Resources among the Tiwi of North Australia', in *American Association for the Advancement of Science Selected Symposium* (Boulder, Colo.: Westview Press, 1982).

A. Grau, Sing a Dance – Dance a Song. The relationship between two types of formalised movements and music among the Tiwi of Melville and Bathurst Islands, North Australia, *Dance Research*, Vol. I(2) (London, 1983).

A. Grau, Dreaming, Dancing, Kinship: The Study of *Yoi*, the Dance of the Tiwi of Melville and Bathurst Islands, North Australia. PhD thesis in Social-Anthropology (Queen's University of Belfast, 1983).

A. Grau, 'New Directions in the Anthropology of Dance', in H. Thomas (ed.), *New Directions in Dance Studies* (London: Ethnographica, 1992).

A. Grau, 'Do the Tiwi Dance their Kinship?', in preparation.

C. W. M. Hart, 'The Sons of Turimpi', *American Anthropologist*, 56 (1954).

C. W. M. Hart and A. Pilling, *The Tiwi of North Australia*, (New York: Holt, Rinehart & Winston, 1960).

C. W. M. Hart, A. Pilling and J. Goodale, *The Tiwi of North Australia*, 3rd edn (New York: Holt, Rinehart & Winston, 1988).

C. Jung, 'Animus and Anima', in *The relations between the Ego and the Unconscious* (London: Routledge & Kegan Paul, 1953).

E. Jung, *Animus and Anima*, (Zürich: Spring Publications, 1957).

J. Mason, Sex and Symbol in the Treatment of Women: The Wedding Rite in a Lybian Oasis Community, *American Ethnologist*, 2(4) (1975).

B. Spencer, *The Native Tribes of the Northern Territory of Australia*, (London: Macmillan, 1914).

R. Steiner, *Cosmic Memory, Prehistory of Earth and Man* (New York: Steiner, 1959).

7 'Saturday Night Fever': An Ethnography of Disco Dancing

DAVID WALSH

Social dancing has always been a leisure pursuit in all societies but, in Western societies, as a result of the highly differentiated and complex structures which characterise them, it takes on a particular form of organisation through the way in which it is conducted in specially provided venues that are designed for dancing as a leisure activity. What at one time in Western society and still in other contemporary and more simple societies would have been a gathering organised on a relatively informal and amateur basis making use of local musicians living in the immediate community has now become a professionally organised activity that takes place in dance-halls that are specially equipped to provide a place and the music for dancing. Moreover, as a place for dancing, the dance hall has traditionally and predominantly acted as a centre of and focus for all the leisure-time activities of adolescents and young unmarried adults, providing them, through social dancing, with the opportunity to mix together and to date one another. In that sense, social dancing, youth leisure time and mating activity are all inextricably bound up with one another and the dance-hall is the social setting which provides the primary site in which they are brought together and interweave with one another. Social dancing then is a form of gathering which brings together a whole series of interests which those who are gathered together have in common with one another – the interest in fun, in companionship and in meeting one another with a view to going out together. But the character of the dance-hall as a kind of venue has changed quite considerably since the end of the 1960s. Before then, the typical dance-hall venue was the local Palais de Danse or, failing that, the Friday or Saturday night dance at the local town hall, both of which involved the professional organisation of the venue pro-

112

vided for dancing. Now it is the discotheque which has become the primary venue for social dancing and the functions it fulfils.

What then is different about the discotheque and why has it replaced the Palais de Danse as the new venue for gathering through social dancing? Largely it is a matter of the ambience which the discotheque deliberately sets out to create, which is one of sophistication and glamour. It extends an invitation to young people to become participants in the 'high life' which the wealth of Western societies has made available to the affluent sections of its population. It belongs, then, with the whole trend of dining out, continental holidays, flash cars, fashionable clothes, etc., which is a major hallmark of Western culture and which has, through a general rise in the standard of living in Western societies, democratised the 'high-life', by bringing it down to an egalitarian level so that more people can share in it. So everything about the discotheque is geared to this self-presentation of glamorous sophistication. To go to one, one needs to dress up. The very names which discotheques call themselves are redolent of glamour – Busby's, Heaven, Jimmy's, Stringfellow's, etc., all of them recall a fashionable place in which to gather as opposed to going to a dance at the local Palais on a Friday or Saturday night. The decor within the discotheque furthers this image, with its elegant fittings, its smart bar or bars, the small but select restaurant which is often attached offering a menu of trendy rather than substantial dishes such as barbecued spare ribs, spicy prawns, sliced parma ham and melon, etc., and a dance-floor which has all the latest lighting effects to guarantee that dancing will be a glamorous and exciting spectacle as well as a pleasure in itself. Most of all, perhaps, it is expensive to spend an evening at the discotheque and this reinforces the image it has created of itself as part of the 'high-life'.

This self-contained world of glamour is carried over into the dancing itself, which is particular to the discotheque as a venue and which can only be properly undertaken under the specific conditions and with the music that characterise discotheques. The music is specifically geared to dancing rather than to listening to since its predominant character lies in the heavy rhythmic beat of the music which carries it along and frequently drowns the voice of the singer and the song lyrics or the repetition of a refrain that echoes the beat itself and reinforces it. The music at the discotheque is for dancing to and sets the scene for the nature of the dancing which takes place there, and particularly its virtuoso character.

Essentially disco-dancing, for all the various fashions or specific styles of dancing that sweep through it on a regular and recurrent basis, is a free-forum kind of dancing. In this again it is unlike the kind of dancing that characterised the old Palais de Danse, in which formal dances predominated (even in rock 'n' roll) in which the male partnered the female in a specific and routinised series of steps and which actually could be and were taught to the respective partners. Typically, in this form of dancing, it was the female who did the display, exhibiting whatever pyrotechnics were available in the specific dance in question and the male, who partnered by providing a kind of steady accompaniment to this display by holding and guiding the female. Now, neither sex is required to guide themselves in relation to the other in a specific sequence of steps that keep them in tandem, except in terms of a general relatedness which is dictated by the rhythm of the music and the fact that the two people have chosen to dance with one another. The result of this absence of a specific partnership, dictated by a particular sequence of dancing steps, is to unloose a kind of virtuoso dancing style in which partners are free to display their own variations on the dance they are doing and in which those variations become constitutive of the dance itself. They are their own masters of what they do and how they do it. Moreover, it is a form of dancing in which men can more actively engage, not only because they are no longer reduced to the role of merely partnering the women who elaborates the dance steps, but because the sheer physicality of the dancing itself creates an image of masculinity which removes the sissyish implications of being able to dance and dancing that inhibited men from joining in when it was the women who did all of the elaborate display in the dance routine. Discotheque dancing, then, has led to the remasculinisation of dancing by helping to give the male a place of eminence in which he can engage in display just as easily as women and without embarrassment as a result. To be able to dance can now be seen by men as a masculine pursuit.

This helps also to understand the important part that the discotheque plays in the homosexual – particularly male homosexual – world. One of the things that can be said about the emergence of the discotheque as the prime site of social dancing is that the gay community has provided an advance guard for its development, often acting as the initial host for discotheque music artistes before they have gained widespread support on the discotheque scene as a whole. Why is this the case? Of course, the demise of a highly specific male–female partnership in discotheque dancing itself makes it much easier for homosexuals to engage in this form of dancing once they do not have to fit into some stereotypical role as one or other of the dance partners but can simply engage in dancing and partnering one another as they wish. Again, as single adolescents or young adults, homosexuals have the financial resources, the time and the lack of responsibilities to go dancing on a regular basis and like any other people of a similar age, they too have an interest in fun, companionship and the possibility of meeting someone whom they date and form a relationship with. But more is at work with regard to gay discotheques than simply those things that parallel the heterosexual world and explain the emergence of the discotheque in that arena. What is particularly crucial with regard to the predominant place of the discotheque in the gay world is the fact that, as a deviant subculture, the homosexual community can only organise a communal life for itself in those areas of society in which it is free to, if you like, 'do its own thing'. Clearly the world of work is not such an area since that remains essentially dominated by the fact that society in general is heterosexual and homosexuals have no choice but to accept and work with this as the reality of the world in which they live. There would be no sense in which homosexuals could create a homosexual world of work since that would have no particular meaning or reality – at most, homosexuals can simply come out at work, but then they will still be doing the work they do irrespective of their homosexuality and in a social context in which the majority of workers are heterosexual. Outside of work and in leisure time, however, it is possible for homosexuals to organise their own world which is specifically for themselves and so of course the pub and the discotheque as focuses for leisure activity become especially important in the creation of a homosexual world where homosexuals can mix freely and be themselves without being pressured to meet the requirements of heterosexual norms. So the discotheque becomes especially important for homosexuals, not simply as a place where they can meet, mate and enjoy their recreation time, but as an actual celebration of the fact that they are gay: there they are being 'out'. In the discotheque they can acknowledge themselves as what they are and make it an occasion for freedom and joyous self-acceptance. So the discotheque, for homosexuals, is part of self-liberation as well as a venue for enjoyment, companionship and meeting.

However, whether it be heterosexual or homosexual, the discotheque still serves one primary function of dance-halls and social dancing, which is that of mating. It remains the main venue for 'chatting up' and dating: here a social etiquette reigns which governs the process by which that is done. Clearly the dance-floor is the initial place from which the process of chatting up begins, but the object of the process is to get the other person to oneself and ultimately to be alone with them. My interest is to chart the moves in this process; in it I leave aside frank introductions by friends to concentrate on how contact is engineered independently of this. The process begins with a survey of who might be potentially available, which requires not just an eye for who one is attracted to, which obviously can be many people and which can be exercised from the point of queuing at the doors of the discotheque through walking by the bar or bars to entering onto the dance-floor itself, but the ability to discern amongst the people who are there which of them is potentially there too with a view to meeting someone. This ability is not so easy to acquire or to exercise, except through practice, since on the surface there are no easy markers with which to engage. In the crowd, it is not necessarily easy to sort out those who are alone and therefore seemingly obviously available from those who are with friends (and may actually be available) from those who are partnered and not available at all (although, to make things more complicated, they may in fact be willing to change partners if the situation arises for doing so). What is needed to exercise discrimination and to select out a potential partner is the practised eye which can pick up subtle signals and treat them as markers of availability. This eye fixes upon things such as the glance that moves from nonchalance to focused attention on oneself and the other and perhaps back to nonchalance again, but the moment of focus is noticed; the half smile of seeming recognition of attention given by the other and its acknowledgement with a similar smile; the holding of the eye of the other person however briefly and in that moment separating them from their immediate activity, be it dancing or talking to friends, that acknowledges an awareness of interest by both parties, even if there is an immediate return to what they were doing before; an admiring stare at someone and particularly their dancing ability, which seemingly switches from observation to sexual interest and back again in an instant; the observant glance at the way people converse or dance together, which gives away in an instant the state of their relationship, their closeness and the character of it, on the basis of an assessment of how they respond to each other physically and emotionally. Of course, the practised eye has to make sure that he or she is available in precisely these same terms, although in the case of heterosexual relations between genders, which requires male dominance, the woman is more likely to act as the pursuant rather than the pursuer. Mistakes of course can be made, but basically it is the use of the practised eye and eye-contact itself which establishes the initial base from which any other kind of move becomes possible.

The next move is to find a way of 'moving-in' on the situation to turn it into an actual meeting-up. The trick, so to speak, is to turn the potential opening into words which will establish a possible relationship; at this point the opening lines, although no doubt idiosyncratic, play upon a continuous variation on the same themes about the nature of the person in question and the reasons why he or she is at the discotheque and with whom. In this, the issue now comes to revolve around the nature of the person imagined in the approach and the actual reality of the person who has been approached. To go any further, these two things must be reconcilable. Should the two mesh, and contact now having been achieved, it becomes possible to move to the next stage which is for one of the persons to ask the other to dance. Through dancing together, contact can be maintained and reinforced, although the nature of discotheque dancing as free-form dancing to loud music means that this can only be achieved through mutual smiling, attempts at bodily coordination between the couple and the occasionally shouted comment. In this respect, the couple are at a disadvantage compared with formal dancing in which they could have held one another and talked as they danced. To continue contact and ensure relationship it is necessary at some point to leave the dance-floor, which is the next step in the process of getting together. Here the issue is for one partner to invite the other or for both partners to decide together to go to the bar for a drink or to move to a quieter place to sit and talk, and it is moving to one of these spots (in part deliberately provided by the discotheque for this purpose) that the chatting-up can begin in earnest. What transpires in the chatting-up stage proper is simply that either the two partners are able to sufficiently engage one another's interest to couple up for the rest of the evening by either remaining at the discotheque and dancing together or drinking together (or possibly now moving back as a couple to be with friends if one or the other has come with friends) or arranging to go off together from the discotheque. Should that take place then dating, at least for the evening, has occurred and the discotheque and social dancing has fulfilled its function in that respect. Of course, at any point in the process of chatting-up, the process can be halted because of lack of interest on the part of either of the two partners, in which case the whole round of moves can start again (and frequently does) if the interest in dating remains a primary concern.

The discotheque, then, creates a glamorous setting in which mainly young people can participate in an egalitarian version of the high life as they come together for social dancing where fun, companionship and the chance of dating are all found in the very same spot and pursued in tandem with each other through dancing.

8 Classical Indian Dance and Women's Status

JUDITH LYNNE HANNA

Recent feminist scholarship on the social and cultural construction of gender and equity enables us to assess the implications worldwide of historically persistent male dominance in dance production.[1] In India a key understanding of the reality of women's subordinate status comes from the traditional and mythical portrayals of women (Ghadially, 1988), some of which are restated in dance.[2]

Explicit feminist perspectives among Indian dancers are new. Chaki-Sircar states in the 1988 brochure of her Dancers' Guild of Calcutta, which performs in Indian cities as well as various countries abroad under Indian government auspices, 'Besides innovation in form, the contemporary dancer here wishes to develop an ethos that questions the traditional one of Brahmanic patriarchy so deeply enmeshed in Shastric classicism'. Elsewhere Chaki-Sircar has written, 'The history of dance in India shows a continuous exploitation of young women either by patriarchal creed . . . or by the Islamic dogma which considered women dancers to be public entertainers for exclusively male audiences'.[3]

India's budding feminist tradition originated in social reform and nationalist groups of the nineteenth century.[4] Bastions of Indian conservatism, such as women's cultures that accept religiously-sanctioned traditional sex-role scripting, recoil from feminist rhetoric. Satisfied with their lot and 'too entrenched in tradition to recognise their oppression',[5] other women dismiss the premise that women as a group are unequal and change is called for.

Liberal feminists believe that non-feminist women are victims of their socialisation or sex-role conditioning; they seek educational reform to eliminate discrimination and to achieve liberty and equality.[6] Whether ritual, social or theatre art, dance has important yet little-recognised potential as a medium of socialisation within a culture's means of conveying information.[7] According to

119

Bandura's social learning theory (1972), an individual tends to reproduce attitudes, acts and emotions exhibited by an observed live or symbolic (for example, film or television) model. It may be mentally registered and used or remain in subconscious memory until a relevant situation activates it. Modelling of gender-related dominance patterns may occur through observations of dance performances that convey information purposely or unintentionally.

Similar to non-human ritualised displays and other human ritual, dance frames messages and thereby bestows power on them. People participate in dance by dancing and watching dance, empathising with performers or fantasising about them. Dance may be understood as a medium through which choreographers/ directors/producers manipulate, interpret, legitimate and reproduce the patterns of gender co-operation and conflict that order their social world. Dance images may lead to reinforcing ongoing models, acquiring new responses, weakening or strengthening inhibitions over fully-elaborated patterns in a person's repertoire, and facilitating performance of previously learned behaviour that was encumbered by restraints. Distanced from the everyday, a dance performance also permits exploration of dangerous challenges to the status quo without the penalties of the quotidian.

Moreover dance has, as does verbal language, vocabulary (locomotion and gestures, steps and phrases), semantics (meaning of movement in the style itself or some reference beyond the movement), and grammar (rules specifying the manner in which movements may be meaningfully combined). With these elements dance spins webs of significance that socialise women and affect their condition. Thematic content speaks to the cultural construction of gender. Traditional stories may be depicted or reinterpreted with a new twist or resolution to an old tale. Novel stories may be told. Dance movement or grammar may replicate patterns of the status quo or break established boundaries. Techniques of presentation, such as lighting, setting, costume and music convey meaningful messages. Departures from convention may be slight or radical transformations.

Diverse and kaleidoscopic, Indian dance is embedded in a context of a specific time, place and situation. Indian dance has an ancient history that extends into the contemporary era and beyond the Indian subcontinent throughout south-east Asia and other communities worldwide where Indians have immigrated. A related complexity is that Indian dance is undergirded by many different religious belief systems and sectarian strands, each with doctrinal, oral and/or written literary, and ritual peculiarities. Buffeted by forces of change, religious adherents may diversely interpret dance over time. Besides there are schools within genres related to the creativity of master teachers. Notwithstanding these factors, an overview of Indian dance does serve to raise questions about the construction of gender roles in the arts and society.

Indian dancers understand their situation and the meaning of dance in terms of 1. religious precepts and context; 2. economic survival beyond the bosom of religious patronage; 3. nationalism with cultural independence from colonialist power and pride in expressions of Indian identity; and 4. current influences outside and within India, including the new aesthetic norm of innovation and feminist perspectives.

DANCE, 'MOUTHPIECE' OF 'MAN'S' RELIGION

Religion often explains and justifies gender relations. Because a significant part of the Indian population was illiterate, the arts became an entrenched dramatic medium used to communicate the Hindu philosophy. High-caste males apparently were primarily responsible for creating the ancient Vedas (sacred texts of Hindu philosophy) and later scriptures, major epics and legends – the texts that dance kinetically visualises. The male gods in these stories, 'like the Greek and Roman deities, are a lecherous bunch constantly seducing the wives of sages and mortals. The sages and monks, surprisingly enough, are also depicted indulging in active sexual pleasure even though living as hermits'.[8]

Hinduism has a pantheon of male and female deities, the supreme all-powerful God manifest primarily through a trio of anthropomorphic gods: Brahma, Vishnu, who appears in one of his incarnations as Lord Krishna of amorous nature, and Shiva, Lord of the Dance who created the universe.

The *Natyasastra* classic treatise on dance and the other arts is said to be the work of a male sage Bharata-Muni some time between 100 BC and AD 200. Receiving instruction from the god Brahma (or Shiva, or his disciple Tandu, depending upon which legend one follows), Bharata-Muni handed it down through his sons.[9] Often called a fifth *Veda*, the treatise specifies that dance enactments of myths and legends would 'give guidance to the people of the future in all their actions'.[10]

During the Epic and Classical periods (440 BC to AD 600), the Upanishad Vedic treatises delineated the role of women. A woman is a 'thing to be possessed'.[11] She should be, and give the appearance of being, subordinate to the men closest to her.

Eight heroines (*nayika*) appear in the *Natyasastra*. Here the plight of the male-defined ideal woman is depicted as longing, hesitation, sorrow, loneliness, anxiety, fear, parting, yearning, pleading, forgiveness, faithfulness, despondency, envy, self-disparagement, depression, derangement, madness, shame, grief, and being rebuked, insulted and mocked by one's family and deceived by one's lover.[12] These many manifestations of love afford dramatic dance themes.

The religion of the literate élite was spread to the illiterate masses through two great popular epics, the *Ramayana* and *Mahabharata*. 'Exemplary' feminine character includes a woman suffering for her husband and family; moreover, as the *Ramayana* unfolds, man makes woman suffer for no fault of her own. Sita the heroine is abducted and subsequently is questioned about her chastity. Dancer Mamata Niyogi-Nakra asked, 'Would a male God's masculinity be questioned with similar trials of doubt?'[13]

While Hinduism supports male dominance it recognises an ideal harmonious union of male and female, spirit and matter, complementary male (*purusa*) and female (*shakti* or *prakriti*) principles or energies within oneself. Indians say, 'Without Shakti [goddess and female energy], Shiva is nothing'. Female dancers become empowered as they play both goddesses and gods. Role-reversal permits a momentary sharing in power. In addition women have power over men through their beauty and seductiveness cast in a spiritual way.

Hinduism also takes notice of the instability of power-relations, goddesses' as well as gods', and goddesses' power and wisdom (for example, Kali and Saraswati). There are some ambiguities, challenges and alternatives to male dominance.[14]

Dhruvarajan (1989) claims that Indians glorify women as mothers but devalue them as persons. The female principle is worshipped; yet in daily life flesh-and-blood females are secondary citizens, humiliated, depersonalised and dominated; 'The more a woman lowers herself, the more she is praised'.[15]

In their fierce forms deities are dangerous. Making a goddess subservient to her husband tames her power. Thus there tends to be an inequality of power structures between male and female deities.

Variants of legends say Shiva and his counterpart the goddess Kali compete in dance contests in which Shiva wins. Shiva performed many dances that Kali was able to imitate perfectly. Out of frustration Shiva exploited her sense of modesty and raised his right foot to the level of his crown and danced in that pose. Although Kali could have emulated this pose, feminine modesty led her to withdraw from the contest. Kali lost not because she was an inferior dancer but because she was a woman and affirmed her subservience in this role.[16] Niyogi-Nakra, at the age of ten, asked her male guru if goddesses could not win over gods; he said no.[17]

High-caste priestly males (Brahmins) designed the scripts enacted in dance and initially choreographed the dance; they and court rulers supported the dance and male professionals, non-Brahmins who came from hereditary families of teachers and musicians (*Nattuvaranas* or *gurus*), taught it to women. As envoys in interpreting and explaining culture, female dancers have been party to the reproduction of patriarchy ensconced in religious sanctification.

PUBLIC WOMEN AND DANCING

The *Rig-Veda* (ancient hymns considered the revealed word of God), epics and ancient laws books speak of unmarried women who offer sexual services. Bharata enumerates in chapter 24 of the *Natyasastra* a number of feminine erotic styles; chapter 25 deals mainly with courtesans who are not excluded from the benefits of religion. The law books however regard prostitution with disfavour. A prestige hierarchy differentiated temple dancers, city courtesans and lowly harlots. According to Gaston (1982), some Indian kings encouraged women dancing in public because it promoted consumption of alcoholic drinks over which the government had a monopoly.

Temple dance, rooted in antiquity and probably firmly established between the ninth and eleventh centuries, prior to the advent of Islamic rule, developed into secular, royal arts of entertainment at the Hindu courts of Rajasthan (Jaipur) and the Muslim courts of Delhi, Oudh, Agra and elsewhere. Through a combination of changed religious practice, pecuniary stringency and disturbed political conditions, the Hindu temples received fewer offerings and the dancer consequently also received less. She had few options to supplement her resources.

Muslim kings, Nawabs and Hindu rajahs who considered themselves rulers by divine right enticed dancers in economic difficulty or used force to requisition their services at court, palace and durbar. At the same time that artistry was some dancers' concern, others (called *nautchwalis, naachivalis, khemtawalis, bhagtanyis* and *bayaderes*) 'realised that their patrons were more interested in the dancers than in the dance, hence to make adjustments, they began to use dance not as an art but as an artifice'.[18]

During the British colonial period there were contradictory attitudes toward prostitution. On the one hand the British rulers debased part of the courtesan profession – practised with widely-reputed skilful music and dance performance – into common prostitution. Concerning the courtesans in the Nawabi capital of Lucknow, 'If the Nawabi had perceived these cultural women as an asset [sons of the urban élite were sent to the salons of the well-known *tawa'ifs* for lessons in etiquette and appreciation of Urdu poetry], the British Raj saw them as a necessary evil, if not a threat and sought to make them an inexpensive answer to the sexual needs of single European soldiers by insisting on clinical standards of personal hygiene'.[19] The soldiers and Indian rural gentry on trips to the capital were uncultured and thus unappreciative of the dance. On the other hand, the British attempted to eliminate prostitution and the dancing assumed to be associated with it. After India achieved political sovereignty classical Indian dance became a symbol of national identity and the decolonised mind and culture.

DEVADASIS

Females called servants or slaves of God, vestal virgins, temple maidens, *devadasis, maharis* in Orissa state and even prostitutes were dedicated to a god in ceremonies in which they became his brides and servants and were given to particular temples. Parents might give their daughter to fulfil a vow, have no male issue (a *devadasi* could inherit) or be too poor to afford a daughter's dowry. A woman could offer herself out of devotion, for the prosperity of her family or out of weariness of her husband or her widowhood. She could sell herself or be enticed.

Because the relation between human and deity is analogous to the relation between a lover and a beloved, the professional temple dancer's requirement of individual service to the deity was incompatible with human marriage and motherhood.[20]

Extraordinary freedom was allowed the temple dancers at a time when wives and daughters lived in a kind of purdah. Besides gaining freedom from the constraints of human marriage and widowhood, the dedicated also learned to read and write, an opportunity denied other women. Furthermore some dancers acquired wealth through gifts from admirers,[21] owned land and made large donations to temples.[22] Allowed to retire from temples as they approached menopause and Brahmin men no longer desired them, the *devadasi* with wealth became her own mistress.

Devadasis usually had high ritual status and lived in the public eye. They danced for the deities inside the temple, outside for festivals involving the larger community and at private parties and at the royal courts, especially for marriages. The temple dancers were regarded as harbingers through which auspiciousness could be attained and were believed to possess power to ward off the effects of ill omens.

Because the temple dance, known as *sadir attam* (in Tamil), *nautch* or *sadir nac*, was a votive offering, rigid rules governed the dancer's training (usually beginning at the age of five to seven) and method of performance. She learned, Kapila Vatsyayan has said, to seek the perfect pose that conveys a sense of timelessness.[23] Simultaneously women's dance movement emphasises the beauty of the body and erotic appeal for an 'other' – god, husband, lover – in all its demanding exactitude.

Traditionally it was socially sanctioned for Brahman male temple servants or other men who fulfilled their marital obligations to have sexual licence with the temple dancers apart from their ritual duties. However, they did not consort with castes lower than themselves.

As noted earlier, men sexually exploited many dancers when their fixed salary for religious duties became small or non-existent. Stories of kidnapping girls for the temple and Brahmans deriving a key source of income from temple dancers' prostitution made the news in India and elsewhere. Furthermore there may have been caste behaviour violations and pollution. In South India in 1881 there were about 11 500 *devadasis*.[24]

Male British rulers and Indian social reformers in tandem waged an 'anti-nautch' campaign at the turn of the century to prohibit temple dancing, the 'dedication' of girls to the temples and the employment of female dancers at public and private festivities. As late as 1912–13 girls were purchased for 2000 rupees each. Campaign efforts in a number of cities helped abolish the practice of dedicating women to a temple and according to L'Armand and L'Armand, (1983) even formally forbade temple dancing.

RE-CREATION

Yet as human history testifies, when dance is suppressed it rises phoenix-like to live again in some transformation. The ethereal beauty of Anna Pavlova's 1929 ballet performance in India helped rekindle enthusiasm for Hindu dance. She included dances based on Indian themes and posed the simple question, 'Where is your dance?'[25] With her Indian-inspired creations modern dancer Ruth St. Denis also stimulated the revival.

Teaching *devadasi* (Bharata Natyam) and other classical dance forms to nondevadasi girls began in the 1930s. In the urban areas intellectual leaders at the forefront of Indian nationalism began to re-evaluate Indian cultural traditions and seek symbols of Indian identity. They so designated dance and consequently catalysed a renaissance of Indian classical dancing.[26] The national integration policy of post-independence India 'promoted the concept that the classical arts helped unite India culturally', while 'fears of unruly and fissiparous regionalism were met by giving particular regional forms of classical arts national recognition'.[27]

Besides giving the dance a regenerated environment in which to be cultivated, the renaissance gave women of the high castes who were previously barred from the art the opportunity to dance and to become dancers. Expertise in dance is a much-prized attribute for a girl of the privileged classes who is seeking a husband. Girls from influential and wealthy families study classical Indian dance as many middle-class girls in the West study ballet. The high school and in diluted form, the cinema, stage and private gatherings have also embraced dance performance. However few married women are permitted to pursue public performance as a career.

Not unexpectedly the primary *gurus* or teachers of the dance renaissance have been male. However economics, traditionally important in the teacher–student relationship, has overshadowed the also critical bond of devotion. Some *gurus* are no longer instructor and parent for many hours of the day. They give group lessons to anyone who can afford classes; dancers may now be from a number of castes or foreign countries. Many of the known *gurus* travel beyond their home areas to key cities and even abroad to teach special courses.

During Jeanes Antze's 1980–1 fieldwork (1982), she learned that one of the main Odissi *gurus* charged 1000 rupees (at seven rupees to the dollar) per student for a month of intensive group classes. Six hundred rupees for a one-hour-a-day class for a month was not uncommon, and *gurus* had seven to ten students. By contrast university lecturers earned about 2000 rupees per month. Gaston (1983), also a student of Indian dance, said that several dancers estimated it cost 10 000 rupees to learn the dance and another 10 000 to 15 000 for the debut recital. Over a period of six years a dance student's family may spend 60 000 rupees or more.

Imparting his own vision and music upon a dance, a *guru* expects respect and credit for a piece he has taught a dancer. Usually accompanying students' performances, he tends to be jealous if one studies with another teacher or creates her own dances. If a dancer wishes to be creative she breaks the dependency mold. Then the dancer has to find and teach another musician to accompany her. According to Gaston, he may leave her for better economic rewards and then she must begin again.

While for those in the homeland classical dance is an expression of Indian identity and esteem, for those who immigrate the dance reflects traditional culture in a changing context. During her study of the Natraj classical Indian dance school in Vancouver, British Columbia, Cunningham was practising the *puja* devotional portion of Bharata Natyam together with Shakuntala, a classmate. Shakuntala's remarks on the meaning of dance echo femininity as a romantic tradition of imposed limitations:

> The religious elements of the dance make it very profound. The role, which is the ideal Indian woman, is linked in India to both God and the family, and the reason that the dance is a play is that my everyday life is the total antithesis of the ideal Indian woman. . . . The dance allows me to act the pleading, teasing, coquettish movements and they imply a female subjugation. . . . So although I couldn't be the person in the dance, in reality I can experience it through the dance'.

It allows Shakuntala a momentary partaking of two contradictory worlds without compromising either.[28]

MEN AS WOMEN

Men as well as women send danced messages of male-dominant gender patterns. In Kathakali, Chhau and the original Kuchipudi, men playing women show their ideals and fantasies about them and in so doing exaggerate female characteristics. Chaki-Sircar and Sircar (1982) suggest that the creators of the powerful and spectacular Kathakali dance-drama staged a public ritual for the entire community; Nayar heroic warriors under the supervision of the Brahman caste, were reacting to foreign aggression. Kathakali was a reaffirmation of the warrior-priest social status and an affirmation of masculine pride in a society where descent and residence are on the maternal side.

In Orissa the custom of small boys performing dressed as girls coexisted with the female temple dancer tradition since the fifteenth century.[29] Since Krishna was male the most effective way of showing devotion was as a female, similar to the *gopis* (milkmaids) who dance their love for Krishna.

Hijras (eunuchs, hermaphrodites and impotent males who identify themselves as female) dance as women.[30] They often perform to film music, improvise and spoof grooms at their weddings. A few may be transsexual. Raymond holds the male-conspiracy view that 'all transsexuals rape women's bodies by reducing the real female form to an artifact, appropriating this body for themselves'.[31] They try to 'co-opt women's power of creativity inherent in female biology'.[32]

FEMALE IMAGES OF THE DIVINE AND MODULATING MALE DOMINANCE

Female images of the divine may empower some women both spiritually and socially to take control of their lives. Perhaps, as in other cultures with rituals of rebellion, powerful goddesses serve to present complementarities, compensation and alternatives to the male dominance models as well as to remind men not to exceed acceptable limits in their behaviour towards women. Implicit is the suggestion that excessive behaviour could cause women to challenge the male-dominant status quo. For example, Kuchipudi, an Andra Pradesh regional variant of Indian classical dance, began with Brahman male dancers and actors, who taught the art to the guilds of male teachers. Then they instructed women.[33] Today, however, women are primarily responsible for its survival and performance.[34]

Chamudeswari Shabdam, an episodic Kuchipudi dance,[35] tells the tale of the unconquerable Goddess Durga and the evil buffalo-headed demon Mahishasura. Durga is a universal spirit with male and female qualities who represents female energy on earth, creativity, motherhood and the potential to destroy evil and bring justice. Saviour of the gods and killer of demons, Durga rules the heavens with Lord Shiva.

CONCLUSION

Until recently men have been the choreographers, ballet masters and producers of Indian classical dance, the mouthpiece of a male-designed religion. Men dictated the dancers' working conditions and economic options. Through thematic movement, content and style both male and female dancers provide gender models for audience members. Common dance motifs are messages of male freedom and dominance counterposed to female subjugation and deference. In addition to danced messages of male dominance, dances about powerful female goddesses may serve to remind men not to abuse their power and to appease women so that they do not rebel. Moreover, Vatsyayan (1968) points out that the messages are reiterated in other art forms accessible to the masses.

Notwithstanding India's state of flux, changing women's roles, a former female prime minister and the prominence of some highly Western-educated, high-caste, upper-class women in various occupations outside the home, including science, medicine, and diplomacy,[36] female low status evinces in the realities of contemporary life in India as elsewhere. Indian women are routinely sold into marriage and brothers are almost invariably favoured over sisters. Successful affluent women are sometimes unaware of the problems of the terrorism of drunken husbands, brutal landlords or the starkness of poverty. Suman Krishan Kant's Women's Grievances Group organisation receives complaints and directs investigations of attacks on women, many of them involving burning and scalding of brides by in-laws who feel they were short-changed on dowries.[37]

Manu's ancient law prescribing the proper role of women in society prevails paradoxically alongside the current Indian constitution that affirms nondiscrimination against any citizen on grounds of sex. Although there are laws to improve the status of women, most women do not know about them.[38]

Indian dance in its heterogeneity reflects regional, ethnic group, religious and social class differences as well as a differential impact of foreign assaults and adaptations. Future research might ask how mythical variants enacted in dance vary in accord with situations and historical periods during which women have had a better quality of life. Do stories of male dominance serve to preserve the status quo? If Western-educated women watch the dance, does the kinetic discourse convey reminders that ancient social traditions are deeply embedded and thus provide a context of sensitivities and behaviour that constrain change?[39] Does observing or participating allow them, as it does Shakuntala, to partake of two worlds? What new meaning is given to the past in the present? What myths and dance enactments will emerge from Indian religious thought, aesthetic values and contemporary experiences? In the past classical dance was for the gods, the élite and the masses in the festival context; for whom and towards what end will dance be performed in the future? Feminists in the United States agree that men use or lose women's ideas and give them no credit. What is women's hidden contribution to Indian dance?

Why do contemporary women collude in the reproduction of female subordination through the performance of male-dictated performances? Different meanings attach to performance. For some dance participants traditional dance preserves the past as an anchor in a sea of uncertainty in modern life. The dance as a symbol of Indian identity has led some women to focus on the preservation and the purity of the approximately 150-year-old aesthetic within the memory of the dance teachers of the 1930s. There is reverence for a reclaimed, reinvented cultural heritage rescued from destruction through the forces of political, social and economic changes due to the invasion and intrusion of outsiders. Feminist perspectives threaten the established religion that scripts social hierarchy; women's economic security is at stake and fear of a backlash constrains feminist action.

Still India manifests novel developments in dance. Some 'dancers and their public are less concerned with rediscovering the ancient glories of our dance forms, and are more with expressing the present, with exploring the future. They wish the dance to expand its possibilities so that it can keep in step with the rest of the changes that have taken place in our society'.[40] Innovation has become a criterion for dance performance. 'Departures from accepted conventions are no longer looked on askance'.[41]

Attempting to revolutionise the very concept of Indian classical dance, Chandralekha, from Madras, 'questions the appropriateness of as basic a convention as the yearning of a female dancer for her male lover, her master, her God'. She wishes to retain the basic vocabulary of Bharata Natyam to create dances with abstract themes. Her dances also include movement idioms from martial arts and American modern dance. 'When she performs a duet during which she straddles a male dancer whose head appears from between her legs, she shocks a middle-class audience comfortable in the premise of female subjugation to the male. The role-reversal she expresses comes not from Western feminist literature, but from the concept of *shakti* as an active female force as opposed to a passive male one. Her movement images evoke the disturbing power of Kali-worship and Tantric cults'.[42] Audiences are shocked, says dancer Nilimma Devi, because the duet's heterosexual physical contact exceeds the bounds of Indian propriety.

Padma Subramanyam composed a dance based on the *Ramayana*, but she gives it a new twist. At the end when Rama asks his wife to go through the fire one more time she shows a range of emotions, from disbelief to anger. Finally she becomes the divine mother standing alone and self-contained.[43]

Viewing the dance language of the classical idiom as exploitive of women, Chaki-Sircar assimilates and synthesises six styles of classical and semi-classical dance: Bharata Natyam, Manipuri, Kathak, Odissi, Kerala martial arts and Yoga postures. Her dances incorporate *mudras*, *ragas*, Sanskrit chanting and traditional footwork and exclude the classical balance and centring. *Gantotri* portrays Shakti not as Shiva's beautiful coy wife as is customary but as energy and power, a beautiful mother and forceful goddess. *Sabala* is about a woman of independence.

Dance not only reflects what is but also suggests what might be. In this process dance generally both mirrors and prefigures shifts in sexual mores and gender roles. Changing dance style and dramatic theme are cultural constructions that respond to an altered environment, encompassing the views and behaviour of women. Now that women are beginning to participate in national political life, become priests,[44] assume guru roles and choreograph and teach their own dances, what gender messages will dance convey?[45]

Notes and References

1. See J. L. Hanna (1988a), (1988b), (1990).
2. See R. Ghadially (1988).
3. M. Chaki-Sircar (1984b), p. 19.
4. M. L. Duley and M. Edwards, eds (1986).
5. S. Chitnis (1988), p. 82.
6. A. M. Jaggar (1983).
7. J. L. Hanna (1987).
8. M. Roy (1972), pp. 117–18.
9. This account is given in the M. G. Ghosh (1950) translation of the *Natyasastra*.
10. Ibid., pp. 1–34.
11. W. D. O'Flaherty (1980), pp. 29, 33.
12. See M. Sarabhai (1965), (1976).
13. The dancer stated this to the author in a personal communication in 1985.
14. See W. D. O'Flaherty, op. cit., pp. 117, 121, 122, 129 and M. Chaki-Sircar (1984a).
15. V. Dhruvarajan (1989), p. 100, see pp. vii–viii.
16. See W. D. O'Flaherty, op. cit., p. 142; M. Khokar (1984), pp. 17–18; and L. E. Gatwood (1985), pp. 66–7.
17. Again, this was stated in a personal communication with the dancer.

18. P. Banerji (1983), p. 144.
19. V. T. Oldenburg (1984), p. 137.
20. In this sense the Hindu ethos is similar to the Christian view of separating the wife/mother from the public woman. By contrast to the *devadasis*, Catholic nuns who marry Jesus deny their sexuality.
21. F. Henriques (1962), p. 183.
22. A.-M. Gaston (1982), p. 10.
23. R. Jeanes-Antze (1979), p. 8.
24. G. A. Oddie (1979), p. 103.
25. F. Bowers (1953), p. 9.
26. M. Chaki-Sircar (1972).
27. J. L. Erdman (1983), p. 262.
28. J. Cunningham (1992).
29. S. Kothari (1968).
30. S. Nanda (1984).
31. J. Raymond (1979), p. 104.
32. Ibid., pp. 207–8.
33. V. A. Rao (1959).
34. M. Khokar, n.d.
35. J. L. Hanna (1983).
36. A. de Souza (1980).
37. See S. Hazarika (1981) and W. Claiborne (1984).
38. See V. Dhruvarajan (1989), p. 36.
39. See A. de Souza, op. cit., pp. 25–26, 28.
40. R. Puri (1986), p. 38.
41. Ibid., p. 40.
42. Ibid., p. 39.
43. This information was conveyed in a personal communication with Roxanne Gupta in June 1988.
44. See S. Hazarika, op. cit.
45. This article is based on material in J. L. Hanna (1988a) and (1992), which have extensive references on India and its dance.

Bibliography

A. Bandura, 'Modeling Theory: Some Traditions, Trends, and Disputes', in R. D. Park (ed.), *Recent Trends in Social Learning Theory* (New York: Academic Press, 1972), pp. 35–61.

P. Banerji, *Erotica in Indian Dance* (Atlantic Highland, NJ: Humanities Press, 1983).

Bharata Muni, see Ghosh.

F. Bowers, *The Dance in India* (New York: Columbia University Press, 1953).

M. Chaki-Sircar, 'Community of Dancers in Calcutta', in S. Sinha (ed.), *Cultural Profile of Calcutta* (Calcutta: Indian Anthropological Society, 1972), pp. 190–8.

——, *Feminism in a Traditional Society: Women of the Manipur Valley* (New Delhi: Shakti Books, 1984a).

——, 'Rabindra Dance Drama in Modern Times', in R. Biswas (ed.), *On Tagore* (New York: Tagore Society of New York, 1984b), pp. 19–24.

—— and P. K. Sircar, 'Indian Dance: Classical Unity and Regional Variation', in A. G. Noble and A. K. Dutt (eds), *India: Cultural Patterns and Processes* (Boulder, Colo.: Westview Press, 1982), pp. 147–64.

S. Chitnis, 'Feminism: Indian Ethos and Indian Convictions', in R. Ghadially (ed.), *Women in Indian Society* (New Delhi/Newbury Park: Sage Publications, 1988), pp. 81–95.

W. Claiborne, 'Dowry Killings Show Social Stress in India', *Washington Post* (September 22, 1984), p. 1.

J. Cunningham, 'Classical Dance of India in Canada: Adaptation, Play and Women', PhD dissertation (William Lyon University, 1992).

A. de Souza, *Women in Contemporary India and South Asia* (New Delhi: Manohar, 1980).

V. Dhruvarajan, *Hindu Women and The Power of Ideology* (Granby, Mass.: Bergin & Garvey, 1989).

M. I. Duley, and M. Edwards (eds), *Cross-cultural Study of Women* (New York: Feminist Press, 1986).

J. L. Erdman, 'Who Should Speak for the Performing Arts? The Case of the Delhi Dancers', *Pacific Affairs* 56(20) (1983) pp. 247–69.

A-M. Gaston, *Siva in Dance, Myth and Iconography* (Oxford: Oxford University Press, 1982).

——, 'The Effect of Changing Social Structures in Indian Classical Dance', in *Contributions to the Sociology of the Arts: Reports from the 10th World Congress of Sociology, Mexico City, 1982* (Sophia, Bulgaria: Research Institute for Culture, 1983), pp. 197–308.

L. E. Gatwood, *Devi and the Spouse Goddess: Women, Sexuality, and Marriages in India* (Riverdale, Md.: Riverdale, 1985).

R. Ghadially, (ed.), *Women in Indian Society* (New Delhi/Newbury Park: Sage Publications, 1988).

M. G. Ghosh (trans.), *Natyasastra* (Calcutta: Royal Asiatic Society of Bengal, 1950).

J. L. Hanna, *The Performer-Audience Connection: Emotion to Metaphor in Dance and Society* (Austin: University of Texas, 1983).

——, *To Dance is Human: A Theory of Nonverbal Communication*, reprint of 1979 with new foreword (Chicago: University of Chicago Press, 1987).

——, *Dance, Sex, and Gender: Signs of Identity, Dominance, Defiance, and Desire* (Chicago: University of Chicago Press, 1988a).

——, *Dance and Stress* (New York: AMS Press, 1988b).

——, 'Dance and Women's Protest in Nigeria and the United States', in G. West and R. L. Blumberg (eds), *Women and Social Protest* (New York: Oxford University Press, 1990), pp. 333–45.

——, 'Feminist Perspectives on Classical Indian Dance: Divine Sexuality, Prostitution, and Erotic Fantasy', in D. Waterhouse (ed.), *Dance of India* (University of Toronto Graduate Centre for South Asian Studies, 1992).

S. Hazarika, 'Past Threatens Future of Indian Women', *New York Times* (6 January 1981), p. E24.

——, 'Age-Old Hindu Barrier Falls: Women are Priests', *New York Times* (3 July 1984), p. A2.

F. Henriques, *Prostitution and Society: A Survey* (New York: Citadel Press, 1962).

A. M. Jaggar, *Feminist Politics and Human Nature* (Totowa, NJ: Rowman & Allanheld, 1983).

R. Jeanes-Antze, 'The World of Indian Dance', *Dance in Canada* (August 1979), pp. 5–9.

——, 'Tradition and Learning in Odissi Dance of India: Guru-Sisya-Parampara', *MFA Dance History and Criticism* (Toronto: York University, 1982).

M. Khokar, 'Bharata Natyam and Kuchipudi' (Mimeograph n.d.).

——, *Traditions of Classical Indian Dance*, rev. and enlarged 1979 edn (New Delhi: Clarion Books, 1984).

S. Kothari, 'Gotipua Dancers of Orissa', *Sangeet Natak*, 8 (1968), pp. 31–43.

K. L'Armand, and A. L'Armand, 'One Hundred Years of Music in Madras: A Case Study in Secondary Urbanization', *Ethnomusicology*, 27(3) (1983) 411–38.

S. Nanda, 'The Hijras of India: A Preliminary Report', *Medicine and Law*, 3 (1984) 59–74.

G. A. Oddie, *Social Protest in India: British Protestant Missionaries and Social Reforms 1850–1900* (New Delhi: Manohar, 1979).

W. D. O'Flaherty, *Women, Androgynes, and Other Mythical Beasts* (Chicago: University of Chicago Press, 1980).

V. T. Oldenburg, *The Making of Colonial Lucknow, 1856–1877* (Princeton: Princeton University Press, 1984).

R. Puri, 'New Directions in Indian Dance', *India Magazine* (June 1986), pp. 36–43.

V. A. Rao, 'Kuchipudi School of Dancing', *Sangeet Natak Akademi Bulletin*, No. 11–12 (April 1959), pp. 1–8.

J. Raymond, *Transsexual Empire* (Boston: Beacon Press, 1979).

M. Roy, *Bengali Women* (Chicago: University of Chicago Press, 1972).

M. Sarabhai, *The Eight Nayikas: Heroines of the Classical Dance of India, Dance Perspectives*, No. 24 (1965).

——, *Longing for the Beloved: Songs to Siva-Nataraja in Bharata Natyam* (Gujarat: Durpana, 1976).

K. Vatsyayan, *Classical Indian Dance in Literature and the Arts* (New Delhi: Sangeet Natak Akademi, 1968).

Part Three
Theory/Criticism

9 Dance, Feminism, and the Critique of the Visual

ROGER COPELAND

One of the most radical and decisive differences between nineteenth-century ballet and early modern dance is so obvious that its far-reaching implications are easily overlooked: the early moderns, almost all of whom began their choreographic careers by creating solos for themselves, were using their *own* unballetic bodies rather than someone else's body as the raw material of their art. It is significant that – at least in conversation – we continue to refer to artists such as Martha Graham or Mary Wigman as modern *dancers* – not modern dance *choreographers*. This habit of speech has the effect of emphasising how often these choreographers tended to perform in their own dances. They didn't stand apart from the choreography and view it as external to themselves. In nineteenth-century ballet by contrast, the choreographer – almost invariably a man – imposed abstract patterns on the bodies of *others* (usually women). There is, after all, no male equivalent for the *corps de ballet*; and the choreographer who manipulates that corps stands apart from his creation.

This distinction – between the nineteenth-century male ballet choreographer who visually 'surveys' his work from a distance and the female modern dance choreographer who rarely 'stands outside of' her own work – provides a striking parallel to the recent writings of those feminist theoreticians who equate analytical detachment with the prerogatives of patriarchy. These writers also assume that a deep, abiding connection exists between patriarchal culture and a tendency to 'privilege' the visual over the tactile. ('Seeing is believing' we often say. Indeed, to exclaim 'I see. I see' is to state – in this culture at least – 'I *understand*'.) The French feminist Luce Irigaray writes that

> Investment in the look is not privileged in women as in men. More than the other senses, the eye objectifies and masters. It sets at a distance, maintains that distance. In our culture, the predominance of the look over smell, taste, touch, and hearing has brought about an impoverishment of bodily relations. The moment the look dominates, the body loses its materiality.[1]

139

This latter notion seems particularly relevant to romantic ballet, where the sylphide is woman dematerialised, existing quite literally (and exclusively) as a sight, an apparition. Our relationship to her is purely 'specular'. As James learns so painfully in *La Sylphide*, she is unattainable; she resists all tactile contact.

By contrast, modern dance placed a much higher premium on kinetic empathy than on visual experience *per se*. Many modern dance choreographers proceeded on the assumption that the visual orientation of ballet (rooted – as we'll see – in the principle of *en dehors* and proscenium framing) precluded the sort of tactile response they wanted dancegoers to experience. Tactility was thought to reduce the physical and psychological distance that the proscenium arch creates, thereby establishing a closer bond – or at least the sensation of such – between performer and perceiver. John Martin, the early partisan of modern dance, has written:

> The modern dancer, instead of employing the cumulative resources of academic tradition, cuts through directly to the source of all dancing . . . Because of the inherent contagion of bodily movement, which makes the onlooker feel sympathetically in his own musculature the exertions he sees in somebody else's musculature, the dancer is able to convey through movement the most intangible emotional experience. This is the prime purpose of modern dance, it is not interested in spectacle . . .[2]

This belief – that the visual and the tactile are at odds with one another – was conveniently summed up in the 1960s by Marshall McLuhan in books like *The Guttenberg Galaxy*. A typical passage reads as follows:

> touch is not so much a separate sense as the very interplay of the senses. That is why it recedes in significance as the visual faculty is given separate and abstract intensity.[3]

In *Love's Body*, McLuhan's associate Norman O. Brown, rhapsodically restates this argument in explicitly *theatrical* terms:

> The garden (of Eden) is polymorphism of the senses, polymorphous perversity, active interplay; and the opposite of polymorphous perversity is the *abstraction of the visual*, obtained by putting to sleep the rest of the life of the body . . . like spectators in the traditional theatre.[4]

And Brown, one of the key intellectual gurus of the 1960s, is advocating a return to ritual, which is presumably more participatory and more tactile than the theatre. One can easily imagine the early modern dance choreographers nodding in agreement as they sing the praises of tactile or kinesthetic experience in opposition to the purely 'visual' impact of ballet. The English word theatre is usually said to derive from the Greek 'theatron' which means literally, 'seeing place', an architectural space that makes specific provisions for spectators, those who sit apart from the action. Everything performed in a theatre is thus expressly designed *to be seen*. (And that is why ballet is often referred to as the most 'theatrical' of all Western dance forms. Balletic turnout promotes the goal of visibility, opening the body up so that it becomes theatrically 'legible' when framed by a proscenium arch.)

Balletic partnering was thought to carry this logic of legibility a step further: As the vogue for pointe work and ethereal characterisations began to dominate nineteenth-century ballet, male dancers were demoted to the status of hydraulic lifts for the lighter-than-air ballerinas. The male dancer's function was thereby to display the female, to put this fully turned-out woman 'on display.' This leads to a provocative question: Had the male dancer actually been demoted – which is what the textbooks tell us? Or did sexual politics dictate that the woman be displayed and that the man do the displaying?

Clearly, recent feminist critiques of 'the visual' can help illuminate some of the deeper differences between nineteenth-century ballet and early twentieth-century modern dance. But is feminist scholarship as useful in accounting for the differences between modern and postmodern dance, both of which, unlike ballet, were pioneered principally by women?

In the early 1980s, two revivals – fortuitously juxtaposed – set me to thinking about the relationship between modern dance, postmodern dance and sexual politics. In April of 1982, at the Brooklyn Academy of Music, Annabelle Gamson performed her reconstructions of several legendary solos by Isadora Duncan. Later that same month at St Marks church in lower Manhattan, a number of early postmodern dances from the mid-60s, including Yvonne Rainer's highly influential *Trio A* were re-staged in conjunction with Bennington College's Judson Project.

At first glance, the work of Duncan and Rainer would seem to have little, if anything, in common. As danced by Annabelle Gamson in her revival of *The Blue Danube*, Duncan's movement sings the song of the body electric: it luxuriates in its own physicality and basks in the gaze of an adoring public. Rainer's movement in *Trio A* by contrast, is considerably less voluptuous. Some would call it puritanical. Certainly it is cold, uninflected, almost 'unperformed' – as if the dancer is merely 'marking it' rather than executing the dance 'full out'. In contrast to Duncan, who races on several occasions toward the audience in an open-armed embrace, Rainer averts her gaze and remains coolly oblivious to those watching.

But despite such stark contrasts (indeed, as a result of them), both dances can be said to reflect the prevailing feminist ideologies of their respective eras. In an age still dominated by the dictates of Victorianism, Duncan dared to dance uncorseted. Dressed in a loose-fitting, free-flowing tunic, she rebelled not only against the corset *per se*, but also against everything it symbolised: the constraints – both physical and psychological – imposed upon women by Victorian culture. Rainer on the other hand is the product of a very different moment in time (ironically, one inspired in large part by the example of Duncan and others like her, but which she rejects rather than embodies): I refer of course to the so-called 'sexual revolution' of the 1960s and 70s.

Unlike the feminists of Duncan's generation who longed for sexual freedom and who viewed puritanical repression as an obstacle to the emancipation of women, many radical feminists of the sixties and seventies eyed the sexual revolution with considerable suspicion, fearful that it hadn't really liberated women, but had simply made them more 'available.' (Even the New Left, at least early on, was not exactly a model of sexual progressivism. Remember the male activists who argued that 'The woman's position in the revolution should be prone'?) According to this argument, the Victorian obligation to be passive had merely been replaced by the contemporary obligation to be sexually alluring. Many feminists began to practise what Midge Decter calls 'the new chastity'.[5] (They began to 'dress down' rather than up; they became suspicious and resentful of what has come to be known as 'the male gaze'. In 1965, Yvonne Rainer published a statement which has since been elevated to the status of a manifesto. It read in part:

No to spectacle no to virtuosity no to transformations and magic and make believe . . . no to seduction of spectator by the wiles of the performer . . .[6]

These words were intended as an aesthetic – not a political – statement. But Rainer's insistence upon saying 'no' to so many of the voyeuristic and erotic pleasures that dance has traditionally offered begins to assume feminist implications when viewed against this ideological backdrop. In this new age of 'the pill and promiscuity', it was feared that women were no longer free *not* to be sexual.

Certainly, the so-called 'dance boom' of the 1960s was very much a part of this sexual revolution. And postmodern dance can be viewed as a reaction against the facile equating of dance and sex that was so central to the dance boom of the sixties and seventies. Rainer in fact, once declared her 'rage at the impoverishment of ideas, narcissism, and disguised sexual exhibitionism of most dancing'.[7] Thus it seems reasonable to suggest that the austere, cerebral, anti-voluptuous quality of the early postmodern dances created by women such as Yvonne Rainer, Trisha Brown, and Lucinda Childs reflects these feminist concerns, if only indirectly.

For many women, theatrical dancing of *any* sort became suspect; for dance has often been regarded as a 'mute' art of pure physical presence in which women are reduced to (and equated with) their bodies. To some, it seemed entirely plausible that women had been 'permitted' to dominate modern dance because it inadvertently perpetuated yet another set of destructive sex-role stereotypes (e.g. Woman as Earth Mother, primal body, natural force, etc.). Gabriele D'Annunzio for example is reported to have declared to Isadora Duncan, 'You are part of the trees, the sky, you are the dominating goddess of Nature'.[8]

By contrast, the women who pioneered postmodern dance were eager to demonstrate that they possessed *minds* as well as bodies. The original title of Yvonne Rainer's *Trio A*, by the way, was *The Mind Is A Muscle, Part I*. This explains in part the prominence of spoken language in much Judson-era postmodern dance, the fascination with abstract thought, the impersonal, objective, mathematically-generated floor-patterns (often based on the 'unnatural', geometric purity of the grid), and the new conception of dance as a mode of 'problem-solving'. Trisha

Brown has said that what attracted her to the elaborate mathematical formulas and diagrams that helped generate the choreography for works such as *Locus* was the desire to demonstrate that women choreographers need not create 'intuitively' or 'instinctively', constructing their dances from movement that 'comes naturally' to the body.

A moment ago, I suggested that postmodern dances often treat choreography as an exercise in problem-solving. One of the central problems addressed by the women who pioneered postmodern dance was how to exhibit the body in public without becoming an exhibitionist. Rainer's provisional solution is evident in her solo version of *Trio A*. She 'averts' her gaze and refuses to directly acknowledge the presence of the audience. ('No to seduction of spectator by the wiles of the performer . . .') Of course, the averted gaze is not an unproblematic solution to this dilemma. The voyeur's sense of power often depends upon invisibility and anonymity. Thus, to openly acknowledge the gaze of the viewer may be more disruptive than to ignore it. Consider Manet's 'Olympia'. What shocked the salon-goers in 1865 was not her nakedness *per se*, but the fact that she stared calmly and collectedly out at the viewer, consciously acknowledging his gaze.

Furthermore, the fear of 'seduction' that Rainer's text speaks of is part and parcel of a more pervasive modernist desire to guarantee the spectator's perceptual freedom, to prevent the spectator from being manipulated by spectacle in a Pavlovian fashion. (Malraux once spoke of the 'lucid horror of seduction'.)

But Yvonne Rainer's use of the word 'seduction' takes on a whole new set of meanings when considered in the light of sexual politics. In fact, much of Rainer's later work plays on the various connotations of the term 'seduction' in life as well as in art. Put another way: the theatrical relationship between performer and audience is analogised to the social relationship between men and women. For example, in the slide-projected text for Rainer's *This is the Story of a Woman Who . . .* we are told that 'social interactions seem to be mostly about seduction'. At another point in the same piece, a projected title reads: 'His very gaze seems to transform her into a performer'. This was 1973, two years before Laura Mulvey published her now classic essay on the male gaze in the cinema, 'Visual Pleasure and Narrative Cinema'. Today of course, considerations of the 'the gaze' are all the rage in feminist studies. Thus Rainer's reference to 'his very gaze' would seem a logical point at which to invest dance writing with some of the energy of recent feminist scholarship, particularly feminist film studies. (And of course, in 1973, Rainer herself was just about to renounce live performance in order to begin work as a film-maker). But we need to be wary of translating Mulvey's ideas from cinema to dance without first considering the enormous differences between the perceptual conditions that prevail in the two media. Indeed, we may even be talking about apples and oranges. Here is one of the most representative (and influential) paragraphs from Mulvey's essay on the gaze:

> In their traditional exhibitionist role women are simultaneously looked at and displayed, with their appearance coded for strong visual and erotic impact so that they can connote *to be looked at ness*. Women displayed as sexual object is the leitmotif of erotic spectacle: from pin-ups to strip-tease, from Ziegfeld to Busby Berkeley, she holds the look, plays to and signifies male desire.[9]

But a few paragraphs later, Mulvey's argument has begun to focus specifically on narrative film:

> Traditionally, the woman displayed has functioned on two levels: as erotic object for the characters within the screen story, and as erotic object for the spectator within the auditorium, with a shifting tension between the looks on either side of the screen. For instance the device of the show girl allows the two looks to be unified technically without any apparent break in the diegesis. A woman performs within the narrative, the gaze of the spectator and that of the male characters in the film are neatly combined without breaking narrative verisimilitude.[10]

These ideas *may* be applicable to the viewing conditions that prevailed at an institution like the Paris Opera in the eighteenth and nineteenth centuries: one thinks of Lancret's famous painting of the lecherous male rakes desirously eyeing Marie Camargo's newly-exposed ankles. And we have already discussed the extent to which the romantic ballerina was put on display by her male consort. (One might also cite Gautier's dance criticism which often borders on soft porn in its obsessive fetishising of the ballerina's body parts, i.e. 'her [Fanny Elssler's] leg, smooth as marble, gleams through the frail mesh of her silk stocking',[11] etc. It is easy to imagine Gautier brandishing his opera glasses so as to zero in on the not-so-obscure object of desire.

But this example notwithstanding, I would caution against too literal a transference of Mulvey's ideas from cinema studies to dance. Mulvey for example is very quick to point out that 'This complex interaction of looks is specific to film'.[12] Elsewhere in the essay, she emphasises the special cinematic conditions that promote this sort of fetishism and voyeurism: '[Film is] a hermetically sealed world which unwinds magically, indifferent to the presence of the audience, producing for them a sense of separation and playing on their voyeuristic phantasy.'[13] In summary, she argues,

> This is what makes cinema quite different in its voyeuristic potential from, say, strip-tease, theatre, show, etc. Going far beyond highlighting a woman's to-be-looked-at-ness, cinema builds the way she is to be looked at into the spectacle itself.[14]

More importantly, these theories of the omnipresent, inescapable male gaze proceed on the assumption that it's *always* the man who holds the camera (or the brush or the pen) and the woman who holds the pose. But in modern and postmodern dance, where so many of the choreographic pioneers have been women, this is hardly the case. Alas, even in the world of twentieth-century ballet, there is no getting around the fact that (heterosexual) male desire plays a much more marginal role than it does in the Hollywood cinema (which is the real focus of Mulvey's essay.) Here – and in the dance world generally – the prominence of the *gay* gaze complicates any attempt to mechanistically assimilate Mulvey's ideas. Of course, gay men can be at least as misogynistic as straight men; but in the dance world, the male gaze is often brought to bear upon the members (pun intended) of one's own sex. Think of all those low angle crotch shots that figure so prominently in a publication like *Dance Magazine*. Here the problem (if indeed it is a problem) is beefcake, not cheesecake.

Indeed, in dance the cinematic notion of the 'male' gaze is less relevant and less useful to the theoretician than a more generalised consideration of the gaze itself, whether male or female, whether heterosexual or homosexual in orientation. We have already seen some of the ways in which dance scholarship can draw upon the recent work of those psychoanalytic feminists who focus on the relative virtues of a visual as opposed to a tactile orientation in the world (the gaze v. the touch, in other words). The writings of feminists such as Luce Irigaray can be very helpful when it comes to illuminating the differences between the detached, visual bias of nineteenth-century ballet and the early modern dancers' emphasis on tactility and kinesthetic experience.

But major problems arise the moment one attempts to apply such concepts to a postmodern choreographer like Rainer. Irigary remember, argued that 'the eye . . . sets at a distance and maintains that distance. But Rainer herself relies heavily on the sort of Brechtian 'alienation effects' that might be said to 'set [the spectacle] at a distance and maintain that distance'. And Rainer remember, is concerned that the *spectator* will be seduced by the wiles of the performer, not that the performers will fall victim to a predatory gaze.

Of course, feminists could argue (and indeed *have* argued) that Rainer's distancing-devices are themselves part of the problem, an unwitting act of complicity with deep patriarchal biases. Listen to the feminist writer Lucy Lippard discussing Rainer's work in the mid-seventies: 'for over a decade now an imposed – perhaps masculine – detachment masquerading as "modernism" has insidiously denigrated feeling'.[15]

Here we encounter, if only indirectly, one of the central conflicts in recent sexual/political theory: the debate over the 'correct' attitude feminists should take toward traditional conceptions of gender difference (e.g. the belief that women are fundamentally instinctive rather than reflective, closer to and more open about their emotional life than men, innately drawn to tactile involvement rather than visual, analytical detachment, and always determined to render their experience holistically rather than to dissect it into fragments). Should feminists set out to demonstrate that these presumably natural differences are nothing but patriarchial prejudices? Or should they turn the inherited hierarchy on its head, celebrating the very characteristics that patriarchy has traditionally denigrated (instinctual modes of knowing, intimacy, fullness of feeling, oneness with nature, etc.) Irigaray, in her *Speculum de l'autre femme* contrasts the values of the maternal womb with the patriarchial logos and comes down firmly on the side of the former.[16]

In a 1975 interview with Rainer, Lucy Lippard tries – rather desperately – to convince the choreographer that fragmentation takes on a different character in her work than it does in the work of male artists, that 'there is a special kind of fragmentation that often surfaces in women's work . . . that quality of pulling together a lot of things . . . while still maintaining continuity'.[17] (In other words, it really aspires toward organic unity.) But Rainer is adamant: 'It's the opposite of the gestalt', she replies, 'Disjunction.'[18]

That response tells us a lot about Rainer, and what it tells us applies as well to Childs, Brown and the other analytically-inclined postmodernist choreographers. They re-claim rather than reject traditional male privileges. They don't celebrate the natural, the maternal, or the holistic. They strive to create movement 'objectively', not by tapping some internal – let alone maternal – instinct. In the so-called 'vacuum cleaner sequence' in Rainer's *Inner Appearances* the slide projected-text read 'Why do women value their insights more than their work,' she thinks. 'Now she is laughing inwardly at her cliché, the old intuition bit.'

The Judson-era postmodern dances of choreographers like Rainer, Brown, and Childs were implicitly feminist precisely because they questioned 'the old intuition bit' and because they emphasised detached visual analysis over tactile, touchie feelie modes of empathy. The attitude toward the visual that character-ised their work in the 1960s and early 70s is the one that Roland Barthes once attributed to Robbe-Grillet in a famous essay called 'Objective Literature'. Barthes forces us to confront the following question: Why should an objective, visually detached examination of things always necessarily be regarded as exploitative and politi-cally regressive? He describes Robbe-Grillet's method of descrip-tion as follows: '[he] apprehends the object as if in a mirror and constitutes it before us as a spectacle'.[19] By contrast, in tradition-al realism, '[the] objects have shapes, but also odors, tactile properties, memories, analogies . . . Instead of this sensurial syncretism . . . Robbe-Grillet imposes a unique order of apprehension: the sense of sight.'[20] All of which might lead one to anticipate a condemnation of visual tyranny à la Mulvey or Irigaray. But Robbe-Grillet is credited with preserving the ob-ject's 'Dasein' or sense of being-there (by sensuously rendering the surface of the object rather than excavating its inner mean-ings.) Robbe-Grillet's writing, says Barthes,

remains on the surface of the object and inspects it impar-
tially . . . language here is not the rape of an abyss, but the
rapture of a surface; it is meant to "paint" the object, in other
words, to caress it.[21]

And this I think is in line with what Rainer was getting at when
she said:

If my rage at the impoverishment of ideas, narcissism, and
disguised sexual exhibitionism of most dancing can be considered puritan moralizing, it is also true that I love the body –
its actual weight, mass and unenhanced physicality.[22]

Notes and References

1. L. Irigaray cited in C. Owens (1985) p. 70.
2. J. Martin in Copeland and Cohen (1983), p. 22.
3. M. McLuhan (1962) p. 83.
4. N. O. Brown (1966) p. 121.
5. M. Decter (1972) p. 1.
6. Y. Rainer (1974) p. 51.
7. Ibid., p. 71.
8. G. D'Annunzio, quoted in M. Green (1976) p. 87.
9. L. Mulvey in Mast and Cohen (1997) p. 750.
10. Ibid., p. 751.
11. T. Gautier (1932) p. 131.
12. L. Mulvey in Mast and Cohen (1992) p. 757.
13. Ibid., p. 756.
14. Ibid.
15. L. Lippard (1976) p. 278.
16. L. Irigaray (1974).
17. L. Lippard (1976) p. 276.
18. Ibid. p. 276.
19. R. Barthes (1972) p. 13.
20. Ibid., p. 16.
21. Ibid., p. 14.
22. Y. Rainer (1974) p. 71.

Bibliography

R. Barthes, *Critical Essays*, trans. Richard Howard, (Evanston, Ill.: Northwest-
ern University Press, 1972).
J. Berger, *Ways of Seeing* (London: BBC and Penguin Books, 1972).

N. O. Brown, *Love's Body* (New York: Vintage Books, 1966).

J. Culler, *On Deconstruction* (Ithaca: Cornell University Press, 1982).

R. Copeland and M. Cohen (eds), *What Is Dance?* (New York: Oxford University Press, 1983).

M. Decter, *The New Chastity and Other Arguments Against Women's Liberation* (New York: Coward, McCann & Deoghegan, 1977).

T. Gautier, *The Romantic Ballet As Seen By Theophile Gautier* (London: C. W. Beaumont, 1932).

M. Green, *Children of the Sun* (New York: Basic Books, 1976).

L. Irigaray, *Speculum, de l'autre femme*, (Paris: Minuit, 1974).

L. Lippard, *From the Center: Feminist Essays on Women's Art* (New York: Dutton, 1976).

G. Mast and M. Cohen, *Film Theory and Criticism*, 4th edn (New York: Oxford University Press, 1972).

M. McLuhan, *The Guttenberg Galaxy* (New York: New American Library, 1962).

L. Mulvey, 'Visual Pleasure and Narrative Cinema', *Screen*, Vol. 16, No. 3, 1975.

C. Owens, 'Feminists and Postmodernism' in H. Foster, *Postmodern Culture* (London: Pluto Press, 1985) pp. 57–82.

Y. Rainer, *Work: 1961–73* (Halifax: Press of the Nova Scotia College of Art and Design, 1974).

10 'You put your left foot in, then you shake it all about . . .'

Excursions and Incursions into Feminism and Bausch's *Tanztheater*

ANA SANCHEZ-COLBERG

Given the recent surge of feminist analysis within various fields of art, particularly film, theatre and literature, it does not come as a surprise that dance has finally come under scrutiny. Considering that dance is a field about and of the body (which in turn has become one of the targeted areas of feminist debate) what does come as a surprise is that this did not happen earlier. For many critics the reason lies in the apparent predominance of women in the field. Visibility has been conveniently equalled with power, dance is assumed to be a feminine field and thus beyond the need of a feminist critique.[1] However, more often than not dance perpetuates – in its training, practices and critical approaches – patriarchal ideology, value judgements and its accompanying ready-made worldview.[2]

Though dance critique is slowly awakening to feminism, dance practice remains a tougher sleeping beauty to awaken,[3] Feminist strategies which have developed into specific methods of production in film-making, literature, criticism and theatre remain neglected in contemporary dance even within the circles of the avant-garde and women choreographers. The process of analysing the old methods from a theoretical/critical point of view has started, but the process of analysing through, from and within the dance practice has yet to begin.

This essay focuses on highlighting strategies of performance/dance making which show potential as methods towards a feminism through dance.[4] It will pay particular attention to

151

strategies as seen in practice within the present production of *Tanztheater*, specifically in the work of Pina Bausch and the Wuppertal Tanztheater.[5]

The study adopts the following premises as points of departure. The aim is not to state 'the ABC of feminism in the dance practice'. The term 'feminist' is not used to prescribe a specific type of production but, rather, particular potentialities open to interpretation. Thus, here the term is embraced with all its unresolved debates and apparent contradictions. The analysis adopts a position of 'difference'[6] and recognises the strength of this aspect of feminism with regard to general socio-cultural transformation. The concern is to open avenues for dialogue within the production of dance adopting the self-critical attitude of feminist critique.

Furthermore, regarding issues of academic methodologies, it is important to note that this study embodies the opinions and subjective interpretations of its author about dance, feminism and Bausch, which have been areas of academic-creative-personal research for various years. The fact that it is a dancer/author seeing/assimilating Bausch from very specific background information on Bausch is relevant to the purposes, nature and aims of this study, whose goal is to link aspects of dance practice – choreography, performance, criticism, aesthetics and politics – within a larger socio-personal context.

BAUSCH AS A SUBJECT FOR FEMINIST ANALYSIS

Bausch's work is a subject which defies simple analysis. The complexity of the work has made it source of numerous writings in theatre, dance, scenic design, dramaturgy, drama criticism. *Tanztheater* has been loved, hated, emulated, copied, mimicked, understood and misunderstood. However, it is generally agreed that *Tanztheater* encapsules a complex and paradoxical production which has openly challenged conventional assumptions in dance.

Bausch does not appropriate the emblem of 'feminism'. In conversations with the audience at the Brooklyn Academy of Music's Next Wave Series in 1985, she became angry when audience members insisted on the 'feminism' of the pieces. She adamantly refuses to give her work a specific classification. It would be contrary to an oeuvre which is fundamentally about the dissolutions of classifications. In this she echoes trends within the feminist writers – particularly the French 'différence' bloc. The resistance to categorise is a methodological choice and regarded as defying 'a phallogocentric drive to stabilise, organise and rationalise our conceptual universe'[7] which, in turn, perpetuates certain binary oppositions which are diametrically opposed to this particular mode of critique.

The reader may ask, given the above, why Bausch as subject of this study? Whether or not she uses the term 'feminism' to name her work is irrelevant. What is of interest here is that certain performance/production/stylistic traits of Bausch's work are akin to aspects of feminist theory. I would venture to say that these features successfully exemplify aspects of feminist discourse within the dance at a structural level as no production has done, even within the circles of feminist dance. On immediate viewing, one can identify a recurrent theme of the antagonism between the sexes which is rooted in gender power relations and patterns of dominance. However, a closer look beyond the thematic into the structural level of Bausch's dancemaking reveals certain choreographic manipulations and stylistic features which posit interesting possibilities within a feminist dance discourse.[8] Bausch operates from a position of subversion and marginality which is manifested through (a) the concern for the body as locus for the dance discourse, (b) the choice of a *poetic language* as a way of presenting the narrative,[9] and (c) the implications of this narrative on the aesthetic/appreciation/criticism of the oeuvre. These analogies are the focus of the analysis that follows.

THE PRODUCTION OF THE WUPPERTAL TANZTHEATER: THE BODY AS FOCUS AND LOCUS

The first parallel between Bausch's and feminist theory is their concern for the nature and shades of human experience. Bausch explores how experience is transmitted via the body.[10] That humans move is taken as a given. The drive to move as well as the spatio-temporal context in which this movement happens shapes the work. The human body, a body which is personal, biological, social, animal, mineral, vegetable, sexual, psychological and an agent of movement, is given a context, a space which is in itself reflective of social, political, cultural, gender, sexual, personal and domestic dynamics. The implications of the interplay between body and space in their diverse and at times incongruent manifestations, give foundation to the production.

Bausch concentrates on the non-intellectual, physical-emotive aspects of human experience. The phrase '. . . what makes us move . . . not how' has been repeated from interview to interview and is accepted as Bausch's leitmotif. The work defines a site to contest the mind/body dualism which assigns preferrential value and empowers the mind (logic-objective-male) and disregards the body (irrational-subjective-female) and thus renders it invisible/marginal/negative. Bausch chooses to communicate 'cette necessité de bouger, de respirer, de manger, de transpirer . . .';[11] aspects of experience which are physically bound and cannot be expressed through any other means. 'Ces choses indicibles'[12] which are part of individual subjectivity and lie beyond and outside the level of logical language. These 'things which cannot be said' are manifested through a vocabulary of ordinary movement and gesture which in the process and content of the pieces (indivisible within Bausch's work) become extraordinary.

Bausch deals with marginal physicality. One of *Tanztheater*'s contributions to the discourse of body/dance lies in bringing aspects of the marginalised body – the hidden, close to the skin, subconscious, psychological, repressed – onto centre stage. Therefore bodies kiss, pinch, pet, slap, stroke, spit, cry, eat, sweat, pant, dress, undress, show their ticks, scars and habits, play with peat, leaves and water. The work assumes a subversive attitude towards the 'official' image of the body. The dramaturgy of the Bauschian body, as Birringer points out, does not reinforce the 'official' image. Rather is at odds with it. More often than not the dancers appear uncomfortable with the roles they inhabit: the women dresses are too tight, too short, they brush their hair a little too hard, the brassiere straps show, heels are too high, shoe sizes too small.

The critique extends to specific aspects of the body in the context of dance. The physical aspects which Bausch chooses for her idiom are not only marginalised in terms of ordinary life but also in the ideal body in dance. Her treatment of the body on stage does not reinforce the predominant youth/body beautiful/

high tech/acrobatic image of the body/dance. In June 1984 the audience at the Brooklyn Academy of Music sat aghast as 24 dancers panted, grunted, sweated their way through the agonies of *Rites of Spring*. By the end of the performance the dancers' body sounds had reached the level of musical poetry and could be said to have been an intrinsic part of Bausch's (I dare not say Stravinsky's) score. The movement vocabulary which she chooses to develop in sections of the dance are surprising. In *Arien*, as Beethoven's Moonlight Sonata plays, a group of men mill in a circle stage right (while the women play 'hokey-cokey' stage left) and begin a spitting competition. They pace around the circle and one by one prepare, aim and spit as far as they can. This is done with rhythmical precision of gesture, step and musical timing. A dance about men spitting is not usually deemed to be an appropriate topic for theatrical dance.

Bausch's treatment of gender warrants further consideration. She takes as her point of departure the existing roles of 'male' and 'female'. The men are assigned the roles of the aggressors, the pursuers, the controllers, regulators, masters of ceremonies, rapists and terrorists. Women, by contrast are the victims. They are pursued, punished, dressed, undressed, raped, terrorised. However, these initial stereotypical gender classification are made to disintegrate throughout the course of the work. Cross-dressing recurs throughout the pieces. In *Kelnen, Arien, Don't be Afraid*, men give up their suits and don similar gowns to the women. At times, as in *Seven Deadly Sins*, women put on men's suits. The cross-dressing goes beyond mere transvestism. The men do not stop being 'men'. However, aspects of the 'other' (female) – which were excluded from the original representation of 'male' – are superimposed. They do not stop doing 'manly' things, for example they continue to partner the women. However, the audience's meaning signs shift via the juxtaposition created by the layering of seemingly incongruous visual signs. Bausch opens up what had previously been closed gender signifiers. The dress (including the institutionalised role defining aspects of the object 'dress') is no longer exclusive to the women, the suit no longer exclusive to men. The boundaries which define the term 'male' (suits) and 'female' (dress) are diffused, and the gender roles lose there fixed value. In *Arien* the men-dressed-as women at times continue to behave as 'men'. At other times they mix with the 'females' into a non-specified grouping of human beings. The gender identity of this hybrid group is strategically defined by their position in space and time, and not essentially defined by biology.

The non-essential character of Bausch's treatment of gender (and therefore individual experience) reveals the socially constructed aspects of experience. Though Bausch speaks of her body's as doing the things 'we naturally do', the term 'natural' undergoes scrutiny. Bausch gestural idiom develops from the interaction between self and social codes and institutions. The display of 'gestus' follows a process of internalisation. Bausch's processual treatment of the action on stage reveals the process of gestural formation. It is uncertain whether the gestus is natural, that is derived from an inner drive, or nurtured, determined by outside circumstance.

In *Arien* the women sit on chairs on the stage apron. Their faces are neutral. The men begin to dash in and out of the wings carrying with them an assortment of costumes and props. They begin to dress the women to the sound of 'A Little Night Music'. The women get dressed in a mish-mash of hats, feathers, furs, inflatable tubes, flippers, skirts, veils, and garish make-up. One man stands behind them, microphone in hand, and begins to ask them 'can you say HA!', One by one the women begin to say 'HA!' As the man coaches them '. . . louder . . . louder, please . . .' the 'HA!s' become louder until they begin to sound like laughter (natural, normal). However, the pitch and speed continues to rise until the laughter becomes shrilled and the 'HAs' sound like crying. By the time the Ha's have increased in momentum, a chain reaction has been set off. The women started the Ha's prompted by the man, however, towards the end of the scene the Ha's have become internalised. They continue to laugh and weep even without prompting. This manipulation of the gesture appears throughout Bausch's repertoire. In *1980*, one of the women announces (in a deadpan way) 'I am tired. . . .', then begins to run around the stage. She repeats this sequence ad infinitum until what was at first an unemotional statement 'I am tired' has turned into 'real' tiredness. She is now tired, out of breath, sweating. After a series of similar scenes it is unclear whether the dancers are moving of their own volition or prompted by someone else (usually in Bausch a male voice-over). Cause and effect in the Bauschian world are not easily distinguished.

The Bauschian body is in constant flux. The body is not presented as a fixed reality. More likely it may be considered a 'plurality, incompleteness and non-linear'.[13] In this the Bauschian body parallels the 'imaginary body' as viewed by the French theorists: the body is a 'collection of sites' with 'multidimensional potentialities'.[14] The contribution of this approach can be summarised as follows:

> There is no individual essence, no single nature to realise. Rather we see that the person is an everexpanding potentiality conceived of as the changing intersections of living structures of meaning, rich in their significatory combinations, plural in their directions, which the individual might take up.[15]

It is Bausch's capacity to demonstrate this within the body/dance which redeems her from the severe criticism which she has been subjected to. Bausch has forced the audience to look past the violence and the chaos. In Bausch's work chaos is not limited to nihilism. The moments of pandemonium are counterpointed with moments of silence where she hints at the existence of potentialities. Through the struggles of the body she embraces human condition with all its tragi-comic contradictions, its beauty, horror, struggle and resignation.

TOWARDS A POETIC LANGUAGE OF THE BODY

Kristeva defines poetic language as 'a double . . . [which] defines an infinity of pairings and combinations [of subject and meaning] . . .'.[16] It deviates from classical grammatical rules by eliminating the thetic[17] combination of subject–verb/beginning–end. It has 'the logic of a carnival . . . a dream logic . . . and transgresses rules of linguistic code and social morality as well'.[18] It does not aim to create specific signification. Rather it generates an accumulation of meanings as a result of the interplay between signs which 'meet, contradict and relativise each other . . .'.[19]

Bausch speaks of her work as 'want[ing] to say something which cannot be said, so we make a poem where one can feel what it is meant . . .'.[20] She agrees that within 'le processus théâtrale ou choréographique, c'est une question de communication . . . mais doit-elle forcément être intellectuelle?'[21] Bausch's

manipulations of dance's spatio/temporal dimensions are analogous to the structures of the poetic language as defined by
Kristeva. *Tanztheater's* choice of a poetic structure rather than a
logical one guarantees the communication at an emotive level
and moreover, allows for plurality and multiplicity of the body's
narrative which it aims for.

Bausch describes her work as arriving from a 'chaos' of material which shapes itself through the rehearsal process into a
performance. Clear distinctions of a beginning a middle or an
end are not applicable:

> Mon travail n'est pas linéaire, J'y reviens constamment pour
> trier, revoir, éliminer, arranger. C'est important pour les dan-
> seurs et également pour ma propre vision. Quand je retrouve
> quelque jours plus tard, une scène que j'avais abandonnée,
> elle a parfois une autre signification et permet de renforcer
> certains thèmes.[22]

This process permeates not only the rehearsals but shapes the
events on stage. The action occurs in a non-sequential parade of
scenes of no chronological order. It makes no attempt to develop
a monologic narrative containing elements such as character,
subject development, exposition, climax, development and de-
noument.

Time in the context of Bausch's production belongs to 'female
time', it 'retains repetition and eternity from among the multiple
modalities of time.[23] It contains paradox inasmuch as the physical imagery repeated through time carries a dialogue between
change and continuity. It allows the image to be seen over and
over again (i.e. 'things haven't changed!'[24]) but it also allows for
its transformation ('You can see it this way, or you can see it that
way'[25]). The image acquires a different meaning through its
changed position in time. Therefore the repetition is never exact
but shifts via free association of past and present images. The
effect is one of juxtaposition of previously assigned meanings,
juxtaposition between the old and the new.

This effect is augmented through the use of temporal choreographic devices such as acceleration, deceleration, slow motion. The image is not presented in its natural 'timing'. For
example in *Arien* a game of hokey-cokey is sung to the tempo of
the *Moonlight Sonata* and not the usual up-beat associated with
the game. This superimposition of different 'times', (a 'cross-

timing' so to speak) is one of Bausch's methods to create ambivalence. In a scene from the film 'Un Jour Pina Bausch a demandé', two dancers exchange what initially appear to be caresses.
The woman touches the man's ear, hair, knees, and embraces
him. As the scene progresses, the tempo accelerates. Caresses
turn into blows, the man gets pushed and pulled, what was an
embrace is now a violent jump into the man's arms. Similarly in
Café Müller, one couple begins to take turns lifting each other
across the room. The lifts gain momentum and speed. The
dancers seem oblivious to the fact that the stage right wall is
getting nearer. By the end of the scene the dancers are slamming
each other against the wall, a romantic duet has transformed
into love-bashing.

Bausch's gaming extends to make Time the subject of her
pieces. Recollections, particularly childhood ones are central to
works like *Arien* and *1980*. There is a concern with history,
specially the personal histories of the dancers which Bausch uses
as 'script'. However, these personal recollections are fragmented
in time. A snippet is given now, another one after a few other
scenes have taken place. The 'present' is not isolated but a con-
tinuum which refers to and makes present and presence of the
past. Bausch interweaves temporal tenses – past becomes present,
present is later past. Clear temporal classifications disappear.

Space undergoes similar transformations. Bausch's treatment
of the space is paradoxical. Settings like those in *Cafe Müller*,
Kontakhof, *1980*, and *Bluebeard* appear to be very real – the walls
are solid (enough to support two hurling dancers as in the case of
Cafe), the grass smells (*1980*). However, throughout there is
always an incongruity. The rooms are filled with dead leaves, the
stage is covered with peat, carnations, and water. Her use of
scenic montage presupposes a fragmentation and ambivalence of
spatial reality. On the one hand montage sets the physical
boundary which defines the dancers spaces. However, it opens
up infinite possibilities by the break in the linguistic boundary of
the space (what that space 'means', e.g. a 'ballroom', a 'castle' a
'stage' and therefore the kinds of action and relationships that
can occur in that space).

Bausch's manipulations of the spatial dimension goes a step
further than Brecht's A-Effect. At the opening of *Arien* the stage
is exposed up to the firewall, exposing the 'theatricality' of the
production. However, when a man begins to hose the stage,

filling it with water, Bausch not only 'defamiliarises' the theatrical experience by showing the convention – the stage – but alienates the convention itself. The stage is still a stage but different from other stages by those inches of water. In this new context, some of the theatrical metaphors are magnified. The stage is transformed into a gigantic mirror which – by means of the glass walls, photographic apparatus, the water, the men's spit, rainfall (yes, it rains during *Arien*), sweat, tears – is fragmented into an explotion of reflections. Seeing and being seen is not just a theme but also a theatrical experience which is transferred into the auditorium as the light refracts on the water and then reflects on the balconies, walls and chandeliers of the Opera house. Bauschian stage breaks its own boundaries.

The stage breaks convention by allowing simultaneous, isolated activity to occur all over with what seems no particular focus or thematic connections. The stage becomes a multiplicity of isolated localities, presented to the audience at the same time. Synchronicity acquires a new meaning. From the dancers point of view each is operating in isolation. However, from the audience's point of view one sees overlapping, collision, random interactions which casts new insight into the dynamics of urban life, determinism and free will.

'YOU CAN SEE IT THIS WAY ... OR YOU CAN SEE IT THAT WAY': THE POLITICS OF INTERPRETATION OF BAUSCH'S TANZTHEATER

The world of *Tanztheater* is a world in constant flux – changing and most importantly changeable. The pieces elude a classical hermeneutic approach to meaning. Once Bausch opens the signifier, it remains open and mutable. She is constantly reflecting upon what are generally accepted first principles – truth, beauty, happiness, love, pain. This has put her under severe criticism of being pessimistic, masochistic, hysterical. She takes away the pleasure of recognition which gives us the economy of physical and emotional expenditure which is associated with classical aesthetic contemplation. The Bauschian world is a constant call to arms: 'by leaving the closure of the meaning unresolved she places on the audience the responsibility of developing and arriving at the solutions.'[26]

Interpretation remains personal and individual. By revealing the process of creation she reveals the mechanisms of authorship. She diagnoses but does not present a cure. Bausch's text is one of many possible texts existing at any one given performance. *Tanztheater*'s carnival is not only linguistically subversive but politically in as much as it denies the existence of an absolute, institutionalised truth. Institutionalised truth is decentralised through difference and diversity. Ideologies which have controlled and regulated experience are perpetuated by their claim to posses this absolute truth, expressed in and through their control of language. Decentralise truth, by making language strategically defined, and you decentralise power. The possibility of a discourse other than patriarchy begins to take shape. *Tanztheater* has begun to transpose the discourse of dance. The marginal body takes centre stage and with it aspects of the oppressed 'feminine'. Bausch and the phenomenon of *tanztheater* is perhaps first in bringing marginal contemporary dance into a large-scale context. We are only just starting to comprehend the full political/social/moral implications of this shift.

POST SCRIPTUM

Just when we thought we had anaesthetised ourselves to Bausch's iconoclasm, she presented *The Sorrow of the Empress* which British audiences were able to see as part of Channel 4's *Dancelines* in the summer of 1989. Once again we were shocked, repulsed, and angry at the images we were made to follow. Children were dangerously suspended from dead trees. Their cries unheard by the adults holding the ropes. The fact that these were dying trees was lost to most of the television viewers. Few knew that it is now common practice of the German Green Party to enumerate and paint white crosses on trees dying as a result of acid rain (which ironically enough comes from England). The image of a child (our future?) suspended from dying trees passed unnoticed as did the white crosses resembling the crosses in many European beaches. Few made any connection. Even less stopped to consider that the violence lies not in the image but in the day-to-day violence – towards children, women, our environment, in fact the whole ecosystem – which is institutionalised and father to that image. Poetic analogy becomes a political alternative? 'We must watch and watch again, and again and again . . .'.[27]

Notes and References

1. Defining the dance field as feminine includes the men who have been considered 'effeminate'.
2. M. Goldberg, 'Ballerinas and Ball Passing', in *Women in Performance* no. 6 (Spring 1988) pp. 7–31.
3. Humphrey speaks of contemporary dancers as asking the 'Sleeping Beauty' to wake up and grow up. She seems to have progressed only into puberty, we need her to continue on to adulthood.
4. I refrain from using the term 'feminist dance' because it presupposes categorisation. Feminism through dance includes both dancemaking through a feminist perspective and also arriving at a feminist framework through dance.
5. It is not assumed that there are no other feminist choreographers. For contemporary feminist choreographers see the journal edited by M. Goldberg (op. cit.). Bausch, however, is unique in bringing marginal dance into a largescale context – a point that is discussed further in the section on 'Politics of Interpretation'.
6. The theoretical armature for this study draws from the works of Julia Kristeva and Helene Cixous, particularly Kristeva's 'Revolution in Poetic Language' in T. Moi, ed. (1985).
7. T. Moi (1985).
8. In a forthcoming study I define dance discourse as ways of constituting knowledge of dance – including the identification of the statement of dance: the identification of the features of the statement; how these differ from other features, and the rules governing the association of these features to constitute the different discourses within 'dance'.
9. Refer to Kristeva in Moi, ed., 1986, pp. 89–136.
10. Bausch's concern with the body as opposed to movement differentiates her work from that of the coeval postmoderns. By giving the body a specific spatio-temporal/cultural context, she avoids the self-referential stance typical of postmodernism.
11. L. Brunel (10 November 1981) p. 43.
12. Ibid., p. 42.
13. A. Caddick (1986) p. 82.
14. Ibid., p. 84.
15. Ibid., p. 85.
16. J. Kristeva, in T. Moi ed. (1986) p. 40.
17. 'Thetic' defines the process of assigning meaning. See Kristeva's 'Revolution in Poetic Language' in Moi, ed., op. cit.
18. Ibid.
19. Ibid., p. 41.
20. J. Berringer (Summer 1980) p. 92.

21. L. Brunel, op. cit., p. 43.
22. Ibid.
23. J. Kristeva in T. Moi ed., op. cit., p. 40.
24. Bausch in conversations with the audience after performance of *Seven Deadly Sins*, Brooklyn Academy of Music, 12 October 1985.
25. Ibid.
26. R. Hoghe (1980) p. 67.
27. Bausch at Brooklyn Academy of Music, 12 October 1985.

Bibliography

J. Berringer, 'Dancing Across Borders', *The Drama Review*, Vol. 30, No. 2, (Summer 1986) pp. 85–97.
L. Brunel, 'Le Point de Vue de Pina Bausch', *Saisons de la Danse*, (10 November 1981).
A. Caddick, 'Feminism and the Body', *Arena*, No. 74, (1986) pp. 60–89.
R. Hoghe, 'The Theatre of Pina Bausch', *The Drama Review* (March 1980) pp. 60–89.
T. Moi (ed.), *The Kristeva Reader*, (Oxford: Blackwell, 1986).
T. Moi, *Sexual/Textual Politics*, (London: Routledge, 1986).
C. Weedon *Feminist Practice and Poststructuralist Theory*, (Oxford: Blackwell, 1987).
Women in Performance, No. 6, (Spring 1988).

Film

C. Ackerman (dir.) *Un Jour Pina Bausch a demandé*. (Antenne Z, France, 1983).

11 'She might pirouette on a daisy and it would not bend'[1]
Images of Femininity and Dance Appreciation

LESLEY-ANNE SAYERS

This paper explores perspectives on the female dancer in dance appreciation and looks at some images of femininity within descriptive writing on dance. It considers how dominant attitudes towards women have affected and channelled responses to dance works into certain ways of seeing and terms of reference. Of course dance criticism does not exist in isolation; from its own nature as criticism it interacts with the forms of the dance itself. Images used by the critic are usually there to evoke the qualities and ideas created by the work. Evocation has been a central aim in the history of art appreciation and particularly so in dance where the art object itself is so ephemeral. So we might say that images of femininity in descriptive dance criticism will simply record in words the images that the dance has produced. Yet this would be misleading as description is a very different thing from observation; it is based on initial acts of selection and focus and imposes a perspective upon the reader. Description is also a far more creative act than it may appear at first glance. The critic brings to a work a viewing context; a set of values and tastes, specialised and general knowledge. With this viewing context, the critic constructs an *interaction* with the work.

Within the confines of a short space on a potentially very broad subject, this paper focuses on a few critical *interactions* that could reasonably be identified as representing common if not 'traditional' responses to women in ballet. Stress is given to the importance of the model of Théophile Gautier at the nineteenth-century Romantic Ballet in Paris and aims to demonstrate how aspects of this model have continued in the twentieth century, interacting with new influences such as the Fokine Principles and the idea of ballet as a collaborative art. This paper makes no attempt to be an historical overview; it aims rather to demonstrate ways in which attitudes towards femininity involved in ballet aesthetics, and which were central to the ideological conflict between Ballet and Free Dance/Modern Dance, emerge in criticism, in ways of viewing dance and dancers. The overall aim of this piece is to show the vitality of dance criticism as a resource, not simply as a record of dance, or of a particular writer, but as an interaction with dance and the broader cultural context of dance history.

Looking at the literature of writing on dance in Britain this century, one could not fail to be struck by the ardency and distinctive style of the first remarkable generation of devotees to the ballet. These balletomane-critics wrote with a passion, they were lovers of a particular conception of ballet that they held to be a peak of aesthetic achievement. Remnants of the grand style and certain aspects of Aestheticism and Romanticism found a niche in what became known as Balletomania. Whatever we may make of this period in terms of criticism, the literature provides a vivid picture of the time, the dance and the viewing context, of the ideals and criteria being established and the attitudes and perspectives that formed them. From the 1920s to the beginning of the period of substantial change in the 1960s, few books were written on the subject of ballet that did not describe falling in love with the art. Most balletomanes were monistic in approach, constructing a hierarchy of criteria in support of their tastes. Arnold Haskell, one of the most widely published and popular of them all, was blatant about the matter, beginning one of his best sellers, *Balletomania*, with a characteristic description of his condition as:

> . . . a man madly, but let us hope not blindly, in love with a certain conception of ballet, and consequently un-interested in, and even hostile to, many other forms of the dance.[2]

Despite the influence of Diaghilev's Ballets Russes with the stress on ballet as a collaborative art form, (which these critics documented and adhered to in terms of stated criteria), many writers harked back in their *approach* to the nineteenth-century models of Classical/Romantic works. One of the most obvious ways that this manifested itself was in the focus of their writings on the ballerina. Diaghilev had re-established the male dancer as a figure of importance in ballet; Nijinsky, for example, was influential in re-establishing masculine beauty in dance, realised in its own right, not simply through triumphant possession of, or heroic supportiveness to the ballerina. Yet the general public for ballet in Britain was used to the art as 'feminine' and as music-hall spectacle rather than as a serious art form compatible with conventional views of masculinity. Despite Diaghilev's impact in London in changing the conception of ballet and bringing the intellegensia to consider it a serious art, of the writers that emerged, those who took a more easily accessible style and concentrated on the dancers, particularly the ballerinas as stars, were the ones that undoubtedly inherited, as well as created, the larger readership.

In discussions of the art form itself we cannot but be aware of the similarity of its categorisation with conceptions of 'feminine' principles. Common dichotomies assumed as absolutes for the ballet are similar in kind to those that have in history assumed the status of truths about women. For example, it has been frequently stated that ballet is an art of the body, of the feelings and emotions and therefore not an art involving the mind. This dichotomy has been a common basis for describing 'feminine' traits and was the basis, for example, of many forms of argument against votes for women and against women's access to higher education. Yet ballet has never been an artistic reinforcement of social forces that worked to restrict women's significance to the domestic environment; its images are rather of perpetual virginity, an idealised and ethereal femininity that reaches for the sky and the domain of the gods, rather than for the earth and its associations with mothering and nature.

The all-pervading influence to both the art of ballet and its viewing context has been Romanticism. The Romantic movement came late to ballet and merged with elements of what became known as the aesthetic movement. It brought a flowering of the form as an expressive art and in terms of criticism it brought the criteria and approach of Theophile Gautier.[3] The ballet became a focus of Gautier's Romantic aesthetics upholding above all principles of grace and beauty. Although Romanticism reflected the decline of the aristocracy in terms of its images, it upheld certain aristocratic ideals, such as grace, and abstracted them from a social ethos. Beauty was of primary importance to Romantic aesthetics and was a focal criterion of Gautier's appreciations. In early Romanticism ideal beauty was of a masculine and virile kind whereas Gautier's writing reflects the dominance of later Romanticism's idealisation of 'feminine' beauty in it's virginal tragi-poetic figures or in the image of the *femme fatale, la belle dame sans merci.* Such types are common figures in ballet. Clear dichotomies of feminine type are also found in ballet criticism, the most famous being Gautier's opposition of the chaste and virginal image of Marie Taglioni as a 'Christian' dancer and the more earthy sensuality of Fanny Elssler as a 'pagan' dancer.[4]

In late Romantic art women were emblematic of an idealised Nature where a unity of body and soul was untouched by discredited intellect. Yeats's treatment of the dancer in his poems is in keeping with Gautier's appreciations and both are manifestations of Romantic ideals. Frank Kermode has pointed out that Yeats's views against the education of women stemmed from his philosophy that intellectual labours destroyed bodily grace and imagination; women, Yeats believed, must think with their bodies and be full of mysterious life. Kermode writes of Yeats's ideals: 'In women, as in poems, the body as a whole must be expressive; there should be no question of the mind operating independently of the whole body'.[5]

The Romantic ethos of Gautier's time rejected any idea of male beauty[6] and Romantic images of the feminine were emblematic of mysterious nature, the world of the imagination which was put forward as a counter to the development of a materialistic and philistine bourgeoisie. The ideals of late Romanticism and of the contemporary bourgeoisie contained equally restrictive attitudes towards women's access to higher education and work, yet Romantic images did at least enable the 'feminine' to be equated with soul in some senses and with a kind of aesthetic purity and power that begins to be comparable to the mysteries of religion. The Romantic image of woman is essentially that of fragile purity or exotic other-worldliness. As such it gave birth to numerous ballets. The Classical/Romantic ballets are interestingly still the most popular aspect of ballet as an art and Romanticism has been a powerful and lasting force on the history of Western culture as a whole.

Lacking the particularities of language, dance often embodies archetypal representations and, in terms of her heritage, the

ballerina has embodied a powerful duality of saint and seductress comparable to the haunting and pallid female figures of
many nineteenth-century paintings. The ethereal image of the
ballerina rising onto pointe and limiting her contact with the
earth, lends her not only an enhanced geometric purity of line
but also a spirituality exploited by many of the leading roles in
the nineteenth-century classics. Yet the backstage status of ballet
dancers in the nineteenth-century, was equatable with that of
courtesans; the Paris Opera was depicted as a 'flesh market' by
the painter Manet for example.[7] In terms of dance criticism this
same duality is revealed in the combination of homage and
voyeurism which formed a dominant and lasting approach to
dancers in appreciation. Many ballet critics have sought to
capture the goddess-like qualities of the ballerina while responding to her as a seductress. This style of ballet criticism again
dates from the passionate prose of Gautier whose work was made
available to British balletomanes in the translations of Cyril
Beaumont. Twentieth-century critics have had a rather different
idea of their role from that of Gautier, gradually becoming a part
of arts specialism within journalism and dancers have come to
enjoy an altogether different status than their nineteenth-century
counterparts, yet as late as 1950 A. H. Franks found it necessary
to comment:

> I think that critics are better able to assess dancers if they keep
> away from backstage. Perhaps it is not impossible to make
> love to a dancer one moment and sum up the value of her
> contribution to a ballet the next, but how many of us can lay
> claim to impartiality in such a marked degree.[8]

Like Franks, dance critic A. V. Coton also inveighed against
backstage associations between critics and artists.[9] The insistence on love as a prerequisite for criticism and a voyeuristic
treatment of the dancer are absent from his writing, and he
worked with a more pluralistic attitude towards dance than was
common in his day. A significant proportion of his writing
however, was directed against such tendencies which are clearly
identified as dominant approaches to the appreciation of dance.
Aside from his direct criticism of 'balletomania', Coton sought to
see the ballerina in terms of her interpretation of a role, in
keeping with the Fokine principles.[10]

Fokine stressed the importance of role and interpretation,

implying technique and craft. This was an important influence on the development of dance criticism affecting approach as well as criteria. A dual heritage from the ideas and approaches of Gautier and Fokine has exercised a central influence of the approach to dance appreciation. The idea of dance as a collaborative art often worked, somewhat incongruously, besides a focus on the 'essentialism' of the ballerina[11] that was in many ways the creation of Gautier and the Romantic movement. In Gautier's writings we catch sight of both the serious aspects of Romantic thought and its more popular and trivialised notions. In the latter vein Gautier describes the nature of dance:

> dancing has no other purpose but to display beautiful bodies in graceful poses and develop lines that are pleasing to the eye. . . . Dancing is ill suited for expressing metaphysical ideas; it expresses only the passions. Love, desire with all its coquetries, the aggressive male and the gently resisting woman – these are the subjects of all primitive dances.[12]

Strange indeed that this should come from the pen that created *Giselle*, a ballet which encapsulates so many Romantic preoccupations and ideas. Gautier goes on to say that in realising this essential fact about dancing, and using her whole body, Fanny Elssler was a true and beautiful ballerina, for whom he recalls 'a volley of applause broke out when her gauze veil parted, allowing us to see the seductive enchantress'.[13]

It was Gautier who first stressed the importance of the smile to the ballerina: 'A dancer's smile should play about her mouth like a bird hovering above a rose, unable to land without damaging it'.[14] It was also Gautier who originated the popular image of the ballerina as being of such gossamer lightness as to make no impression on the petals of flowers.[15] His concentration on the essentialism of the ballerina was in many ways more in evidence in popular attitudes towards ballet during at least the first half of the twentieth century than Fokine's famous Principles ever were. In 1950 for example, Haskell wrote of Irene Skorik:

> I first noticed her in the role of Leda . . . The dancer's build was perfect, magnificent feet and legs supporting a well-formed body with a small head ideally set on the shoulders and beautifully rounded arms . . . And then there was the smile. And how much the smile is a part of the dancer as our

great Gautier has stressed. This was a shy smile, the smile of someone with a secret that she is enjoying.[16]

The critic here cites himself as the active one in the area of selection and seeing, but passive in the sense in which he is captivated and acted on by the dancer's charms. In both cases the critic's state of stimulation remains a central focus of the description. In his essay on Skorik, Haskell tells the reader that he selected this ballerina for his attention because she enchanted him, sometimes irritated him but never bored him and never allowed his attention to wander. The contrast between Haskell's approach and that of American critic Walter Terry, writing in the same book as Haskell's article on Skorik, is stark and notable. Terry selects dancer Nora Kaye and his piece focuses on her approach to work and her *use* of movement, her *use* of abilities and attributes:

> Too many neglect the 'why' but Miss Kaye, because she purposely or instinctively asks 'why' and digs up the answer, is better equipped to face the 'how' of a role or a movement that those who remain incurious about the reasons for and the motivations of those patterns of action which must be given stage life.[17]

The language itself expresses a completely different ethos and viewing context from that of Haskell. Terry's words such as 'digs up', 'why,' 'how', 'motivations', 'reasons', suggest thought and hard work. He concentrates on Kaye's investigative qualities in being able to get to grips with a role. Whereas the excerpt from Haskell stresses himself as the active one, 'I first noticed her', he writes and he goes on to revel in her build and smile without showing how she has used these attributes in her realisation of the role of Leda. The smile that hovers mysteriously on her lips is about being a ballerina in Haskell's conception of ballet, not necessarily about interpreting Leda. Skorik is seen by Haskell as an embodiment of certain ideal traits; we experience her voyeuristically, through Haskell's gaze, detached from her work and interpretation.

A central ideal of the classical technique is the masking of technique and strength, particularly so in the case of the ballerina where a display of strength would be inappropriate to the ideology that informs it. Similarly critics, like lithographers, most often colluded with the illusion of the work in this respect. Interestingly 'charming' is probably the most commonly applied adjective of praise used to describe ballerinas in the history of dance criticism and words taken from the sensual enjoyment of food, such as 'delicious' are also common.

Haskell was the most successful of his generation in speaking to the popular imagination in terms of the ballerina and the art of ballet. His books were widely read and often ran into many editions. In focusing accessibly on the aspects of ballet that captured this imagination he was able to educate in terms of ballet history, technique and aesthetics. He has also left us with a particularly vivid repository of attitudes towards dance and dancers in his era. His approach could in many ways be said to be a trivialised form of Romanticism, but his attitudes towards gender were in keeping with predominant postwar attitudes towards women of the 1950s. In the glossary of *What is Ballet*, 1965, Haskell defines the critic almost solely in terms of his relationship to the female dancer:

> *CRITIC*: An angel when he praises an artist, a villain when he dislikes her, and the very devil when he praises her rival. Has an important function in ballet, holding a watching brief for the totality of the arts, at times even defending ballet against the increasing monopoly of the dancers.[18]

As light-hearted as Haskell's intention here undoubtedly is, he relies on the reader's recognition and tacit acceptance of the idea that ballet is really about ballerinas and draws on commonly held ideas of 'feminine' psychological traits, a model of narcissism and vanity accompanied by jealousy and rivalry (a common theme of comedy films of the era). On a paternalistic note he implies that critics are responsible people whereas dancers are not, but we have only the 'feminine' imagery above by which to judge why they may be so irresponsible.[19]

The link between cultural attitudes, aesthetic ideals, approaches to criticism and descriptive language, is clear; what is more difficult is to explain the potency of particular images and ideas. In *Tonight the Ballet*, 1934, rather than simply evoking the illusion of the work and responding to it as one enraptured, critic Adrian Stokes takes his rapture as the starting point for a penetrating analysis of the significance of the image:

> The ballerina's body is etherealised. She seems scarcely to rest
> upon the ground. She is, as it were, suspended just slightly
> above the earth so that we may see her better. She seems cut
> off from the sources of her being, or rather, those dark internal
> sources are shown by her as something light and white, brittle
> as are all baubles, all playthings that we can utterly examine;
> yet at the same time, so perfect is her geometry that we feel
> this plaything which our minds may utterly possess, to be as
> well the veriest essence.[20]

Stokes's associations here are quite disturbing. The ballerina's
body, etherealised and suspended, so that he, as the viewer, can
see her better, is cut off from the sources of her being which are
seen as dark and internal. In this state of severance from her
being, she becomes like a bauble and a plaything, she can be
utterly examined and utterly possessed. Yet she is an essence,
and therefore remains, despite his penetrating gaze, alluringly
unobtainable. Through technique the image has become safe for
examination and possession; yet we are aware of Stokes's fear of a
shadow side, of her 'dark internal' nature that needs to be transformed by her into a light, white, bauble, a plaything so that he can
possess her within the safe distance of his enchanted gaze.[21]

In keeping with the European tradition of the female nude in
art, painted so often without body hair,[22] Stokes's vision of the
ballerina in this excerpt is without signifiers of her own desires,
or sexual potency, unless they be realised narcissistically, in
being looked at and desired. In terms of female archetypes she
resembles the innocent and passive Psyche rather than the earlier potent and alchemical goddess, Aphrodite. The representation of Psyche is described by one Jungian interpreter as 'a king's
daughter – too lovely, too perfect, too deep for the ordinary
world'.[23] A description that could be applied to many of the
heroines of ballet. An archetype perhaps more suitable and less
threatening to patriarchal social and cultural organisation than
is Aphrodite. Critic Rayner Heppenstaal describes the ballerina
on pointe in a similar way to that of Stokes:[24]

> a woman on her points, because of change in significant line
> and stress and action, ceases to be significantly a woman. She
> becomes an idealised and stylised creature of the Theatre. And
> there is a kind of eternal virginity about her. She is inaccess-
> ible. She remains unravished.

There is undoubtedly much in this imagery of potent significance to female as well as male psychology. Of the legions of girls who seek to become ballet dancers many appear to aspire to becoming the embodiment of a particular image that the Classical/ Romantic ballet has established and which has had a lasting and deep appeal. Like Dr L. M. Vincent in his book, *In Pursuit of the Sylph*, dancer Gelsey Kirkland in her autobiography draws attention to elements of misogyny and narcissism that are visible in certain aspects of ballet; Kirkland also gives us a brutal and honest account of her own addiction to the images she felt impelled to adhere to in her profession. Agnes de Mille wrote: 'The forces which impelled women to the austerity of the church operate to form the great dancer. In a strange transmutation dancing is a form of asceticism – almost a form of celibacy.'[25]

Analyses of image-making in other media have most often concentrated on images of women created by men, and stress the importance of considering the nature of the male unconscious in reading these images.[26] The real complexity of male and female psychological involvement in image-making is perhaps both clearer and more complex in dance and points to the importance of considering the appeal of images *of* women *to* women. Unlike the passive model in painting, the dancer actively forms the creator's vision, she colludes with it, aspires to it and realises it. The model of male artist/female model for male viewer, sometimes applied to the fine arts, can be revealing but is in the end of limited value in understanding the basis upon which such relationships work.

Early opponents to ballet in the free and modern dance styles often stressed a fundamental ideological opposition to the ballet, which in terms of the free dance at least, often focused on a need for other representations of women. Maud Allan, like Isadora Duncan, found the images of the ballet lacked truthfulness. In her autobiography, 1908, she describes ballet as a brainless child to which the world pays homage leaving its beautiful mother, the true dance, to die unhonoured.[27] Duncan had spoken of dance and ballet in similar terms in 1902/3 saying that her reforms were a question of:

the development of the female sex to beauty and health, of the return to the original strength and to natural movements of woman's body. It is a question of the development of perfect

mothers and the birth of the healthy and beautiful children.
The dancing school of the future is to develop and to show the
ideal form of woman . . .[28]

Duncan clamoured against the pouring of ideas of femininity
into restrictive moulds; for her the very technique, as well as the
images, represented the human spirit in bondage. Although her
work was markedly different from ballet, it was often seen in
comparison with ballet and frequently Duncan herself was the
focus of similar perspectives to those in which the ballerina was
viewed; perspectives which applied the criteria and ideals of
ballet and sought to detach an essential 'Her' from her work.
Critic Rayner Heppenstaal wrote about Duncan at length (without ever having seen her dance) and he takes as his focus-point
Duncan the woman as she was seen by many critics:

> With such a woman, you must either be outraged, or laugh, or
> fall cataclysmically in love;. . . I fancy I should have fallen in
> love. . . . The art was the woman. It was the embellishment
> and justification of her extraordinary womanhood. And the
> woman – which is to say the little girl – was born under
> Aphrodite . . .
>   She was a whole woman, most whole, perhaps, in her grand-
> manner follies and vulgarities, and she responded wholly to her
> blood's images of Aphrodite and Apollo, Dionysus, Minerva,
> Zeus . . . Stupidly, perhaps, and certainly with a great deal of
> confusion, she was submitting herself with all the profundity
> of her womanhood, to a real if forgotten splendour . . . But . . .
> She had no intellectual control over her experience.[29]

Duncan is seen here as both goddess and silly misguided child.
Heppenstaal would have fallen in love with her for she was
wholly woman, but most womanly in her ostentation and vulgar-
ity. Aphrodite is used to reinforce a vision of Duncan's potent
femaleness, of her work as blood's images, profound and splen-
did but without intellectual control, of an archetype of female
sexuality well removed from the ideals of femininity enshrined
by the ballet. For Heppenstaal, Duncan's 'dark internal sources'
(to borrow Stokes's terms), are in control and therefore she is out
of control; she is 'self-expressing' rather than giving a socialised
aesthetic, a culturally-formed and controlled exposition that the
technique of Classical ballet represents. Her self-expression (the

art was merely the woman, to paraphrase Heppenstaal) is a term of disparagement here. Yet applied to a ballerina it was not always so. Haskell wrote for example: 'A dancer of genius, however, can sometimes hold her audience entranced by creating something out of nothing, that is merely by expressing herself.'[30]

It is not just a question of abstract form and aesthetics however; Heppenstaal's language refers to images that Duncan represents and these form a stark contrast to the type of characterisations of the ballet. According to Heppenstaal Duncan was a 'glamorous matriarch, affirming, in herself, the glory of the primeval womb'. Yet he goes on to judge that her work was 'merely an art of sexual display, and I stress the merely'.[31] Finally he dismisses her in a condescending fashion as 'a bit of a feminist', who 'wasted' a lot of time on issues such as emancipation which he judges had nothing to do with dancing. Clearly for Isadora emancipation had everything to do with dance and Heppenstaal's own analysis and his terms of reference certainly demonstrate why this should be. Duncan certainly lacked the technique and models of an established art form, but Heppenstaal applies a set of aesthetic criteria, and most importantly a way of viewing her, that rest on a set of values related to conceptions of women as much, if not more so, than they do on aesthetic principles.

Heppenstaal's opinion of Duncan and his basic aesthetic criteria do not differ markedly from those of critic Andre Levinson, who judged Duncan's contribution to dance as 'scant and feeble'.[32] What is different is the manner of treatment. Where Heppenstaal concentrates on the woman, Levinson looks at her creation of images, is notably less voyeuristic and attempts to set her *work* in an appropriate context. He writes for example:

> Duncan has that vividness of form, that absence of chiaroscuro, that concreteness of style that characterises quattrocento painting. In her *Ange avec Violon*, in her poetic *Primavera* there is all the healthy strength of the good Lorenzo di Credi, softened by Botticelli's fragile intellectualism . . . She has that idyllic note, that inability to capture the monumental and hieratic such as we see in the work of a Pietro di Cosimo, whose Venus reposes amidst the multicoloured flowers of a Tuscan glade while a butterfly momentarily alights on her bared knee.[33]

Heppenstaal views Duncan as if she *is* Aphrodite in some essential way, for Levinson *she creates the image* of a particular style of Venus; there is a vital and important difference in manner of treatment. In general it was quite rare for dance critics of the time of Levinson to break away from the basic idea that in art women become and embody, men create. Yet, ironically, Heppenstaal gets closer to the significance of Isadora's dance, in terms of its sexual politics, almost by becoming a part of it, in revealing the terms of his spectatorship.

How Duncan relates to ideas of femininity however, interests Levinson as much as her essential womanliness preoccupies Heppenstaal. Interestingly, for Levinson Duncan's image 'unites ripe femininity with ephebic masculinity' and he concludes that 'there is no real femininity' in her for 'unpremeditated grace mingles with strength'. He goes on to describe her as an 'androgynous performer'.[34] It is a curious description when compared to the powerful images of Duncan's womanliness evoked by Heppenstaal's description. It is also remarkably similar to an earlier and equally beguiling description of a clearly seductive and sensual dancer, Fanny Elssler, as androgynous. Gautier revelled on many occasions in the sensuality and sexual attractiveness of his pagan dancer, Fanny Elssler; yet he clearly describes the experience of her beauty as intensified by its sexual ambiguity:

> Beneath the amorous languor, the intoxicating sensuality that yields to the heat of passion, and the feminine sweetness and all the gentle fascination of a ballerina, can be sensed the agility, the sudden speed and the steely muscles of a young athlete.[35]

He notes that her hips and breasts were undeveloped and that 'she could equally well be a charming woman and the most charming boy in the world'.[36]

Archetypal ideas of woman and femininity affect not only how female dancers are presented and present themselves but also how they are viewed. Dance critics have continued to face challenges in 'seeing' new work and new embodiments or definitions in the context of established models. For example, American critic Marcia Siegel tried to reach the qualities of Graham's women characters in *Primitive Mysteries* by referring to dominant models of femininity which these creations departed from. She wrote in response to the film version of 1964:

> One can hardly think of the dancers in *Primitive Mysteries* as
> anything other than vessels, instruments for the divine mes-
> sage they are acting out. They must not express or interpret
> the movement individually; they must not stand out from the
> group. In fact, if they are women at all, they are a breed apart.
> They have not taken up dancing to be looked at as beautiful,
> sexually attractive, ingratiating, or in any way idealised or
> "feminine" figures. Yet the fact that they *are* women, fully
> capable of conducting a religious observance, that they do not
> need male priests or teachers to channel their worship or
> intercede for them with God, is one of the boldest of *Primitive
> Mysteries*' many achievements.[37]

They are 'vessels', an ancient definition of femininity, but they
are not like dancers – there to be looked at, beautiful, sexually
attractive and idealised (and to this critic 'ingratiating'), so they
are *not* feminine; yet they *are* women, she goes on, and it is that
challenge that is the 'boldest' aspect of the work. Instead of a
collusive aim to render the illusion of the work, Siegel does not
surrender her detachment from the work's perspective; we are
aware of its effect on her and of her as a critic. In other words the
passage is descriptive in terms, but the function of the description is to serve the interpretation and analysis and this is overt
rather than concealed behind description as *apparently* straightforward reporting.

In the two passages that follow, two different critics, Marcia
Segel and Richard Buckle, are responding to similar movement
qualities in Jerome Robbin's silent, non-narrative work, *Moves*.
They have different approaches to criticism: where Siegel is more
directly analytical, Buckle aims to mediate between work and
audience, drawing on his experience and associations to the work
as a way into 'seeing' it. Yet most obviously they have adopted
differing perspectives and that difference hinges on response to
the treatment of the female dancer in terms of the images produced. Siegel writes:

> The man lifts her by the armpits . . . He grabs her wrists and
> pulls her hands behind her back. Slowly, almost sadistically,
> he puts one hand on her forehead and bends her head way

back . . . These poses are two of many things the women do in *Moves* that make them seem remote, mechanical. Robbins arranges them to exploit their physical beauty – the curve of the calf, the length of the neck, the sinuosity of the upper torso – while limiting their mobility or their capacity for change.[38]

The use of the phrase 'the man lifts her by the armpits' is so clinical as to be subversive to the dominant treatment of this image in dance. We are made aware that her reading of the work is not in keeping with Robbins's own intention of how it should be viewed by the phrase 'Robbins arranges them to exploit their physical beauty . . .'. We do not get a response to the physical beauty but are pointed instead to regard it critically, as an exploitation and limitation. Richard Buckle's perspective is quite different. He writes:

> In this pas de deux a man, bending a woman into different shapes like a sculptor, seems to learn from her limbs about the conjunctions of love. . . .
> The men admire and arrange the women. I think of that series of drawings Picasso did in '54, two hundred in three months, all about the old painter and his goddess-model – so many, many variations on the theme.[39]

Marcia Siegel's description is from the point of view of the one who is manipulated, whereas Buckle sees from the point of view of the manipulator, giving us a suggestion of what the male dancer was experiencing, learning 'from her limbs about the conjunctions of love'. In Buckle's rendition we are only aware of this one perspective; it is taken as the natural one and this is supported by reference to other such images in other arts. Siegel makes us aware of this dominant perspective but she subverts it so we become aware of another viewpoint. Yet importantly both critics impose a viewpoint; even when a perspective is based on the same viewing assumptions as the work itself, as in Buckle's rendition, the critic is still selecting that viewpoint as the perspective of his description.

The values and ideologies that make up dance aesthetics and appreciation have a history not just in terms of dance; ways of viewing draw on complex cultural and social contexts. In terms of ways of seeing women in dance appreciation we can frequently see the evidence of the past in the present, particularly when a critic has to say what a dance or dancer is not doing in order to try and reach some appropriate description of what they are doing. This is seen particularly with challenging new work and was very much the case when the Modern Dance departed from the predominant criteria of ballet appreciation; the literature is full of descriptions of what the dance was not. With descriptions of the Modern Dance of Kurt Jooss for example, Stokes spends most of his descriptive language in *Tonight the Ballet* on what he misses from ballet and what is missed includes a particular kind of 'feminine' imagery, the 'glamour', 'the blithe ballet face', the pointe work, the classical line and 'the look into the distance that is practiced even at the barre'.[40]

To take one more recent, and extreme example, in 1983 the the *Sunday Telegraph*'s coverage of Dance Umbrella brought back into focus many of the ideological conflicts between ballet and Modern Dance as well as drawing on ideas of beauty and femininity in women. Contemporary dancers were described as 'the sort of unshapely ladies who congregate like lemmings for modern dance'. The critic went on to state:

> Too many barefoot dancers are a bit like those prehistoric plesiosaurs 'who make up for their tiny minds by having extra large behinds', and I sometimes watch unbelievingly as a building quakes before the daunting onslaught of large bosomed, wide haunched, well padded amazons, seemingly only too ready to act out their aggressions in public.[41]

These amazons (who in mythology cut off a breast to facilitate the carriage of weapons) have, ironically perhaps, a similar lineage in terms of appreciation to Heppenstaal's matriarch born under Aphrodite. These dancers are 'wholly women' clearly, as attention is particularly drawn to their big bosoms and wide hips, yet they are judged to be less than conventionally feminine. Their weight is used here basically as a sign of their unattractiveness; yet lightness, a valued 'feminine' attribute and particularly so for ballerinas, is not without adverse cultural value in terms of women's history. It was, after all, the comparative lightness of women's brains that was put forward in the nineteenth century as an argument that women were less suited to intellectual labour than men, and formed the basis for an opposition of cerebral activity and femininity.[42]

The central paradox perhaps is that for the implied ideal model, ballet dancers reportedly often suffer from such insufficiencies of body fat as to undermine their oestrogen level to the extent of creating a state of infertility. Agnes de Mille has drawn attention to the fact that few ballerinas develop the bodies of mature women, retaining instead the lean-hipped and flat-breasted look of adolescence. She also notes that 'the women best capable of communicating sensuous satisfaction are in their bodies the least sensual'.[43] Similarly, Dr L. M. Vincent points out that ballet schools prefer female students who mature sexually later than the general female population, whereas this is not the case with males. He points out that the selection criteria and demands of ballet are in opposition to normal female development, running a 'collision course with hormones' whereas this is not the case for male dancers.[44] Again the duality of the saintly and the disparaged emerges even in terms of the interaction of dancer with her own body; she can obtain an ideal state and be worshipped as a star but she must necessarily restrict those 'dark internal' forces that are her natural state. It seems not so much to be idealisation and denigration as separate entities but a constant discourse between the two, as interrelated, and interdependent opposites. In such paradoxes and dualities we can glimpse the complexity of ideas of femininity which, in association with ideas of masculinity, evolve in social, psychological and cultural contexts to form and influence aesthetics. Dance, as an art involving body-image where women have been in central positions in some respects at least, is a rich source for understanding gender issues in the arts and society. In reading dance criticism we can look beyond individual stylistics and peculiarities to dominant ways of seeing dance and dancers and to the relationship between those ways of seeing and the nature of the dance itself.

Notes and References

1. A description of Adeline Genée, *Dancing Times* (London: November 1911).
2. A. L. Haskell (1934), p. 15.
3. Theophile Gautier was an influential aesthetician, poet, writer and art critic. Author of *Mademoiselle du Maupin* which was influential on the

aesthetics of his day. The author also of the ballet *Giselle*, his reviews covered many years of the Romantic Ballet in Paris from the 1830s to the 1870s.

4. I. Guest, ed. (1986), p. 15–16.
5. F. Kermode (1971), p. 66–7.
6. Gautier made many references to male 'ugliness' in dancing. See for example I. Guest, ed., op. cit., p. 5.
7. 'Ball at the Opera', Edouard Manet, 1873. Described as representing a 'Flesh Market' by Julius Meier-Graefe. See L. Nochlin (1989), p. 12.
8. A. H. Franks, 'Alicia Markova' in C. Swinson, ed. (1950), p. 40.
9. A. V. Coton (January 1950), p. 19. See also A. V. Coton's Introduction to his first book, *A Prejudice for Ballet*, written in 1938.
10. Fokine's principles for dance were published in a letter to *The Times*, 6 July 1914, p. 6. They stressed that style should be appropriate to the nature of the ballet's themes; that dancing and gesture have no meaning unless they serve the expression of the action and must not be used in isolation from the ballet itself and the importance of total expressiveness in the dancer's body and in group work.
11. I use the term 'essentialism' to refer here to conceptions of the innate nature of a ballerina regardless of role. This aspect has been a focal point of ballet appreciation resulting in statements of ideas such as a ballerina is born not made.
12. T. Gautier in I. Guest, ed., op. cit., p. 16.
13. Ibid., p. 15.
14. Ibid., p. 38.
15. Ibid., p. 16.
16. A. L. Haskell, 'Irene Skorik' in C. Swinson ed. (1950), p. 46.
17. W. Terry, 'Nora Kaye' in C. Swinson, ed., op. cit., p. 70.
18. A. L. Haskell (1965), p. 13.
19. For a discussion of the historical basis of attitudes towards the feminine, see J. Sayers (1982).
20. A. Stokes (1942), p. 81.
21. Psychoanalyst Karen Horney drew attention to the dichotomy of the saintly and the disparaged in attitudes towards women in her paper 'The Dread of Woman', 1932. She writes:

> The attitude of love and adoration signifies: "There is no need for me to dread a being so wonderful, so beautiful, nay, so saintly". That of disparagement implies: "It would be too ridiculous to dread a creature who, if you take her all round, is such a poor thing".

See K. Horney in H. Kelman, ed. (1967), p. 136.
22. See J. Berger (1972), chapter 3. His analysis of ways of depicting the nude in Western art has been influential on similar studies in the other arts. It may have a lot to offer the understanding of treatments of the body and gender in Western dance.
23. R. A. Johnson (1976), p. 10.
24. R. Heppenstaal (1936), pp. 105–6.
25. G. Kirkland (1987).

26. L. Mulvey in 'You Don't Know What Is Happening Do You Mr. Jones?' in R. Parker and G. Pollock, eds (1987), pp. 127–31 writes that:

> Women are constantly confronted with their own image in one form or another, but what they see bears little relation or relevance to their own conscious fantasies, their own hidden fears and desires . . . The parade has nothing to do with woman, everything to do with man . . .

It is also important to consider women's collusiveness in terms of spectatorship and their introjection of the kind of images Mulvey is identifying.

27. M. Allan (1908), pp. 46–7.
28. I. Duncan, 'The Dance of the Future' (1902/3), in R. Copeland and M. Cohen, eds. (1983), p. 264.
29. R. Heppenstaal, op. cit. pp. 93–4.
30. A. L. Haskell, 'The Dancer' in C. Brahams, ed. (1936), p. 4.
31. R. Heppenstaal, op. cit. pp. 103, 108.
32. A. Levinson (1982), p. 32.
33. Ibid., p. 28.
34. Ibid., p. 32.
35. T. Gautier, op. cit. p. 32.
36. Ibid., p. 24.
37. M. Siegel (1979), pp. 57–8.
38. Ibid., p. 257.
39. R. Buckle, 'At the Saville' (30 August 1961), in R. Buckle (1980), p. 60.
40. A. Stokes, op. cit. p. 107.
41. The *Sunday Telegraph*, (Oct./Nov. 1983). Quoted in 'Revealing the Reviews', *Dance Theatre Journal*, Vol. 2, No. 1, (1984), pp. 6–8.
42. See J. Sayers (1982), p. 89, in which she quotes Topinard (1894) who argued that womens brains were lighter than mens because their duties in life required less cerebral activity and that the weight of the brain increased with the use made of the organ.

The comparative smallness and lightness of womens brains to that of men was a popular basis, in the nineteenth century, for arguing that it would be wrong, and destructive to essential 'femininity', to give women equal educational opportunities with men.

43. A. de Mille, 'And Promenade Home', quoted in L. M. Vincent (1979), p. 9.
44. Ibid., p. 100.

Bibliography

M. Allan, *My Life and Dancing*, (London: Everett, 1908).
J. Berger, *Ways of Seeing*, (London: BBC and Penguin Books, 1972).
R. Betterton (ed.), *Looking On*, (London: Pandora Press, 1987).
R. Buckle, *Buckle at the Ballet*, (London: Dance Books, 1980).
A. V. Coton, *A Prejudice for Ballet*, (London: Methuen, 1938).
A. V. Coton, 'Two Points of View', *Dance Magazine*, January (1950), p. 19.

I. Duncan, 'The Dance of the Future' (1902/3) in R. Copeland and M. Cohen (eds.), *What is Dance?*, (Oxford University Press, 1983).

I. Guest (ed.), *Gautier on Dance*, (London: Dance Books, 1986).

A. L. Haskell, *Balletomania*, (London: Victor Gollancz, 1934).

A. L. Haskell, 'The Dancer', in C. Brahms (ed.), *Footnotes to the Ballet*, London: Lovat Dickson, 1936).

A. L. Haskell, *What is Ballet?*, (London: Macdonald, 1965).

R. Heppenstaal, *Apology for Dancing*, (London: Faber & Faber, 1936).

K. Horney, 'The Dread of Woman' (1932) in H. Kelman (ed.), *Feminine Psychology*, (New York: Norton 1967).

R. A. Johnson, *She: Understanding Feminine Psychology*, (USA: Religious Publishing Company, 1976).

F. Kermode, *Romantic Image*, (London: Fontana, 1971).

G. Kirkland, *Dancing On My Grave*, (Garden City, NY: Doubleday, 1986; Jove Books edition, 1987).

A. Levinson, *Ballet Old and New*, trans. Susan Cook Summer, (New York: Dance Horizons, 1982).

L. Nochlin, *Women, Art and Power and Other Essays*, (London: Thames & Hudson, 1989).

R. Parker and G. Pollock (eds), *Framing Feminism*, (London: Pandora Press, 1987).

J. Sayers, *Biological Politics*, (London: Tavistock Press, 1982).

M. B. Siegel, *The Shapes of Change*, (New York: Avon Books, 1979).

A. Stokes, *Tonight the Ballet*, (London: Faber & Faber, 1942).

C. Swinson (ed.), *Dancers and Critics*, (London: Black, 1950).

L. M. Vincent, *Competing With the Sylph: Dancers in Pursuit of the Ideal Body Form*, (Kansas City: Andrews & McMeel, 1979).

12 Still Dancing Downwards and Talking Back

ZAGBA OYORTEY

The sound of feet pounding the ground becomes the rhythm of the music whose notes are in turn transformed into dance steps . . .
Francis Bebey, *African Music, A People's Art*

There are many misconceptions about African people's dance, most of which, if not all, derive unfortunately from the framework within which Europe has interacted with Africa. A linear mode of interpreting history and human activity ensured that the early European anthropologists studied African and indeed the cultures of all other subjugated peoples within an evolutionist discourse. There was the assumption therefore, that these were transitory cultures that would in due course follow Europe into an industrialised and 'scientific culture'. It is my contention that the inability of the majority of Europeans to take on the full significance and meaning of African dance derives from this original misconception. In the kind of dispensation where one culture was seen as 'primitive' and the other 'modern', African dance, if it had any value at all, was something to be indulged in moments of hedonism.[1]

In a broader context of, say, African visual arts, its 'primitivist' value was enhanced if it was reworked by a Picasso or a Braque. That neither the arrogance of the anthropologist and colonialist nor the 'borrowings' of European artists have altered the nature of African arts is symbolic of the resilience and inherent dynamism of African culture.

African people's dance has continued to thrive, preserving not only its canons but recreating extensive vocabularies of expression to document the synthesis between European and African cultures.[2] For its practitioners, African dance is a source of joy, an educational experience in social mores, a therapeutic exercise and a religious expression. The enduring appeal of African peo-

184

ple's dance derives therefore from what one might call its functional completeness and the wealth of knowledge it continuously yields to all those who seek its treasures.

Today in the 1990s, a random sample of reviews on African dance in Britain reveals a dearth of knowledge about the subject. This in no way does justice to the groundswell of popular participation by Europeans in African dance.[3] Surely enough work has been done by anthropologists, choreographers[4] and 'Africanists' of all persuasions to offer, if not any valuable theoretical insights, at least descriptive accounts to which any conscientious critic could refer.

In the course of this essay, I will highlight some of the principles of African people's dance and show how this informs the work of practitioners in Britain. I will also look at the critical concerns raised by this practice and discuss which, if any, European critical categories are applicable to African people's dance. Such a course is motivated by the absence of adequate space for discussing the meaning and sources of African dance. Furthermore, I believe that a discussion of African dance in the parameters of gender and culture, while being relevant, assumes that African dance enjoys an equal status with European dances and that there are not any more pressing issues of concern. M. Salmon (1987) and K. Owusu (1986) have demonstrated what some of the factors impinging on African arts and dance are in Britain. I believe that until such a time when enough information on African dance has filtered down to all British enthusiasts, any *ad minutiae* decoding would be superfluous.

In terms of definitions, I use African peoples in this paper to represent sub-Saharan and diasporan cultures. In Britain diasporan African becomes specifically those African/Caribbean artists who first created spaces for African and African Caribbean dance in Britain. The exclusion of North Africa is due to that part of the continent being largely inhabited by Berbers and Arabs who have more cultural affinity with Middle Eastern and Oriental cultures. This said, however, the aim is not to present Africa as a monolithic whole. Far from being a homogeneous whole, Africa has hundreds of languages with varying customs and cultural practices. Yet, out of this diversity, historians have traced broad migratory patterns showing common origins and destinations. Similarly, ethnolinguists have grouped languages spoken by Africans into specific and general families.

One feature that unites the diversity of African cultures more forcefully though is a common conception of the supernatural and attitudes to what one might call religion. No African language group has a name for religion and this is precisely because religion pervades all things although this is not to be confused with names of cults or divinities (gods and goddesses). In all African societies there is the concept of a supreme being/ presence as one that can only be reached through the mediation of lesser divinities.[5] I will return later to aspects of African religious thought and how these are seen in dance.

It is quite possible to construe a theory of social organisation from the allocation of gender roles and styles from a given African dance. It is not my intention to pursue such a line of enquiry here. I consider that it is more worthwhile to discuss the ideals from which the dances emanate. We must therefore begin with the worldview and conceptions of reality which are mirrored in dance.

The separation between matter and spirit/intuition and rationality that is common in European philosophy is absent in African thought.[6] Outside the margins of Islam and Christianity, conceptual and applied thought in mainstream African society stresses a holism in which matter and spirit exist simultaneously. C. Kamalu (1990) refers to this as a 'concert of opposites'. In cultural/artistic terms, this becomes what A. Euba (1989) refers to as the 'clustered' nature of African arts – where a performance would present music, theatre and visual arts as one thing.

Within that expanded framework, to read the non-aggressive dance postures of a woman as suppliant only gets us off to a false start. Men and women typify different aspects of the force of creation. Women are not adjuncts of men, or for that matter created out of some fictional 'spare rib' as they are within the Western Christian tradition. The position men occupy as heads of households is often more titular than real. There are and always have been, however, abuses of women and it is arguable that the new socio-economic relations introduced by colonialism might have in certain cases facilitated the exploitation of women.[7]

In stressing the organic/collectivist features of African arts, one does not do so at the expense of ignoring the marked disparities in the economic propensities of Africans. At least 70 per cent of all Africans live away from the urban areas and it is this majority who, by their lifestyles and practices, become the 'custodians' of the traditional arts. This is in no way a suggestion that by merely relocating to the urban areas, the traditional ways of 'seeing and doing' are lost. Such a view would belie the resonance of 'folk arts' to be seen in Harare, Accra, Banjul or any other major African city.

Members of the various ethnic groups who relocate to the cities often form language-based associations through which they enjoy and pass down their songs and dances. In the city, new forms emerge out of the throwing together of language groups: some of these forms aggregate through conscious planning into national forms. The Ghana National Dance Ensemble and Les Ballets Africains du Guinea are two examples of groups whose repertoires are based on careful selections of national dances. Both of these national companies see themselves as ambassadors who tour the world promoting intra-cultural dialogue.

African dance fulfils this role because of the status it enjoys in its own society. Together with song and music, dance could easily be seen as the highest art forms in sub-Sahara Africa. This is because the two are employed in almost every aspect of African life – from birth to death and in the interval between. Furthermore, African dance utilises all other art forms in its expression and thus becomes the site for other kinds of artistry. A. M. Opoku summarises the importance of dance in Africa in the following words:

> To us life with its rhythms and cycles is dance and dance is life. The dance is life expressed in dramatic terms. The most important events in the community have special dances to infuse further meaning into the significance of these events. . . . The dance is to us what conventional theatre is to other races.[8]

In his book, *The Bluesman*, J. Finn describes African dance as 'at once the internalisation of everyday events and the externalisation of the drama within'.[9] Behind this seemingly simplistic description lies a conception of the world, nature and the role of artistry. Placed within the dynamics of time and space, art and in this instance dance, becomes a record of history, a means of communication and the expression of individual agency or creativity. Because it aims to be true to life as it is conceived and lived, African dance becomes an avenue for total expression. The whole body is therefore capable of being 'danced' and mimicry of animals is not unknown. The animal world as part of the natural environment becomes part of the artistic imagination.

A general notion of art as a means of making the invisible concrete, extends to show dancing as demonstrative of being alive to forces other than the immediately perceptible. 'Aliveness' or the living quality of an entity is not, of course, confined to animate things. Apart from the human ability to make things move, there is also a counterpoint to Newton's law of motion which is worth referring to here.[10] Both the animate and inanimate are manifestations of a higher consciousness or force. It is this interaction between material/spiritual; seen/unseen; living/not living, that defines the parameters of activity and consciousness.

R. F. Thompson[11] makes reference to the Tiv (Nigerian) word '*vine*' (to dance) which 'additionally unites dance with further artistic happenings and is not confined to the human body, but can combine in certain contexts with things and objects granting them autonomy in art'.[12] A further inference from this point is the interconnectedness of things and the dimensions of conceptual thought which gives much credence and legitimacy to both the visible and the invisible.

In their movements, therefore, African dancers may make use of certain acrobatic dances, some of which seem almost to defy gravity. These could be understood as part of the extra-physical dimension of the 'infinite catalogue' of African dance which expresses *inter alia* 'ambition, spiritual awareness and physical and mental prowess'.[13] Some of the best examples of this kind of dancing are done by the Foula of Guinea in West Africa. The 'Leoudiere' dance of the Foula which uses 360 degree 'swivels' and 180 degree 'splits' could easily be seen as the progenitors of breakdance.[14]

There is no simplistic delineation between the sacred and the secular in African dance. For example, an illustration of this may be where the raising of hands in supplication can exist comfortably with the shaking of hips and gyrations of the waist. Although this may contradict certain notions of propriety in European classical ballet, to the sub-Saharan African dancer it is anything but inappropriate. J. Finn explains this difference succinctly by arguing that morality cannot be defined in any set terms but could be expanded to contain artistic truth or the absence of it:

> Its [African dance's] one goal is to be true to its subject: otherwise it would belie its purpose, which is to present a true-to-life picture of the event it has undertaken to pronounce upon. It has no other aim than this, and does not concern itself with western ideas of morality. Its 'morality' is inextricably bound up with its purpose. Its ends are achieved if the spirit invoked descends upon performers and spectators.[15]

Finn deals further with the issue of propriety in words that need no amplification:

> The whites' notion of the art was diametrically opposed to this. Raised on an unhealthy diet of religious bigotry, the main cause of which was Original Sin – whites fell victim to the malady of hypochondria.[16]

In light of the above, it is clear that African dance has an almost inexhaustible catalogue. Given the variety of subjects that African dance accommodates and the sheer diversity of sub-Saharan African cultures, the task of discussing African dance becomes daunting. That notwithstanding, a schematic approach that begins by a familial grouping of the dances seems to be the most appropriate approach. While K. Nketia (1986) uses two categories – drama of worship and social drama, P. Harper (1967) groups African dances into three broad categories – religious or ritualistic, social organisational and recreational. Both schema are useful. The advantage of Nketia's scheme, however, is in its delineation of religion/worship/memorial as one category, and the condensing of all other forms under the category of the social, religion's all-pervading influence surfacing even in the social dances. Harper's is best for the novitiate who would need a wider window into African dance. Some of the conclusions in that study are, however, contentious and I shall touch briefly on them later.

Religious dances or drama of worship are a central feature of traditional religion and are main means through which supplicants achieve communion with the supreme being or any of the mediating deities. In this sense, the dance is itself an act of worship performed by members of a particular cult. These

dances are often coded and participation is through appren-
ticeship and tuition led by priestesses or priests. The dance forms
and patterns are more of a canonical kind and are geared towards specific ends. The elaborate nature of some of these is
underscored by Nketia's observation of the 12 drum suites, each
with its movement sequences that are utilised in the Akɔn
worship drama of the Ashanti.

Harper's discussion of the Shango (God of Thunder) dance of
the Yoruba, confirms the scope given to the individual in the
execution of the canonical work which holds true for all African
dances, confirming the relationship between the individual and
society. Harper observes that:

> A performer is expected to improvise within the range of
> accepted patterns of movement for a particular dance. . . .
> Each dancer begins his own interpretation of the style of the
> dance to his performance. . . . Shango priests perform the
> same movements in their ritual dance but each expresses a
> different aspect of the personality with which he performs the
> movements.[17]

In the broader context of the African diaspora, the best examples
of religious dances are to be seen in the Haitian Vodoun, the
Cuban Santeria and the Candomble in Brazil. In all these
dances, the high point and essence of the congregation is 'possession' or, properly speaking, the descent of the invoked deity/
power into the supplicant. This is achieved through the power of
drumming and singing/chanting. Messages are then relayed
through coded language from the divinity and interpreted by a
consecrated person. Thompson (1984) provides examples of the
iconography or image making which accompanies these descents
of deities in Haiti. Here, the notion of art as making the visible
apparent are perhaps better illustrated.

Social dances, unlike the above, are performed by all members
of a given society although with the more commemorative kind
such as the Akɔn funeral dances Nketia (1986) observed and
described, the particular drama may only be performed by the
immediate relatives or affiliates of trained dancers. A good number of dances in this category have religious overtones precisely
because of the central place religion occupies in the life of the
community. For instance, the Dipo dance of the Krobo of eastern Ghana is social in so far as it marks the initiation of girls into

womanhood but the various rites that precede the outdooring of the girls/women are of a religious kind. The same goes for the Poro initiation rites for young men in Sierra Leone.

Dance as expression of social order, according to Harper 'safeguards the traditional established social political hierarchy and consequently, the standards of behaviour and morality within the society.'[18] This observation, which is borne out by many researchers, is the main plank in the arguments of scholars of the functionalist school. The problem with it is that quite often this functionalism is given as the defining characteristic of African dance at the expense of, for instance, how artistry is deployed and the leeway that tradition affords individual creativity.

The catalogue of recreational dances is less finite and covers a wide spectrum. Dances in this category often arise out of particular incidents or express particular historical periods, for example, the Kpanlogo of the Ga people in Accra.[19] This dance which is made up of movements from traditionâl dances like Kolomashi, Tumbe and Okpee, came to prominence during the period after independence in Ghana. Its name is a combination of the names of Kpani and Logoshi, and Otu Lincoln is credited for formalising many of its movements. The fluidity and dynamism of African dance is best illustrated in this category where new ideas are moulded constantly into dances using movements that are both indigenous and relatively 'foreign'.[20] The gumboot dance of South Africa which came out of the migration of Africans into urban areas for work may be a recreational dance but the intention behind it is quite serious. The gumboot dance is one example of transmutation of the harrowing city life and regimentation of manual labour into an art form.

There are a variety of settings within which dance occurs in Africa: religious dances in or near shrines, social dances during festivals or on occasion and recreational dances which could occur anywhere. If any one thing can be said to be a common feature of all these dances, it would be in the different emphasis given to movements men and women make in executing these dances. While male dances tend to be more of an athletic or physical kind, women tend to perform rounded and fluid dance figures. Could this be seen as stereotyping women, hence sexist? This would be viewed as such in certain European contexts, specifically in those feminist circles where this difference could be construed to mean that women were weaker. Such an interpretation, however, would run counter to the grain of African philosophy.

Men and women, the African would argue, express different aspects of life and are mutually interdependent. Biological and social factors have determined that while men may express themselves in quick bursts of action, a woman's strength is more likely to be perceived in its resilience. These seemingly contradictory attributes are believed to be harmonised in interdependence and do not mean natural superiority of one gender over the other. In traditional thought, women are the cornerstone of the family and society; they bring forth children, nourish them and run homes. Furthermore, the earth – the source of sustenance for life – is believed in many African communities to be a feminine principle, for example, Ala the earth goddess of the Ibo. With the Ashanti, the earth is referred to as '*Asase Yaa*': *Yaa* being the name given to females born on Thursdays. Similarly, the Krobo refer to the spirit of 'Zugbazu' which is the female component of divine creativity. The importance of the earth/land as source/sustenance reflects a deep-seated respect for reproduction which is personified in women. Another fact that has relevance to this discussion is the absence of gender-specific pronouns in all African languages. If language is a primal act of human affirmation, then this point could shed some light on the issue of egalitarianism.

The above example illustrates that Africans do not believe women are inherently inferior. The debate as to when and why the matriarchal age was eclipsed by the universal patriarchal system is of course outside the concerns of this essay. Suffice it to say that negative attitudes arise out of social interactions and are often given some dubious legitimacy by history. This is not uniquely African, it is a global problem. Practitioners of African dance in Britain, however, often find themselves having to answer to charges of sexism or stereotyping women.[21] These are charges which may not be out of place in European culture where de-gendering of personalities and androgyny are becoming more acceptable.

There are, however, grounds on which the practice of African dance in Britain could be accused of sexism. Bolaji Adeola[22] believes that the overwhelmingly disproportionate number of male choreographers to female ones could be one such case. This is an issue which derives from the initiators of most dance companies being male – Barry Anderson, George Dzikunu, Felix Cobson, Chester Morrison and Peter Badejo, to name but a few. There is no intrinsic reason why, as African dance activity increases and becomes part of the fabric of British society, women choreographers should not increase. The charge of sexism could be made more irrefutably in the case of African 'popular' music.[23] Many of these groups often embellish their acts with women who do not play instruments but who come on to do lewd and sexually provocative dances. Sexism or charges of it are not the biggest barriers between African dance and its European audiences. Critical interpretation or the lack of it would, in my view, be a more pertinent issue.

Many European commentators on African people's dance have observed that Africans tend to dance flat-footed and from a crouching position.[24] What these signify is, however, seldom explained. For purely physiological reasons it would seem that starting a dance movement from a flat-footed position would be the most natural. In addition, equilibrium of the body is enhanced. The 'crouch' is explained by Professor C. K. Ladzekpo[25] to mean seeking and achieving a 'low centre of gravity' which is comparable to the dominant beat in the percussion ensemble. In the flat-footed position, the dancer 'centres' his/her being to receive/absorb the music before literally exploding outward in centrifugal-like force. This would, for a start, conflict with the contra-gravitational ethos of European ballet seen perhaps in the celebration of the female dancer's *en pointe*. If any one figure could be said to represent African dance, it would be the figure of the circle which is seen in both choreographic patterns and the 90, 180 and 360 degree rotations that African dancers make. It is important that these postures and movement sequences are understood as reflective of shared ideals of collectivity and a cyclical notion of history. In contrast, the lines and angles of European ballet should suggest a linear conception of time and an over-preponderous contrivance of the body into human movement positions which are normally difficult to attain. When these two dissimilar art forms are placed together, the immediate starting points for criticism should be differing notions of history, time, artistry, and how these inform uses of the body for the dramatic purposes of dance. These different conceptions of dance and uses of the body need not be antagonistic or even mutually exclusive, as many in the field of contemporary and modern dance know.[26] Yet, if any one thing can be said to be a bane of African dance in Europe, it would be the 'non-art' status given to it and the consequent dismissive tones in which European critics tend to discuss African dance.

As recently as September 1990, Jeffrey Taylor and Nadine Meisner writing in the *Mail on Sunday* and the *Sunday Correspondent* respectively wrote in a language that would shame Geoffrey Gorer (1935). Taylor, in the piece headlined 'Stepping in the wrong direction', refers to the production of Les Ballets Africains du Guinea, as having 'limited choreographic detail . . . the steps are the same and so are the rhythms'. For her part, Meisner referred to the music in the same production as 'noise, pounding percussion'.

Quite clearly, the critics mentioned above viewed these dances and music from an essentially eurocentric standpoint. Since the dancers were not performing an item from European ballet, from what standpoint could they be said to be stepping in the wrong direction? Art in general may be said to be about the human condition: in this sense, art is universal. But as Gombrich (1967) has argued, in each place art, among other things, is shaped by specific historical, social and climatic conditions. This being the case, the least one expects of criticism is an acknowledgement of a different culturally tuned sensibility and an attempt at explaining the differences and finding the common human language that transcends all true art. None of the critics who went through the ritual slaying of the show could claim to be unaware of the large numbers of African artists who could have been interviewed or the various studies done on African dance.

The characteristics of African dance are not such that would make the subject unknowable. This is a view shared by African/American dance notator, Jean Johnson Jones.[27] She believes that the Labanotation system can accommodate the complex cadences of African dance and she has demonstrated it several times in her work. Jones's conviction rests on the fact that the Laban system is based on the principles of human movement and can therefore account for the multiple possibilities of the movements the human body can make in time and space. By not being dance-specific like other forms of notation, and given that it moves from general to specific descriptions, Labanotation caters for the variety of movements that constitute African dance. Through this kind of work, a body of knowledge is gradually becoming available for a 'scientific' understanding of African dance.

Nicholas Dromgole, in one carefully balanced review in the *Sunday Telegraph* in September 1990, accepted that perhaps 'the untrained western ear' could not appreciate the rhythmic complexities of African music. African dance music, which is often led by percussion, seldom has a single rhythm. It operates on the basis of multiple rhythmic patterns which are structured to reflect the complexity of life. The 'structural interdependence' between music and dance which Nketia (1986) refers to means that the drummers would lead by creating a complex range of tones and textures to which the dancers would execute a variety of movement cadences. The relationship between dance and music in the African context means that all the African dance groups in Britain have resident musicians who provide live music. When they are not performing, these groups hold workshops in schools and community centres.[28] This kind of work is also positively shaping European understanding of African music.

Arguably, there has been a perceptive change in the responses to African and African-derived arts in Britain. There are two reasons for this. One is the work of African/Caribbeans who, in the sixties, made demands for the recognition of their specific socio-economic needs and respect for their cultural differences.[29] The second reason for the shifting climate of thought towards African dance has to do with the increased proliferation of African dance groups in Britain today. This is a reflection of both the efforts of artists and the interest that Europeans are showing in African dance. It is important that this is sustained. However, for a fuller understanding of African dance to take place, a more informed discussion of the basics of African dance is required. Not all aspects of African dance can be easily transposed to the stages in Europe. The differences of theatrical and performance conventions in Africa and Britain imply that in one society a performance may be seen as a spectacle or decorative and audience participation may be minimal. In the other society, art often functions as ritual and hence is overwhelmingly functional, with the demarcation between audience and performers being broken down. Such differences have to be explored and explained in greater depth. For example, the reality of a worship drama can never be presented authentically on the stage. What is possible, however, as G. Dzikunu says, 'is to use the context of the European performance space to signal and highlight the peculiarities of such a ritual'.[30] In the worship drama there is no such thing as a spectator, rather there is a congregation of similar faith and worldview.

But, on the whole, the vocabularies and resources of African dance could be understood in any context if the African artist him/herself is fully grounded in his/her tradition. Where the artist is skilled, he/she would be able to make a judicious selection to facilitate whatever intentions are meant to be conveyed.

The need to institute African dance in Britain is about more than a meeting of the educational and recreational needs of diasporan African communities. It is also about learning more about the world and allowing large numbers of Europeans to form a first-hand impression about other arts. The functional completeness I intimated in the beginning of this essay includes a whole range of corrective orthopaedic movements which will have more relevance as more people turn to alternative medicine. African culture, contrary to current opinion, is not in any danger of being overwhelmed by European ways of life. On the continent of Africa, there are syncretic movements that combine the best of both worlds. These operate at the subliminal level of 'whatever threatens the sanctity of our body politic, we domesticate and transmute'. Behind these fusions is the inexhaustible reservoir of cultural resources rooted in a different way of looking at the world. Not, however, without its own contradictions, but certainly, one which has in its own context worked its answers to its role in the universe.

The fears expressed in the conclusions of Gorer (1935) and Harper (1967) about the threat and effects posed by Western culture to Africa are no more real now than then.[31] Ladzekpo's summary of African dance as the means through which the culture is 'saturated with the myths that sustain it',[32] means that as long as we can dance and play our music we refer to resources that provide guidelines even in our changed circumstances. The flat-footed African dancer who shuffles and glides is, after all, only putting into another form the art of verbal circumlocution. Life is not met head-on and one learns to swim with the tide and fly with the wind.

Notes and References

1. This is comparable in certain respects to the level at which many Parisians related to the jazz music of African/Americans who passed through or settled in Paris in the first decades of the twentieth century.
2. Beyond the arts, this point has applicability in many areas of social, economic and political life.
3. Most cities in England and particularly in London have resident African dance and music groups which are patronised by large groups of Europeans. Jenako Arts in Hackney is one example of a venue which arranges for tutors in African dance and music to teach both children and adults.
4. Corrine Bougard, Artistic Director of Union Dance, a London-based contemporary dance group, uses African dance movements in her work.
5. Direct access to the Supreme Being or through the mediation of only one agency is unknown in sub-Saharan African religions. Instead, there are a plurality of 'minor gods' who, on 'licence' from the Supreme, cater for human needs or requirement. Hence, the gods of war, goddesses of fertility, etc. See, for example, S. Booth, ed. (1977). See also Bibliography of the same.
6. The gap between Hegel and Marx typify the perennial Western dilemma over what takes precedence – matter or spirit?
7. The African woman, whether in the pre-colonial or post-colonial context, has always been a producer. In addition to her duties as a mother and a wife, she has always had to earn a living. Colonisation might have, with its introduction of Western-style education and employment, created opportunities for the social advancement of African women. This cannot, however, be an all-embracing change. The early bias towards educating male children has still not been totally eradicated and men still occupy a disproportionate area in the professions. In such a case, one could say that cleavages of inequality were deepened rather than closed. Without being conclusive, one might say with a degree of scepticism that changes affecting women in Africa may have been qualitative in terms of access to health facilities but not quantitative in terms of improving the lot of women to a point where they are at a par with men.
8. Quoted in K. Nketia (1986), chapter 19.
9. J. Finn 1986), p. 91.
10. See C. Kamalu (1990), p. 81.
11. R. F. Thompson (1984).
12. Ibid., p. xxii.
13. J. Finn, op. cit.
14. Z. Oyortey (1990).
15. J. Finn, op. cit.
16. Ibid.
17. P. Harper (1967), p. 79.
18. Ibid., p. 12.
19. Information on Kpanlogo was given to me by George Dzikunu.
20. 'Foreign' is used here in reference to forms that do not derive directly from an ethnic group. It is also used to qualify forms that accrue from cross national contacts.

21. Although women musicians are not unknown in Africa, the overwhelming majority of drummers and other instrument players in any traditional context are men. This situation which transfers to Britain in the works of practitioners of African dance is often a point latched onto by critics.
22. Bolaji Adeola is a dancer with Adzido Pan African Dance Ensemble, the foremost African dance group in Britain. Her views were recorded in an interview with Z. Oyortey.
23. 'Popular' music refers to the dance-hall-type music which is often traditional music played with electric instruments and very common in urban areas. 'Highlife', 'Juju' or 'Soukous' are some of these forms. The need to increase audiences and to 'hype up' African music as sensuous, often lead to the use of women in this manner. It is a common feature of African 'popular' music, both in Africa and the West.
24. See the Introduction to M. Stearn and J. Stearn (1979).
25. Personal communication with Professor C. K. Ladzekpo at the 1989 Black Dance Development Trust's Summer School, Birmingham, England.
26. Pearl Primus and Berto Pasuka, African/American and African/Caribbean dancers and choreographers working earlier in this century are two examples of such artists.
27. Jean Johnson Jones is a Labanotation Officer at the University of Surrey.
28. Under the now defunct Inner London Educational Authority, many African dance groups were assisted to hold workshops in many London schools. Through this kind of work, people within the educational system and pupils particularly, received early contact with African arts.
29. See K. Owusu (1986) for a discussion of the problems facing black artists in Britain.
30. Personal communication with George Dzikunu, Artistic Director of Adzido Pan African Dance Ensemble.
31. Gorer and Harper, in their works which have been cited in this essay, conclude with fears of Africa losing its traditional arts in the face of increasing 'Westernisation'. Since African art is not only seen in forms but also in an understanding of conceptions of the universe, it is not far-fetched to say that although 'Westernisation' may change certain outward forms, the ideas which inhere or with which these are fashioned would remain African. Compare this with Japanese culture which, despite its heavy technological/computerised facility, still retains a sense of itself as Japanese.
32. C. K. Ladzekpo, at inaugural lecture at the formation of the Black Dance Development Trust, Commonwealth Institute, London, 1985.

Bibliography

N. S. Booth Jr, *African Religions*, (New York: Nok Publishers International, 1977).
A. Euba, *Essays on Music in Africa*, (Bayreuth Universität: Iwalewa-haus, 1989).
J. Finn, *The Bluesman*, (London: Quartet, 1986).
E. H. Gombrich, *The Story of Art*, (London: Phaidon, 1967).

G. Gorer, *Africa Dances* (London: originally published 1935; Harmondsworth: Penguin, reprint 1983).

P. Harper, 'Dance in Africa', *Journal of African Arts*, Vol. 1, No. 1 (Los Angeles, Calif.: African Studies Centre, 1967).

C. Kamalu, *Foundations of African Thought*, (London: Karnak, 1990).

K. Nketia, *The Music of Africa*, (London: Gollancz, 1986).

K. Owusu, *The Struggle for Black Arts in Britain*, (London: Comedia, 1986).

Z. Oyortey, 'African Magic', Review of Ballet Africain in *West Africa Magazine*, August 1990.

M. Salmon, *Ethnic Minority and Black Arts Policies in Britain and their Influence on the Development of Black Dance Since the 1940's*, BA dissertation, Roehampton Institute (1987).

M. Stearn and J. Stearn, *Jazz Dance*, (New York: Schirmer, 1979).

R. F. Thompson, *African Art in Motion*, (Los Angeles, Berkeley and London: University of California Press, 1974).

R. F. Thompson, *Flash of the Spirit*, (London: Vintage, 1984).

13 The Anxiety of Dance Performance

VALERIE RIMMER

The concern of this paper is to address the ways in which dance performance as an ideological, representational vehicle derives its power and transforms ideology into actions and beliefs. In addition, the aim is to address the ways in which the nature of subjectivity is challenged by psychoanalytic theory leading to a further understanding of the constitution of female subjectivity and the impossibility of imposing a sexually differentiated schemata as a fully rounded acquisition. By taking a brief analysis of *Swan Lake* I will demonstrate the relevance of Lacanian psychoanalytic theory, showing the ways in which it highlights questions regarding the difficulties of spectatorship for women – questions that are particularly apt when asked in relation to the content, structure and style of *Swan Lake.*

Any critical writing that expresses its intention to examine dance performance from the perspective of reading as a woman, without challenging the construction of the category 'woman', can only attempt a continuity between the women's experience of herself and her experience as reader. This is because, however that concern is articulated, it will necessarily lead to the reduction of meaning to a version of experience – a reduction that will focus on the narrative content of a work, offering woman as theme, i.e. as the expression of attitudes to women, images of women or the psychological motivation of female characters, etc. The construction of the work and its sustaining concepts can then be placed in a secondary position to the concerns of female-represented experience which is privileged as the 'proper' matter of the female reader and which can be validated and reinstated against further readings of the text. As understanding or reading the performance text is attempted via learnt codes and conventions relating to reference and rhetoric, meaning can be located, in a non-problematic way, as whatever is present to the experience of reading. However it is essential for any study relating to female spectatorship/readership, that the structure of an experience that is defined as belonging to 'woman' is explored as a way of intervening in what is given as an unproblematic version of a fixed and residual textual meaning. Otherwise the achieved result from this position will be, at its best, an attempt to place a male-dominated, critical tradition, whose focus has been on male themes, characters and fantasies, etc., within a more equalising framework. To develop a category of female reading places as unproblematic the relation between woman's experience of herself and her experience as reader. In order to address this relation it is necessary to challenge the construction of subjectivity, particularly the constitution of the condition 'woman'. Without doing this the experience of reading as a woman can be offered as achievable – provided one possesses the 'right' knowledge – and as an experience that can be differentiated from the male condition. Thus reading as a sex-coded, gender-inflected strategy of interpretation, continues to privilege male experience as human and total and defines woman's as secondary and derived in relation to it. From within this position therefore women can only be shown to be working against their own experiences and interests.

Using psychoanalytic theory, particularly the writings of Jacques Lacan, a space can be designated in which the constitution and maintenance of a sexually differentiated identity can be described and understood in such a way that neither category can be defined or fixed in a fantasy relation. Psychoanalytic theory offers an explanation of the way in which women's experience is constructed foregrounding sexuality as the site of conflict and fantasy. In his reworking of Freud's concept of the unconscious, Lacan shows that woman's experience of herself is neither complete nor simply achieved, and that sexual difference as a structuring device is constantly in conflict with this experience. Lacan offers an explanation of subjectivity that is in conflict with itself and as such places sexuality in a problematic position. By linking the concepts of sexuality and the unconscious, Lacan not only challenges as meaningful differentiated images of sexual difference that privilege male and exclude female, but he shows that the actual construction of meaning is potentially threatened.

Subjectivity as a logocentric category of thought is sustained at the level of metaphysical law by phallocentrism. The fantasy of sexual difference is dependent on a binary opposition that by its nature prevents a free play of meaning, defining woman as the underprivileged secondary term that provides the conditional truth of male dominance and privilege. Phallocentrism provides the underlying structure of the whole order of representational space across which there is an ongoing dissemination of subjectivity which fantasises woman as otherness. She stands for an absence of male presence, as the fact on which male ownership and control relies, and in this fantasy relation allows the dominance of the duplicitious nature of logocentrism.

By disrupting the subject of certainty Lacan's conceptualisation of the unconscious moves towards a greater understanding of the fictional status of categories of sexual difference to which every individual is subjected. Lacan continues Freud's work on the constitution of identity via his formulation of the *stade du miroir* which states the process by which the individual internalises himself and, as a source of all later identifications, is central in articulating the fantasy relation which sustains versions of subjectivity. The mirror stage is a process by which the individual learns to control his/her own image giving him/her a corporeal form that has otherwise, until this point of development, been denied them and that is essential for the proper development of perceptual relationships with others. But the 'moi' that the individual recognises at this stage, and that is confirmed through the image of the parents and cultural representations, is an imaginary construct, a misrecognition. At this point in its development the child is an alienated subject, a 'moi' that will only achieve true subjectivity in the symbolic order of language.

Language is given to the individual from the other when s/he learns to speak and therefore s/he is appropriated as an identified symbolic subject – ordered by language. But for Lacan, if identity is given only in language, language speaks for the lack that is behind that first moment of symbolisation. Lacan uses the '*fort/da*' game to articulate the absence or lack within the signifying chain that the individual attempts to fill at the level of the signifier through symbolisation. Symbolically the repetition of the sounds 'fort/da' designate the concepts of presence and absence as the child throws his/her cotton reel out of sight and has it returned to him/her. Present or absent the toy stands for the absent mother, and by implication the lost breast. The game therefore becomes a symbolic enactment of the desire for wholeness.

In terms of the psyche the partial object conveys a lack and it is this lack that stimulates a desire for unity which in turn stimulates the movement towards identification. In this sense absence provides the condition of possibility for presence. At the *stade du miroir* the recognition of the child outside itself as a whole image is a misrecognition that is based on a primary moment of lack. This is because the child can only attain identity in language and cannot exist as a fixed irreducible reality outside of language. The subject then becomes the subject of speech whose identity is given via shifters – pronouns I, you, me – that do not refer to a fixed, knowable category but are meaningful in relation to whoever is being referred to at the moment of speech. The child that recognises itself as '*moi*' at the mirror stage therefore misrecognises itself in an essential moment of division that will constantly be repeated at the level of language in the sliding pronoun. The mirror image then is the category that allows the subject to operate as 'I' and is the model for the ego function which constitutes identity and which itself is constituted as a splitting or division.

The order of language for Lacan is the symbolic order and the order of the ego and its identifications is the imaginary order and there is subsequently in his work a stress on the symbol and the image. Both of which imply the process of substitution for a lost object. Lacan also refers to the Real – what is real for the subject – and it is in the third order of the real that both the imaginary and symbolic co-exist, linking the subject to the world and others.

It is the loss of the first object that is hidden at the level of the imaginary order that the subject seeks to replenish at the level of signifier – in language. But the subject can only operate in language by repeating that essential moment of division. It is therefore in this gap of re-presentation that all fantasies will be expressed.

The demand of the child, to return to Lacan's writings, will be in an ongoing relationship to something other than what can give it satisfaction because the 'demand for' will always contain this something other that will never be satisfied by anything the mother can say or do. This something other that is left over Lacan calls Desire and it is always produced within a context but has no context of its own – it is left over as lack, as the original impossibility.

Lacan's formulation of desire questions accounts of sexuality that can be referred back to a level of demand, that can be satisfied. His conceptualisation of sexuality necessarily contains an unattainable element that denies its complete satisfaction and refers back to fundamental division articulated in the constitutive processes of identity. The subject, in addressing its demand to the Other, fantasises the other as a place of wholeness of unity which will reflect its truth. This is a misrecognition that slides over the irreducible moment of loss described in Lacan's account of the *stade du miroir*. And this is a version of sexuality that is located at the level of fantasy because it is registered at the level of demand (desire is misrecognised) and is addressed to a sexually differentiated other.

The division of male and female which rests on genital difference hides the problematic of sexuality via the fantasy that articulates a complementary relationship between the two terms. Lacan's explication of the concept of the Drive illuminates this further. The drive is not a concept that is biologically defined as an instinctual drive that, associated with genital identity, matures and achieves a fulfilment of need. It challenges any concept of satisfaction as a fulfilled response to need. For Lacan the process of the drive and not its end result is crucial. This process articulates the loss of the object around which it revolves – a loss that characterises the individual's relationship to the Other. In this way the drive can be called representational. The drive is inhabited by what Lacan calls *jouissance*. An excess of pleasure that also contains the characteristics of insistence and aggression and which can easily take it beyond an economy of pleasure. It always is striving towards something other than the relationship on which it is focused. In referring to the drive as representational Lacan asks that an analogy be made between the limits that representation imposes, and the subject's constitutive, sexually differentiated identity, his ordering in language. Also by identifying its process as crucial Lacan is placing meaning, as an ongoing and arbitrary process, in an analogous relationship with the drive. It is the structure and identity of the drive that challenges normative accounts of sexuality that relies on the fantasy of an identification of the heterosexual subject who is made complete through another.

For Lacan the purpose of the analytic encounter is to show that the imaginary identification of the subject with another is dependant on a third term – the symbolic naming of the subject in language via shifters. The Oedipus complex and the concept of castration can only be understood in their referral to a wider symbolic order which is beyond the interactions of the analytic relationship, although it is within this encounter that these are played out. The castration complex which has its emphasis on paternal law is defined in relation to the concept of desire. There is a prohibition on the child's desire to be what the mother desires in that the mother cannot be wholly for the child and fulfil its desires because of her own. The symbolic barrier between the child and the mother is the phallus which is representative of the father's place. It stands for prohibition as it is a barrier to the desire to be the exclusive desire of the other. The phallus figures the mother's lack via her own desire and prevents the desire of the child to be what the mother desires. The phallus therefore starts the order of sexual exchange and refers the child's desire beyond the mother. The status of the phallus as the desire and satisfaction of the mother is both imaginary and symbolic.

Lacan reformulates the concept of the father in relation to desire as paternal metaphor in which the act of substitution, the law by which metaphor works, allows the phallus as the prohibition of the father to stand for the absence of the mother. For the child therefore desire always contains a lack. It also refers to the father as a function that refers to a law and not the presence or absence of the real father. The imaginary figure, which symbolises the absent mother, in the status of the phallus is differentiated from any conception of the role of father by this concept of paternal metaphor. The phallus becomes the place where the imaginary coupling of mother/child breaks in its reference to the father as a function that refers to a law.

Until Lacan's reformulation of it the Oedipus complex defined the predominance of the father, figured in the phallus, as natural but Lacan argues that this predominance should be redefined as normative. It is only if the fantasy of the mother/child dualism is maintained that the assertion of male privilege via the phallus can be presented as natural and unproblematic. He feels that it is the emphasis on the mother/child relationship in psychoanalytic theory that displaces the concept of the unconscious and bisexuality, and which articulates a failure to grasp the importance of the symbolic. It is only in societal terms that this privileging of

the father locating the mother as 'privileged site of prohibitions'[1]
can occur.

The privileging of the phallus and the resultant sexually differentiated ordering is shown by Lacan to be given in the order of
the symbolic and therefore cannot be reduced to any unproblematic, natural account of sexuality. The concept of desire and
the recognition by the individual of his lack in the place of the
other is the difficulty that resides in the state of subjectivity and
that is given at the level of the symbolic. Lacan shows that sexual
difference is a legislative difference that reduces being to a division of genital difference but at the same time attributing a value
to that division. The famous example constantly cited is of two
identical doors that are differentiated linguistically by the words
Ladies and Gents. The words articulate a genital difference that
symbolises the having, or having not, of the phallus. This means
that to enter any door correctly the user has to take their place in
a sexually differentiated, symbolic division. Genital difference
then becomes visibly and figuratively representative of sexual
difference via the words 'Ladies' and 'Gents', assigning a meaning to the possession or not of the phallus. The moment of lack,
when a woman choses her assigned place via the word 'Ladies'
belongs not to the natural or the real but to the symbolic, the
order in which this lack-in-being is given a meaning.

The phallus can only play its role as veiled. Like the signifier it
has no value in itself other than as a symbol that signifies, and
therefore can only represent, something that has already been
accredited value. The symbolic ordering of women's sexuality
then becomes inseparable from the representations through
which it is produced but these representations, as the site of
fantasy, will always evoke the loss on which they are fantasised.
Sexuality is characterised by a meaning that, like the unconscious, is always slipping away as an enactment of the initial
division of being in the subject.

For Lacan men and women are signifiers bound to a common
use of language and female sexuality can only be understood in
terms of its construction which articulates the binary opposition
male/female privileging the first term. Questions of the relationship of women to that language remain still to be answered,
but what is achieved from the Lacanian perspective in questioning sexuality and its constitution is to make visible the order of
organisation that underlies definitions of woman. We can de-

velop an account of how the legitimated phallic term in relation to sexual difference, offers a definition of woman as a symptom of itself, the phallus occasioning femininity as masquerade.

The difficulties involved in addressing the problems of sexuality in relation to danced representations, and the relationship between spectator and scene(seen), have to be centred around the exposition of the sexually differentiated subject of certainty as an imaginary subjected identity. This has led to a focus on repetition, not as a secondary term defined in relation to an original – its poor relation – but as a process that repeats an elision which pressurises self-contained representations as images where identification of a sexually differentiated self takes place.

The body is a major signifier that is restricted by the eye ('I') in Western culture and in dance, where it is aesthetically captured as form, what is enabled is the maintainance of a particularly repressive mode of sexual recognition. With all representations there is a demand on the part of the spectator to look for their truth, or their coherence in a referential sense, but Lacan shows that at the moment of seeing fundamental questions are being asked of the way the spectator recognises and responds to their own subjectivity.

A version of the self has been developed in Lacanian theory that is fundamentally linked to a notion of exteriority, in which the '*moi*' becomes increasingly dependent on an alienated other. This perspective is developed further in Lacan's account of the 'gaze'. Initially the gaze is experienced in a space that is external to the subject operating in the first instance at the moment when the mother unites in the imaginary order infant and mirror image. And at other times it is confused with actual looks. The subject can indirectly feel as if it is operating the gaze from the distance of seeing itself, as it experiences the effects of a gaze that is in operation in and on the self as all-pervasive, without an actual looking taking place. Seeing oneself being seen is a repetition of the moment of the subject's misrecognition at the mirror stage.

In relation to Lacan's formulation of the gaze we must ask ourselves, what is the guilt of dance performance that is coterminous with the lack of being in the subject of desire? What is being suppressed that necessitates the desexualisation of the dancing body in order that the performance can be (scene) seen? Using a voyeuristic example Lacan situates the gaze outside. It is when the subject places its eye to the keyhole that it is most likely to find itself subordinated to the gaze which will overwhelm the subject and reduce it to shame. It is at this moment that the subject sustains itself in the function of desire as the gaze remains outside of desire and the look within.

The dancing body in presenting itself as the embodiment of performance representation to be looked at, represents a subject that is objectified operating from an imagined position of self-consciousness. The conventions of performance actively work to support the process of objectification by taking an untrained, everyday body and, via technique and training, mark it off from the utilitarian body as an image that is fit for the consumption of the spectator. The spectator by taking up his/her place in the reciprocal relationship confirms the dancing bodies as objectified aesthetic bodies. Both dancing bodies and spectator derealise themselves as the relations of dance performance place them in terms of seeing and being seen (being imagined as scene). To be is then to be perceived as dancing representation, a certain type of being that is dependent on a misrecognition of the subject as a full subject in the imaginary order.

Lacan likens the gaze to a camera, as an instrument that embodies light, and through which the subject is photographed and constituted as subject. This is what he calls the alterity of the gaze. The subject enters the visible through the gaze and it is from the gaze that s/he receives its effects. If for a moment we think about the dance critical text we can see, particularly in the works of Denby (1949, p. 37) and Clement Crisp (1983, p. 4) that dance criticism gives itself the task of producing a picture of what went on. It freezes a danced moment in language and offers it as a representation of performance. The critic is then acknowledged in the role of other constituting the subject (the dance performance) for the reader.

Dance performance has the status of specular extravaganza. It foregrounds the image and naturalises identity by concealing its external support. This can happen because the relationship between the gaze and the look is structural in the sense that the gaze is supported by the look. Lacan stresses the otherness of the gaze, that it can masquerade as the look, and yet it is distinct from the eye ('I') that looks. The characteristic of the gaze is that it can issue from all sides whereas the eye sees from only one point. Also the gaze cannot be apprehended or made self-present. In this aspect the relationship between the eye (look) and the gaze is similar to that between penis and phallus. The former can stand in for the latter but can never become it. This has important ramifications for discussions about sexual difference. Who possesses the gaze in relation to dance performance and how central is the look to the circulation of the visual field?

In feminist film-theory an argument has been made in respect of a male voyeurism incorporated into the gaze that structures the look, manipulating the spectator to identify with the male look as it objectifies the female figure. As has already been shown above, the woman functions as the site (sight) of male insufficiency by being defined in terms of her lack of phallus. As the object of the male look and the site where he can deposit his lack (a defence against castration anxiety) the woman is made subservient to a look that is structured by sexual difference. Dance performance posits the woman as object of the male look and she functions in this place as symptom at the level of both structure and content. An imagined identity is then brought into existence whereby lack in being is supported by lack of phallus. This allows the sexually differentiated subject as a certain type of meaning to be constructed in which the gaze, as its confirmation, and the look are brought together. The look substituting for the gaze, denying its lack. The spectator can then sustain himself in relation to the performance in a misrecognised function of desire.

By redefining Freud's writings on castration-anxiety away from the physical term, the phallus, Lacan relocates lack at the level of the symbolic order. In relation to the gaze he shows that its alterity is symbolic of the lack that is placed at the level of the eye and constitutive of castration anxiety. In dance performance what occurs is that the eye focuses on the body as object of the look and not on the look itself which allows a definition of subjectivity at the level of phallic anatomical reference.

The performing body acts as a place where the audience fantasises at the level of represented image using it as a type of mirror that allows for the transformation of the everyday body. The external representation is then the place to which the audience constantly refers to sustain their identity. The female body, as a desexualised representation, can then portray a version of subjectivity that is cause and support of that stance. Behind that representation is a conception of the exemplary male subject as adequate to the paternal function which is dependent on a negation at the heart of subjectivity – the lack that is fundamental to the constitution of identity in the symbolic order which is compounded by culturally defined representations. Although the male dancing body is highly conventionalised and exemplarised (Prince Siegfried in *Swan Lake*) it is dependent on being treated as if it were devoid of desire, achieving desiring status only via its place in the representation and not visibly via the tumescent penis. This lack is transformed through a demonstrated technical virtuosity as indicator of masculinity and difference maintaining focus on the subjected female dancing body. Woman are used as the place to which the lack in the male look is assigned and as we can see in *Swan Lake* there is an attempt to pass this look off as the gaze. Male desire is thus systematically covered with projection and control and to attempt to understand this position it is essential to differentiate between the look and the gaze. This will produce a framework from which to examine the ways in which social meanings are attributed to the phallicised dancing body and the forms which this differentiation assumes.

In *Swan Lake* the gaze, defined as male, is located on the side of law and authority within a framework of male heterosexual desire. Structurally dance performance focuses audience attention on what is seen (scene) – the object of the look – away from the look itself, and through an equation between the masquerader's gaze and the male subject/body. The female subject/body is represented as the spectacle that captures the look and is subjugated by it. As stated above, the look can masquerade as the gaze – the eye can stand in for the gaze – but this is a misrecognition as the gaze cannot be equated with any particular viewer but is pervasive and intangible, emanating from all sides – the eye can never approximate it.

The narrative of *Swan Lake* progresses via a theme of transformation in which the figure of the hero, Prince Siegfried, crosses the boundaries and penetrates the space of the other. A representation of this is given in terms of physical environments. Both Siegfried and Odette/Odile inhabit different orders. The Prince as the subject of consciousness is experienced as a rationally ordered subject who is distinguished by knowledge (signified by the role of the tutor), wealth (palace and garden which display an ordered extravagance, etc.) and authority (the main character of the work is a prince celebrating his coming of age demonstrating his suitability to be leader of his kingdom). These effects all produce an evident self-consciousness or substantiality. Whereas the Swan Queen is both conceived and constrained by the sorcery of Von Rothbart. She inhabits the mysterious landscapes of the sky and the dark forests and lake and to achieve her true identity as woman she needs the male other. Distinguished as a human male body, Siegfried becomes the active principle of culture and the creator of differences. The female body – the Swan Queen – is the site of obstacle, and as a swan by day and a woman between the hours of midnight and dawn, Odette is the culturally constructed ideal of femininity figured by the enigmatically beautiful swan. She signifies a faultless, spotless innocence both morally and spiritually and as such is imaged, by the spectator, as the proper object of the prince's, and by extension their desire.

When Siegfried first sees Odette he observes her from a distance. He is the eye ('I') in this voyeuristic transaction and will offer her an identity via the register of his desire. Enchanted by her, during the progression of the narrative Siegfried captures her by taking charge of her desire. He articulates Odette both bodily via the movement and narratively, defining her identity in relation to his desire. During the course of their love duets Siegfried at first holds Odette by the wrists, leaving her hands free as a reference to her otherness – her freedom to inhabit a world characterised by flight – a world that has as its basis a deception – the Swan Queen is conceived from her mother's tears by sorcery. As the love-duets continue so does the amount of support (to her arabesques and the high lifts) that Siegfried offers until finally Odette is completely held by him. He holds her arms close to her body behind her back. Gradually her movements are constrained by him, her power to take flight is overtaken and literally and symbolically Siegfried has taken control of her body. 'Siegfried lifts Odette high in his arms . . . effortlessly to the demands of the theme'. (Balanchine and Mason, *Swan Lake*, 1978)

Subjectivity in *Swan Lake* is seen to depend on a visual agency. Captured by Siegfried's look which articulates his fantasy of her, Odette is given her being as woman and she must maintain the fidelity of that look to guarantee her difference. Within the ballet the act of looking is emphasised both as a challenge to the duplicitous nature of representation and as its solution, the Swan Queen becoming the proper image through which the problems of matter and form can be conceptualised and thought.

Odile as the black swan becomes the place where anxiety is located in terms of male lack. She stands as the image of the white swan. As the re-presentation of Odette, the black swan shows the underside of femininity, presenting a real danger to Siegfried's rational self-presence. And although she will be subsumed by the phallocentric demands of representation she momentarily surfaces to threaten a version of psychic integration and an ordering of sexuality and difference as the real threat of dance performance – the subversive everyday body that can disrupt the aesthetic constraints that serve to conventionalise the body of performance. The black swan, symbolic of the subterranean forces of danger and death, conceived totally from within Von Rothbart's desire for revenge, and structurally via concerns about the validity of representation, underpins the fantasy of the marriageable virgin Swan Queen as the suitable choice for the exemplary prince. To locate Siegfried as the locus of truth he must not be seen to be infected by the wrong choice of love-object based on the demands of the penis. Therefore the exhilaratingly beautiful black swan must be constrained by a version of feminine that is portrayed as excessive. For him to be deceived by sorcery (a re-presentation of Odette) would demonstrate an irrational inability to evince the truth of present to consciousness that his identification as a male, and narratively as the prince, would demand. In many versions of *Swan Lake* the prince has to die as a way of keeping the male subject pure, sanctifying phallocentrism as the basis of subjectivity. His suicide can then demonstrate his own moral vigilance and his positioning as true subject of certainty. Visually he enacts the reverse of the Cartesian subject of certainty 'I think therefore I am', becoming 'I am tricked by the irrational and therefore I am not'. By crossing the boundaries between rationality and excess the prince has then to take the right action to safeguard the rational ordering of society, truth and knowledge. The black swan as excess is aesthetic trouble to the dance performance, demonstrating the vigilance that is needed to protect against the danger of being deceived by a representation and not being in touch with original truth and knowledge. In his writings referring to the gaze Lacan shows that the gaze cannot in itself constitute subjectivity. It is a 'point of light' that needs the intervention of what Lacan calls the screen, as the image through which identity is constructed. The screen has a particular status in Lacanian theory as a culturally determined image or set of images through which all subjects are classified in terms of their class, gender, race, etc. It has a masking function and as an alienating image is placed over the subject and takes the place of identity offering the subject a constitution based on a separated form of itself (precisely the role of the black swan). In likening it to a disembodied source of light Lacan emphasises the characteristic of the gaze as being its dispersability. The gaze, located at the sight of the object of vision, gives a perception to the object that it seizes and in doing so raises as an issue the fusion of gaze and spectacle. The pervasive quality of the gaze means that it always photographs us even as we look and therefore all visual transactions between spectator and object are infected by this quality. The look cannot therefore function as gaze for the spectator but it can function as gaze in relation to the performance even at the moment that the spectator assumes the status of object to the performance. What this means in terms of dance performance is that the subject, the body of performance, is dependent for its definition on Lacan's screen as a way of hiding its subversive potentially threatening sexuality. Identity is given via the screen and the subject is inscribed within it, but simultaneously it can function within the image as subject of the representation. This protective clothing that desexualises the body is based on a misrecognition – of both the gaze and the object – which posits the impossibility of any unmediated relationship existing between spectator and dance performance.

Lacan in his formulation of the gaze moves attention away from the gaze to the place of cultural representation – the place of the constitution of seeing and being seen (scene), and it is here that questions central to the reading of dance performance as woman will address themselves. Shown above are various areas of concern fundamental to this problem:

a. Subjectivity is totally dependant for its status on misrecognition at the site of the screen via the gaze, and the look in its characteristic mask is posited within the scene (seen) of performance.

b. The look derives its support from the gaze in the same way that the phallus derives its material support from the penis therefore locating a problem at the level of corporeal representation.

c. In dance performance male and female bodies are the site of economic, social and sexual oppression but they are represented structurally as bodies that are free of conflict. However at the level of narrative positive images can be attempted but these often work to resubstantialise identity, resituating the phallus as the referential definition of subjectivity, locating the '*moi*' in a fantasised place of misrecognition in the imaginary order.

In *Swan Lake* the aesthetic space is conceptualised in terms of sexual difference and versions of femininity are placed within that as fantasies that articulate the male castration anxiety. The fundamental drama that, via the theme of representation splits the image of femininity in two becoming both its guarantee (via the white swan) and its threat (figured by the black swan), becomes one and the same mystification of an identity that is constructed for the female in relation to phallocentrism. Siegfried has unleashed an anxiety, in his eventual choice of wife that is based on a misrecognition, that returns to a construction of femininity that informs the relation between aesthetic form and sexual difference. A relation that is based on misrecognition and which is dependent on the fantasies of a rounded, original identity. As Lacan shows, to conceive of woman as a symbol of a cultural ordering is to sustain that order with little attention given to the image of woman that it offers. The problematics of subjectivity and particularly of the relation of the woman to the danced text can then be suppressed and relocated so as to appear non-threatening, removing dance performance from its anxious relation to itself.

Note

1. J. Rose (1986) p. 36.

Bibliography

G. Balanchine and F. Mason, *Balanchine's Festival of Ballet* (London: W. H. Allen, 1978).

C. Crisp, 'The Nature of Dance Scholarship: The Critic's Task', *Dance Research, the Journal for the Society of Dance Research*, Vol. 1, No. 1, Spring (1983).

E. Denby, 'Dance Criticism', *Dance Encyclopaedia*, A. Chujoy, ed. (New York: Barnes, 1949).

J. Lacan, *The Four Fundamental Concepts of Psychoanalysis* (Harmondsworth: Penguin, 1979).

J. Lacan, *Speech and Language in Psychoanalysis*, Notes and translation by A. Wilden (London: Johns Hopkins Press, 1981).

J. Rose, *Sexuality in the Field of Vision* (London: Verso, 1986).

K. Silverman, 'Fassbinder and Lacan: A Reconsideration of the Gaze, Look, Image', *Camera Obscura*, A Journal of Feminist Film Theory, Johns Hopkins University Press, 19 January 1989.

Index